Affluenza

How Overconsumption Is Killing Us—And How We Can Fight Back

John de Graaf
David Wann
Thomas H. Naylor

16pt

Copyright Page from the Original Book

Affluenza

Copyright © 2014 by John de Graaf, David Wann, Thomas H. Naylor

All rights reserved. No part of this publication may be reproduced, distributed, or transmitted in any form or by any means, including photocopying, recording, or other electronic or mechanical methods, without the prior written permission of the publisher, except in the case of brief quotations embodied in critical reviews and certain other noncommercial uses permitted by copyright law. For permission requests, write to the publisher, addressed "Attention: Permissions Coordinator," at the address below.

Berrett-Koehler Publishers, Inc.
235 Montgomery Street, Suite 650
San Francisco, California 94104-2916
Tel: (415) 288-0260, Fax: (415) 362-2512
www.bkconnection.com

Ordering information for print editions

Quantity sales. Special discounts are available on quantity purchases by corporations, associations, and others. For details, contact the "Special Sales Department" at the Berrett-Koehler address above.

Individual sales. Berrett-Koehler publications are available through most bookstores. They can also be ordered directly from Berrett-Koehler: Tel: (800) 929-2929; Fax: (802) 864-7626; www.bkconnection.com

Orders for college textbook/course adoption use. Please contact Berrett-Koehler: Tel: (800) 929-2929; Fax: (802) 864-7626.

Orders by U.S. trade bookstores and wholesalers. Please contact Ingram Publisher Services, Tel: (800) 509-4887; Fax: (800) 838-1149; E-mail: customer.service@ingrampublisherservices.com; or visit www.ingrampublisherservices.com/Ordering for details about electronic ordering.

Berrett-Koehler and the BK logo are registered trademarks of Berrett-Koehler Publishers, Inc.

Third Edition
Paperback print edition ISBN 978-1-60994-927-3
PDF e-book ISBN 978-1-60994-928-0
IDPF e-book ISBN 978-1-60994-929-7

2013-1

Interior design and composition: Seventeenth Street Studios

Cover design: Mark van Bronkhorst, MvB Design

Copyeditor: Karen Seriguchi

Proofreader: Laurie Dunne

Indexer: Richard Evans

Page 4: illustration by Joel Pett. Pages 14, 36, 49, 54, 62, 71, 98, 111, 135, 151, 208: illustrations by David Horsey. Pages 30, 79, 90, 120, 129, 142, 167, 170, 178, 189, 197, 221: illustrations by Michael Swofford © Postconsumers.com.

Photo, page 162: The Surrender of the Joneses, Francine Strickwerda

TABLE OF CONTENTS

More Praise for Affluenza	i
FOREWORD	v
Introduction	viii
PART ONE: Symptoms	
CHAPTER 1: Feverish expectations	3
CHAPTER 2: All Stuffed Up	30
CHAPTER 3: Stressed to kill	40
CHAPTER 4: Family fractures	54
CHAPTER 5: Community chills	71
CHAPTER 6: Heart failure	85
CHAPTER 7: Social scars	99
CHAPTER 8: Resource exhaustion	113
CHAPTER 9: Industrial diarrhea	132
CHAPTER 10: A cancerous culture	147
PART TWO: Causes	
CHAPTER 11: Early infections	167
CHAPTER 12: An ounce of prevention	178
CHAPTER 13: The road not taken	189
CHAPTER 14: An emerging epidemic	206
CHAPTER 15: The Age of Affluenza	218
CHAPTER 16: Spin doctors	232
PART THREE: Cures	
CHAPTER 17: Diagnostic test	251
CHAPTER 18: Bed rest	258
CHAPTER 19: Affluholics anonymous	269
CHAPTER 20: Fresh air	281
CHAPTER 21: Back to work	296
CHAPTER 22: Building immunity	316
CHAPTER 23: Policy prescriptions	330
CHAPTER 24: Vital signs	353
CHAPTER 25: The glow of health	375
ACKNOWLEDGMENTS	391

NOTES	393
BIBLIOGRAPHY	435
ABOUT THE AUTHORS	466
Index	473

More Praise for Affluenza

"This witty yet hard-hitting book provides evidence of the social problems caused by the American obsession with acquiring 'stuff' and proposes solutions for living more sustainably. Highly recommended."
—*Library Journal*

"Now here is a good reason to go shopping! The wonderful book that made consumerism the issue it should be, *Affluenza,* is here in a third, fully updated edition. The story of the Joneses, of 'keeping up with the Joneses' fame, is itself worth the very modest price you will have to pay to enjoy this classic, now new and improved."
—**James Gustave Speth, author of America the Possible and former director, Yale University School of Forestry and Environmental Studies**

"If ever there was a right book at the right time, *Affluenza* is it. This country needs this book."
—**Lester R. Brown, President, Earth Policy Institute, author of Plan B 4.0 and Full Planet, Empty Plates**

"*Affluenza* makes us take a hard look at how the drive to excessive consumerism is personally, socially, and environmentally disastrous and then takes us on an exciting path to deeper happiness and satisfaction. It is a must-read for all who strive to create more healthy, just, and secure communities."
—**Anthony D. Cortese, former Commissioner, Massachusetts Department of Environmental Protection, and founder, American College & University Presidents' Climate Commitment**

"De Graaf, Wann, and Naylor have achieved something special with *Affluenza*. They take an unflinching look at the train wreck of America's consumer culture and then extricate us from the wreckage by providing practical policies and achievable actions for building a healthier society. *Affluenza* is also a great read; it contains the hopeful ideas we need to reach a livable future."
—**Rob Dietz, coauthor of Enough Is Enough**

"The programs offered at the end of the book work on many levels, from making personal choices to changing the rules of the game to reward all actions moving us toward a thriving, just, and sustainable future. So enjoy! This is a great book about a tough-to-face set of problems."

—**Vicki Robin, coauthor of *Your Money or Your Life* and author of *Blessing the Hands That Feed Us***

"*Affluenza* is an engagingly conversational, thought-provoking look at where we have perverted the American dream. Though the nature of books like these is to preach to the converted, *Affluenza* offers enough support to the arguments and enough depth to the solutions to have a good chance of reaching the unconvinced."
—***Detroit Free Press***

In memory of Dr. Henry J. Frundt
(1940–2010)

In loving memory of Marjorie Southworth
Wann (1926–2012)

FOREWORD

When *Affluenza* was first published in 2001, its diagnosis of the sickness in consumer society and its prescriptions for the cure stood in marked contrast to the nation's prevailing optimism. The American economy was at a postwar peak. The stock market had tripled in the previous decade, topping the once-unimaginable 10,000 level. Soaring housing values were making ordinary homeowners rich (on paper, at least). The first dot-com boom was minting young millionaires and billionaires in the high-tech entrepreneurial class.

Then the World Trade Center attacks sent the stock market plunging, triggering a recession and exposing the hollowness of a system whose leaders advised us that the patriotic response to terrorism was to go shopping. In the years following, the dot-com boom went bust, and the near-collapse of corrupt financial institutions plunged millions of homeowners into debt and foreclosure. Today, even as the economists tell us the Great Recession has ended, the real unemployment rate—those without work, those who need more work, and those who have stopped looking—remains scandalously high. The Occupy movement has sharpened awareness of the inherent inequities of an economy in which the wealthiest get richer and richer while most of the rest of us work longer hours with less job security, health insurance, and retirement security just to keep our heads above water.

But if *Affluenza* was ahead of its time, more than ever its time is now.

From book groups to congregations to classrooms, *Affluenza* has become an enduring classic—not only for its insight into the emptiness and unsustainability of a system based on ever-expanding consumption but also for boldly pointing a way out. Its ultimately hopeful message—that it is possible to build a society based on not *more* but *better*, not selfishness but sharing, not competition but community—has inspired millions to rethink their lives and question the status quo. Its very title has become a part of the language, an indispensable tool for describing the ills of a society where, to paraphrase the personal-finance guru Dave Ramsey, we work too much to buy things we don't need with money we don't have to impress people we don't even know. It has played an immeasurable role in informing my own work on *The Story of Stuff* films, which the authors so generously cite in chapter 22.

The third edition of *Affluenza* is in many ways a new book. The first edition was an outgrowth of a PBS TV special of the same name; this revision goes deeper in its analysis, providing a somewhat more serious discussion of the issues. The data and references cited in the text and footnotes have been extensively updated to reflect the many changes that have rocked the world in the past thirteen years. The authors want this book to contribute to the rich and exciting discussions that are taking place everywhere about community, citizenship, and voluntary simplicity. If we take their lessons to heart, perhaps a future edition will be a history of how we found a cure for the plague of affluenza.

    Annie Leonard, author of *The Story of Stuff*
    Berkeley, California
    July 2013

Introduction

AFFLUENZA (n.)—a painful, contagious, socially transmitted condition of overload, debt, anxiety, and waste resulting from the dogged pursuit of more.

In his office, a doctor offers his diagnosis to an attractive, expensively dressed female patient. "There's nothing physically wrong with you," he says. His patient is incredulous. "Then why do I feel so awful?" she asks. "So bloated and sluggish. I've got a big new house, a brand-new car, a new wardrobe, and I just got a big raise at work. Why am I so miserable, Doctor? Isn't there some pill you can give me?" The doctor shakes his head. "I'm afraid not," he replies. "There's no pill for what's wrong with you." "What is it, Doctor?" she asks, alarmed. "Affluenza," he answers gravely. "It's the new epidemic. It's extremely contagious. It can be cured, but not easily."

Of course, the scene is an imaginary one, but the epidemic is real. A powerful virus has infected American society, threatening our wallets, our friendships, our families, our communities, and our environment. We call the virus *affluenza*. And because the United States has become the economic model for most of the world, the virus is now loose on every continent.

Affluenza's costs and consequences are immense, though often concealed. Untreated, the disease can cause permanent discontent. In our view, the affluenza epidemic is rooted in the obsessive, almost religious quest for economic expansion that has become the core principle of what is called the American dream. It's rooted in the fact that our supreme measure of national progress is that quarterly ring of the cash register we call the gross domestic product. It's rooted in the idea that every generation will be materially wealthier than its predecessor and that, somehow, each of us can pursue that single-minded end without damaging the countless other things we hold dear.

It doesn't work that way. The contention of this book is that if we don't begin to reject our culture's incessant demands to "buy now," we will "pay later" in ways we can scarcely imagine. The bill is already coming due. At its most extreme, affluenza threatens to exhaust the earth itself. As the corporate critic Jeremy Rifkin told John some years back, "We human beings have been producing and consuming at a rate that far exceeds the ability of the planet to absorb our pollution or replenish the stock."

Scientists say we'd need several more planets if everyone on earth were to suddenly adopt the American standard of living.

Welcome to the third edition of *Affluenza,* fully updated with a different subtitle. Much water has run under the bridge since the first edition was published in 2001, following a period of galloping economic prosperity in America. The book quickly became a hit and has been translated into nine languages while selling nearly 150,000 copies. A second edition was published in 2005, when signs were clear that the prosperity we discussed in the first edition was beginning to falter.

Now eight more years have passed, and during those years the chickens have come home to roost and the hubristic assumptions of 2001 have crumbled. The flaws in the affluenza economic model we described then, coupled with glaringly stupid policy decisions encouraging rampant financial speculation, brought the whole show to a crash in 2008. Since then we have been picking up the pieces all over the world. Personal bankruptcies exceeded 1.5 million the following year, the most ever. Even in 2012, there were 1.4 million such declarations in the United States, about equal to the number of students earning bachelor's degrees.

In this book, we bring theory and data up to date. There have been many changes since 2001, perhaps equally positive and negative. But the overall impact of the disease called affluenza has not diminished, and the stakes are higher, given the realities of climate change, technological unemployment, and the massive shift toward inequality that began emerging in the United States in the 1980s and exploded after 2001.

AFFLUENZA: THE FILM

Most movies start with a book, but this book started with a movie. John, a coauthor of this book, and Vivia Boe produced a documentary in 1996 about the subject of overconsumption and its many not-so-benign consequences for American society. Their research told them the subject was a huge one, touching our lives as Americans in more ways than any other social or environmental issue. But how to make sense of it? How to present the issue so that viewers could see that multiple problems were caused by our consuming passion and were all connected to one another?

After videotaping more than two-thirds of the program, John and Vivia were still wondering how to weave together the wide range of material they had collected. Then, on a flight from Seattle to Washington, DC, to do still more videotaping, John happened to see the word *affluenza* used in passing in an article he was reading. It was like that moment in cartoons when the light bulb goes on over someone's head. That was it: *affluenza*. A single word that not only made a catchy (pun intended) TV title but also suggested a disease resulting from overconsumption.

Here was a way to make the impacts of overconsuming more clearly understandable—as symptoms of a virus that, in the United States at least, had reached epidemic proportions. They could then look at the history of this disease, trying to understand how and why it spread, what its carriers and hot zones were, and finally, how it could be treated.

From that point on, they began to use the term, asking interviewees if the idea made sense to them. And indeed, physicians told John and Vivia they could see symptoms of affluenza in many of their patients, symptoms often manifesting themselves physically. A psychologist offered his observation that many of his clients "suffer from affluenza, but very few know that that's what they're suffering from."

The documentary, *Affluenza,* premiered on PBS on September 15, 1997, and was greeted with an outpouring of audience calls and letters from every part of the United States. Clearly, it had touched a deep nerve of concern. Viewers as old as ninety-three wrote to express their fears for their grandchildren, while twenty-year-olds recounted sad tales from the lower depths of credit card debt. A cover story in the *Washington Post* Sunday magazine about people trying to simplify their lives introduced them as they were watching the program. A teacher in rural North Carolina showed it to her class of sixth graders and said they wanted to talk about it for the next two weeks. On average, the kids thought they had three times as much "stuff" as they needed. One girl said she could no longer close her closet door. "I've just got too many things, clothes I never wear," she explained. "I can't get rid of them."

CROSSING POLITICAL LINES

Though past criticisms of consumerism have come mostly from the liberal side of the political spectrum, *Affluenza* spoke to Americans of all political persuasions. The head of one statewide conservative family organization wrote saying, "This issue is so important for families." Ratings and audience response were as high in conservative cities like Salt Lake and Houston as they were in liberal San Francisco or Minneapolis. In colleges, the program was more popular at Brigham Young than at Berkeley. At Appalachian State University in Boone, North Carolina, students and faculty showed it to audiences in both poor mountain communities and upscale churches, recording audience comments and producing a video of their own called *Escaping Affluenza in the Mountains*.

THE WHOLE WORLD IS WATCHING

We've become convinced that this is an issue that troubles people *throughout the world*. We've heard from countries where we couldn't imagine anyone would be concerned about affluenza—Thailand, Estonia, Russia, Nigeria, for example—but where, indeed, citizens hoped to adopt what was good about the American lifestyle and avoid what was harmful.

An Islamic business magazine in Sri Lanka asked us for a short article about the disease. Activists in rural northern Burma translated the TV program into the local Kachin dialect. A sixteen-year-old Israeli girl sought permission to project it onto the wall of a Tel Aviv shopping center. Seeing overconsumption as a disease, they said, helped them understand it better and explain it to others.

A SOCIAL DISEASE

Often, writers speak of "affluenza" with different emphases. Some have used the term primarily with reference to the spoiled children of the super-rich. Defined as such, it loses the sociopolitical message we put forward and becomes a matter of purely personal behavior. In our view, however, the virus is not confined to the upper classes but has found its way throughout our society. Its symptoms affect the poor as well as the rich, and our two-tiered system (with rich getting richer and poor poorer) punishes the poor twice: they are conditioned to want the good life but given very little possibility of attaining it. Affluenza infects all of us, though in different ways.

AFFLUENZA: THE BOOK

Television, even at its most informative, is a superficial medium; you simply can't put that much material into an hour. And that's the reason this book was written: to explain affluenza in more depth, with more examples, more symptoms, more evidence, more thorough exposition. If you've seen the video, you'll recognize a few of the characters and stories.

The first edition arrived on the market just before the terrible tragedy of September 11, 2001. Families and friends suddenly seemed more important than things and work. But then, the consumption propaganda machine kicked into high gear again. If you want to be patriotic, President George W. Bush told Americans, go to the malls and shop. Buy to fight terror.

From Democrats, the message was the same. San Francisco mayor Willie Brown had a million shopping bags printed with big flags on them and bold words: AMERICA: OPEN FOR BUSINESS. Washington senator Patty Murray proposed "Let's go shopping" legislation that would have removed the sales tax on products during the 2001 holiday shopping season. Almost no one dared to mention that anger and envy over the profligate spending of Americans might encourage sympathy for terrorists in developing countries.

Since the first edition of *Affluenza* was published, it's been used widely by book groups and in university classes. We had hoped *affluenza* would become a household word, and that seems to be happening. An Internet search before our PBS broadcast turned up about two hundred cases of the word on the Web—all of them in Italian, where *affluenza* simply means affluence. In 2005, a check of the word on Google found 232,000 references to it (!), referring, in the vast majority of cases, to overconsumption. A similar check in 2013 found 2.3 million references, a leap of an order of magnitude. London's *Independent* newspaper picked it as one of its most popular new words for the year 2003, and dictionaries are considering including it in the next few years.

Moreover, use of the term continues to grow: a popular play called *Affluenza*, by James Sherman, has been touring the country for several years. Clive Hamilton wrote a fine book by the same title in Australia in 2007, graciously asking us to borrow the title. Oliver James, a British psychologist, also wrote a good book with the same name in 2009, when there were already one million references to *affluenza* on the Internet, but unlike Hamilton, James suggested that he had invented the word!

SYMPTOMS

We have divided the book into three sections. The first explores many of the symptoms of affluenza, each—only half whimsically—compared to a real flu symptom. Think of how you feel when you've got a bug. You're likely to be running a temperature. You're congested. Your body is achy. You may have chills. Your stomach is upset. You're weak. You might have swollen glands, even a rash.

In the Age of Affluenza, America as a society shows all of these symptoms, metaphorically at least. We present each as a chapter. We start with individual symptoms, then move to the social conditions, and finally turn to the environmental impacts of affluenza.

Some chapters may greet you with the shock of self-recognition—"Honey, that's me!" You might notice the conditions discussed here taking hold of your friends. You might find some more troubling than others and worry more about your children than about your Mother Earth. You might be well off materially but feel stressed out or empty, as though your life lacks purpose or meaning. Or you might be poor, and angry at your inability to give your children what marketers say they "gotta have" to fit in. Or you have watched bulldozers destroy the only open space left around your community to make room for row upon row of identical tract homes with three-car garages. If you're elderly, you may have noticed your children's inability to balance their budget, and you may worry for their children as well.

If you're young, you may be anxious about your own future.

Wherever you're coming from, we believe you'll clearly recognize that at least some of the symptoms of affluenza affect you. Then, as you read on, you'll begin to see how they're connected to others less obvious from your vantage point.

GENESIS OF THE DISEASE

In Part Two of this book, we look beneath the symptoms to search for causes. Is affluenza simply human nature, as some would suggest? What was the genesis of this powerful virus? How has it mutated throughout history, and when did it begin to reach epidemic proportions? What choices did we make as a society (between free time and stuff, for example) that deepened our infection? We look carefully at warnings from across time and cultures and at early efforts to eradicate the disease with controls and quarantines.

Then we discover how the spread of the disease has become not only socially acceptable but actively encouraged by all the powerful electronic carriers our technological civilization keeps perfecting. We suggest that affluenza promises to meet our needs—but does so in inefficient and destructive ways. And we contend that an entire industry of pseudo physicians, handsomely rewarded by those with a huge stake in the perpetuation of affluenza, conspire to keep the diagnosis of the disease and the extent of its symptoms from reaching the general public.

CURING AFFLUENZA

But far be it from our intent to leave you permanently depressed. Affluenza *can* be treated, and millions of ordinary Americans are already taking steps in that direction. A 2004 poll by the Center for a New American Dream (www.newdream.org) found that 49 percent of Americans had claimed to have cut back on their spending.[1]

The same poll also revealed that 85 percent of Americans think our priorities as a society are out of whack; 93 percent feel Americans are too focused on working and making money; 91 percent believe we buy and consume far more than we need; 81 percent think we'll need to make major changes in the way we live to protect the environment; and 87 percent feel our current consumer culture makes it harder to instill positive values in our children.

Several cultural indicators seem to show that Americans are building their immunity to affluenza. For example, the number of golfers (an enjoyable sport but a costly one) is down while home gardening is up, and some courses are being converted to parks and other recreational areas. Sales of smaller hybrid cars have jumped in the United States, while SUV sales have fallen somewhat, and total driving in the US leveled out in 2005 and has begun to decline. Reports from cities like Seattle show that many young millennials prefer to rent cars from companies like Zipcar and Car2Go, or to walk, bike, and use public transit. They also seem to be putting off getting driver's licenses until college age or older.

For the first time in many years, there are more farms rather than fewer, indicating the entry of small, often organic farmers into agriculture and a great new interest among the young in wholesome, unprocessed food. Trends like these are reported in Part Three of the book, along with many natural, technical, and even social remedies for beating affluenza. As with symptoms, we look at treatments, starting with the personal and advancing to the social and political. Our treatments, too, employ the medical metaphor.

We encourage a restored interest in fresh air and the natural world, with its remarkable healing powers. We agree with the futurist Gerald Celente, author of *Trends 2000*. "There's this commercial out," he says, "and it shows this middle-aged man walking through the woods pumping his arms, and all of a sudden in the next cut, there he is on the back porch, woods in the background, walking on this treadmill that must have cost a fortune. It doesn't make sense. It was so much nicer walking through the woods, and it cost nothing at all."

We suggest strategies for rebuilding families and communities, and for respecting and restoring the earth and its biological rules. We offer "policy prescriptions," with the belief that some well-considered legislation can help create a less affluenza-friendly social environment and make it easier for individuals to get well and stay that way.

We also present preventive approaches, including vaccines and vitamins that can strengthen our personal and social immune systems. And we suggest an annual checkup of our vital signs. Ours comes in three phases:

1. You can take a little test to see how you're doing personally in staying well (see Chapter 17).
2. We find a useful substitute for our current outmoded measure of national health, the gross domestic product (GDP). We

recommend an index called the *Genuine Progress Indicator* (GPI), currently being fine-tuned in several American states. Using multiple indices to discover how we're doing, the GPI paints a different picture of our success as a society. While GDP has risen steadily throughout our history, the GPI has been falling since 1973 in the United States, and since 1978 globally, because "bads" like pollution are subtracted rather than added to its index.

3. Finally, using the "gross national happiness index"—an idea that comes from the Himalayan kingdom of Bhutan—we can begin to take stock of how satisfied we really are with our lives and what we might do to be more content with less stuff.

CHANGES IN OUR THINKING

We've gotten a lot of feedback from readers since we wrote the first edition of this book—hundreds of personal reviews and some excellent journalistic assessments as well. Much of the feedback has been contradictory, so we've had to go with what made most sense to us. Criticisms of the book have taken two lines. Our accessible, sometimes flippant, writing style has been praised, and even used to teach writing in college English classes, but other readers have felt it engaging to the point of superficiality—"It feels like a television program" was how some put it. While trying to maintain the book's light quality, we have also responded to this criticism by taking out some of the silliest stuff, and we have substituted deeper analysis for some of our storytelling. We think this makes this edition a more serious book and hope that it will be seen that way, though we know these changes will not please everyone.

The second major criticism of the first two editions is that we were "too political." Many readers said that they agreed with our criticisms of consumerism and overspending, but they thought these were personal problems and that we should have stuck to giving people tips to live more frugally and not gotten into dreaded politics. The fact that our historical section includes some ideas from Karl Marx (though it also includes ideas from several prominent conservative economists) waved a red flag for some readers. But we do not apologize for looking to a broad range of ideas. A current Russian joke is illustrative. It goes like this: "Everything Marx said about communism was false. Unfortunately, everything he said about capitalism was true." If we are to get a handle on affluenza, we must be open to all ideas, not just those deemed "American."

Moreover, we believe that, if anything, our first editions, and the TV program on which they were based, *underestimated* the importance of policy while focusing too much on personal behavior. Many of the drivers of affluenza are structural—our economy, as the activist Michael Jacobson put it, is simplicity unfriendly and "structurally opposed to simpler living." We can see this in the financial crisis, driven in part by personal spending beyond our means but greatly exacerbated by public policies rewarding greed and speculation. So we won't back down on this one; indeed, this version of the book calls greater attention to the need for better policies.

We want to make clear from the outset that much spending in the United States is driven not by some special American greed, but by reasonable fear and a desire for basic financial security. As we will argue, the insecurity and inequality central to life in the United States are greater drivers of this virus than the gross desire to consume.

LET'S BEGIN A DIALOGUE

This book contains little truly new information, yet the issue in this "information age" isn't more information. It's how to make sense of what we already know and how to use values, not just information, as a lever for getting healthy again. We offer a way of understanding seemingly disconnected personal, social, and environmental problems that makes sense to us—as symptoms of a perilous epidemic that threatens our future and that of generations to come. Our intention is to encourage a national dialogue about the American consumer dream so that whatever choices each of us makes about consumption—and the choices we make as a society through policy change—are made with a clearer understanding of their possible consequences.

The underlying message of this book isn't to stop buying; it's to buy carefully and consciously with full attention to the real benefits and costs of our purchases, remembering, always, that the best things in life aren't things.

A NOTE ON NOTES: As we have updated our endnotes from the previous volume, it has become clear to us how quickly numbers change. And in some cases, we offer statistics that are best understood by looking at trends. Occasionally, therefore, we point to sources of multiple data and to more that can be useful to you, rather than simply the source for the number we mention. Moreover, since far more people now get their information online, we have chosen where possible to direct you to supporting material that can be accessed online rather than simply the names of hard-copy articles. We have occasionally cited *Wikipedia* as a source, knowing that might encourage scolding from some quarters. But the advantage is that *Wikipedia* pages point readers to many other sources and references, allowing them to dig far deeper into a subject. It is our hope that by opening up more sources for information, we can encourage you to better explore the complex issues surrounding this subject. Finally, where we have not cited the source of quotations, they have all come from personal conversations with the authors.

Happy reading!

PART ONE
Symptoms

CHAPTER I

Feverish expectations

Let's put it bluntly: we can't grow on like this. In these pages, we'll argue that affluenza has overheated our economy and our planet while leaving us feverish with desire for ever more consumer products. Never before has so much meant so little to so many. In the blink of an eye, geologically speaking, our feverish expectations are changing our planet beyond recognition, with little thought for those who will come after us.

The late, great environmentalist David Brower, who turned the Sierra Club from a tiny California hiking society into America's most powerful conservation organization, used to give what he called his sermon as part of his many speeches. He compressed the age of Earth, estimated by scientists at some 4.6 billion years, into seven days, the biblical week of creation, if you will. When you do this, a day represents about 650 million years, an hour 27 million years, a minute about 450,000 years, and a second 7,500 years.

On Sunday morning, Earth congeals from cosmic gases. In the next few hours, land masses and oceans begin to form, and by Tuesday afternoon, the first tiny "protocells" of life emerge, probably from scalding primordial vents in the bottom of the oceans. In the next few days, life forms become larger, more complex, and more wondrous. Shortly before dawn on the last day—Saturday—trilobites and other strangely shaped creatures swim by the millions in the Cambrian seas. Half a billion years later, in real time, we will be amazed by their fossils, scattered about the globe.

Around the middle of the very last day of the week, those gargantuans, the great reptiles, some mild, some menacing, thunder across the land and fill the sky. The dinosaurs enjoy a long run, commanding the earth's stage for more than four hours, until a monstrous meteorite, landing in the Gulf of Mexico, makes the climate too cold and ends their reign. By the late afternoon and evening on Saturday, mammals, furry, warm-blooded, and able to withstand a colder world, flourish and evolve, until, a few minutes before midnight on that final night of the week, *Homo sapiens,* walking erect on two legs, learns to speak, use fire, and create increasingly complex forms of organization.

Only about ten thousand years ago in real time, less than two seconds before midnight in our metaphor, humans develop agriculture and start building cities. At a third of a second before midnight, the Buddha is born; at a quarter of second, Christ. Only a thirtieth of a second before midnight, we launch the Industrial Revolution, and after World War II, perhaps a hundredth of a second before midnight in our week of creation—again, on the final night—the age of consumerism begins, the age of stuff, the Age of Affluenza.

In that hundredth of a second, Brower and others have pointed out, we have managed to consume more resources than did all human beings all together in all of previous history. We have diminished our soil, fisheries, fossil fuels (which took hundreds of millions of years to form), and who knows what other resources, by half. We have caused the extinction of countless other species, and we have changed the climate. Think about it; try to grasp in your mind what it means to have done all of this in this blink of the geological eye.

There are people, Brower went on to say, who believe that what we have been doing for that last one-hundredth of a second can go on indefinitely. If they even think about the issue, they believe, without evidence, that science and new technologies will allow our continued hyperexploitation of the planet's resources. They are considered normal, reasonable, intelligent people—indeed, they run our corporations and our governments. But in reality, they are stark, raving mad. They are like Frankenstein's monster. They are rampaging all over the globe now, but as a race they were born in the USA.[1]

It will be hard to change their mind, hard to change our practices, but not nearly as hard as it would be to change the laws of physics. We can't grow on like this.

CONSUMER MANIA

Since World War II, Americans have been engaged in an unprecedented consumer spending binge. We now spend 71 percent of our $15 trillion economy on consumer goods. For example, we spend more on shoes, jewelry, and watches than on higher education.[2] We spend as much on auto maintenance as on religious and welfare activities. In 1986, America still had more high schools than shopping centers. Less than twenty years later, in 2005, we had more than twice as many shopping centers (46,438) as high schools (22,180). In the Age of Affluenza (as we believe the century following World War II will eventually be called), shopping centers have supplanted churches as a symbol of cultural values. In fact, 70 percent of us visit malls each week, more than attend houses of worship.[3]

Until recently, our most profitable shopping centers were megamalls. Typically, they cover areas of fertile farmland that formerly produced bumper crops instead of traffic jams. Indeed, sixty-nine acres of prime American farmland are lost to "development" every hour. When a new megamall opens, the pomp and ceremony rival anything Notre Dame or Chartres might have witnessed in medieval times.

The Super Mall in Auburn, Washington, opened to a stampede of a hundred thousand shoppers in October 1995. The crowd gathered under an imitation of the state's 14,410-foot Mount Rainier. Rising above the Super Mall's front entrance, the imitation mountain provided one show which the real thing could not: a display of fireworks, set off as soon as the ribbon-cutting ceremony was over.

In a spirit of boosterism that would have impressed Sinclair Lewis's Babbitt, speaker after speaker extolled the wonders of the new shopping center, the biggest in the state. "The number of shoppers expected to visit here over the next year exceeds 1.2 million," burbled Auburn's mayor, adding that "committed shoppers can shop till they drop in 1.2 million square feet of shopping space." Along with a new racetrack and casino in the area, the mall was expected to become a "destination attraction" for vacationers from the entire western United States and Canada. It would, they said, create four thousand jobs and "improve the quality of life throughout the region." Thirty percent of the expected business would come from tourists who would each spend about five hours and more than $200 at the mall.[4]

FUN FOR THE WHOLE FAMILY

The thousands of eager shoppers on hand for the opening wore bored and impatient expressions during the speeches but pushed eagerly through the open doors when the rhetoric stopped. One woman said she was "really excited about the mall because this is something we haven't had in this part of Washington. We were waiting for something like this."

"We said, 'If we build it, they will come,' and they did," gushed a happy shopkeeper. Another explained that its hardwood floors "add a little sense of excitement to the mall. They're much easier than walking on tile or granite and make the Super Mall really special." She hoped children would enjoy it, "because shopping has become such a family experience that's really important."

"Shopping malls have really become the centers of many communities," says Michael Jacobson, founder of the Center for the Study of Commercialism in Washington, DC. "Children as well as adults see a shopping center as just the natural destination to fill a bored life."[5]

WHAT ELSE MATTERS?

The host of the TV program *Affluenza*, Scott Simon, visited Potomac Mills, a large Virginia shopping mall, during production of the program. Shoppers were eager to answer his questions about where they came from and what they thought of the mall. None of the people Simon talked to were sweating profusely. But all seemed infected by feverish expectations, often the first symptom of affluenza.

Two women from Dallas, Texas, said they'd been at the mall for three days straight, while their husbands golfed nearby. "We're always looking for a bargain. You've got to know the brands, and we have experience, we're proud to say," they proclaimed. "I didn't need anything. I just went to shop," said a man with a cart full of merchandise. "Whatever I like, I buy." "I bought a lot more than I planned to," another woman admitted. "You just see so much."

Yes, you do, and that's the idea. Seeing so much leads to impulse buying, the key to mall profitability and to the success of big-box stores like Wal-Mart. Impulse: a devilish little snake that cajoles first, then bites later, when the credit card bill comes due. Only a quarter of mall shoppers come with a specific product in mind. The rest come just to shop. "What else matters?" asked one of the ladies from Dallas at Potomac Mills, only half in jest.

"I came here with one overriding interest, to spend money," said a proud teenage girl, who was getting rid of the hundred dollars her mother had given her for this particular spree. "I like to shop," she explained. She's not alone. One poll found that 93 percent of teenage American girls rate shopping as their favorite activity.[6]

An older couple passed by with a shopping cart piled to the brim. "This is only half of what we've purchased," the man said cheerfully. "We brought a long list of things to buy," his wife added, "and then we bought a lot of stuff that wasn't on the list."

But Potomac Mills is a mere mini-mall compared to the Mall of America in Bloomington, Minnesota. With 4.2 million square feet of shopping space (100 acres), the country's biggest mall ("Where It's Always 72 Degrees!") spreads over an area the size of seven Yankee Stadiums and will soon double in size. It employs twelve thousand people and attracts forty million visitors a year. The Mall of America is more than metaphorically a cathedral; some people get married there. It is also a world-class affluenza hot zone.

A WORLD PHENOMENON

Today, the malls of America have rivals in other countries. The Phoenix City Market Mall in Mumbai, India, is only slightly smaller than the Mall of America, and the New South China Mall is nearly twice as big, while the Dubai Mall has become the world's most visited leisure and shopping destination, with sixty-five million annual visitors.[7]

But the malling of the world may be starting to lose steam. The big Indian and Chinese malls are full of vacant space, as many of India's and China's poor, unable to afford the products, come only to look, not to buy. In an even more promising development, recent demonstrations in Turkey began when the government announced plans to demolish Istanbul's popular Taksim Gezi Park and build a shopping mall in its place, striking a powerful blow against affluenza.[8]

In the United States, too, many malls are losing tenants. Retail experts predict that a tenth of the approximately one thousand megamalls in the US will close their doors within the decade. Part of this downturn was the result of the recent recession. But much of it can be blamed on greater consumer spending options.

HOME SHOPPING

While many malls, and vast discount megastores like Wal-Mart and Costco, still boast growing sales (and still drive smaller, locally owned stores out of business), Americans are now doing a whole lot of shopping right from their couches. Nearly twenty *billion* mail-order catalogs (more than fifty million trees' worth of paper) flood our homes each year,[9] about seventy for every one of us, selling everything from soup to nuts (to refrigerators to underwear). "Buy Now, Pay Later!" they shout. While some resent their arrival, most Americans eagerly await them and order from them with abandon. In some cases, we even pay for the catalogs (such as Sears's) so that we can pay for what's in them. Then there are the home shopping channels. Critics mock them as presenting a continual succession of baubles on bimbos, but for a sizable minority of Americans, they're the highlight of the cable TV systems, and highly profitable. And to think someone once called TV "a vast wasteland." That was before the shopping channels, of course.

Mail-order catalogs and shopping channels carry a lot more than products. They are highly contagious carriers of affluenza.

In the past several years, a new affluenza carrier has entered the mix in a big way. In time, it threatens to someday outdraw malls, catalogs, and shopping channels combined. The intense frenzy with which the ubiquitous Internet has been embraced as a shopping center can be compared only to that which followed the discovery of gold in California and Alaska, or to the Texas oil boom. Americans now spend an average of thirteen hours a week online, and much of that time is spent shopping, since a majority of Internet sites are selling something.

Ten years ago, consumers spent $50 billion online, nearly double what they had spent four years earlier. By 2012, online sales had topped $200 billion, and they continue to double every four years. Though they are still only a fraction of total retail sales ($4.4 trillion), the trend is clear.[10]

A BIT OF BACKGROUND

Take a walk down memory lane. Way down. If you're as old as the authors, your memories carry you back to the 1950s at least. World War II and the Great Depression were over, and America was on the move. Suburban houses were going up everywhere. New cars were rolling from the assembly lines and onto new pavement. Ground breaking began for the National Defense Interstate Highway System, soon to stretch from sea to shining sea. A TV dinner (introduced in 1953) came from every oven.

"It's a great life, eh Bob?" a man in a '50s commercial intones as a young couple and their towheaded son sit on a couch watching the tube. "And tomorrow will be even better, for you and for all the people." Of course, the great life wasn't great for the millions who were poor or discriminated against. And even for middle-class

America, it wasn't worry-free. On the same day in 1957 (October 4) that *Leave It to Beaver* premiered on American television, those pesky Russians shot Sputnik into space. Nikita Khrushchev promised to bury us "in the peaceful field of economic competition." We know how that came out.

But 1957 was important for another, less heralded reason. It was the year the percentage of Americans describing themselves as "very happy" reached a plateau never exceeded and seldom matched since then. The following year, a year when Americans bought two hundred million Hula-Hoops, the economist John Kenneth Galbraith published an influential book calling the United States "the affluent society."

We *felt* richer then than we do now. Most Americans today don't think of themselves as affluent, says the psychologist Paul Wachtel, "even though in terms of gross national product we have more than twice as much as we did then. Everybody's house has twice as much stuff in it. But the feeling of affluence, the experience of well-being, is no higher and perhaps even lower." Liberal economists argue that since about 1973 the real wages earned by middle-class Americans haven't risen much and, for many workers, have declined. Young couples talk of not being able to afford what their parents had. But one thing is incontestable: *We have a lot more stuff and much higher material expectations than previous generations did.*

STARTER CASTLES

Take housing. The average size of new homes is now more than double what it was in the 1950s, while families are smaller. Right after World War II, 750 square feet was just right (in Levittown, for example). By the '50s, 950 square feet was the norm; by the '60s, 1,100 square feet was typical; and by the '70s, 1,350. Now it's 2,500.[11]

In recent years, before the housing bubble burst, homes became a symbol of conspicuous consumption, as beneficiaries of the '90s stock market boom began to buy real estate, bulldoze existing (and perfectly functional) homes, and replace them with megahouses of 10,000 square feet and more. Starter castles, some have named them. Others call them monster homes. In places like the spectacular mountain towns of the West, many such megahomes are actually *second homes,* mere vacation destinations for the newly rich.

CAR WARS

As with homes, so with cars. Until 2000, the eighteen-foot-long Chevy Suburban set the standard for gigantism. Then, not to be outdone, Ford introduced the Excursion, a seven-thousand-pound titan that was a foot longer than the Suburban. Ford Motors chairman William Ford even apologized for making so many SUVs, calling his Excursion "the Ford Valdez" for its propensity to consume fuel. He condemned SUVs as wasteful and polluting but said Ford would continue to manufacture them anyway because they were extremely profitable.

"For a lot of people an SUV is a status symbol," says car salesman Mike Sillivan. "So they're willing to pay the thirty-to forty-odd thousand dollars to drive one of these vehicles."

Never one to give up without a fight, General Motors came charging back at Ford, acquiring ownership of the Hummer, a more luxurious version of the military transport vehicle used during the Gulf War. GM is "placing a big bet that the decade-long trend toward ever larger and more aggressive-looking sport utility vehicles would continue," according to the *New York Times*.[12] "It's like a tank with fashion," says one teenager quoted by the *Times*. The kid says he loves the Hummer because "I like something where I can look down into another car and give that knowing smile that says 'I'm bigger than you.' It makes me feel powerful."

A Hummer dealer website (www.lynchhummer.com) features a link to "Stupid Hummer Tricks." The link offers photos of, among other things, a Hummer in a standoff against a buffalo, another proudly knocking aside trees as it plows up an incline in a forest, and a third nearly submerged in a pretty mountain stream. Now what will Ford counter with, an even bigger SUV called The Extinction?

LET'S DO LUNCH

We've talked about houses and cars. Now consider food. The '50s did give us TV dinners. Turkey, peas, and mashed potatoes in a throwaway tray for sixty-nine cents—thank you, Swanson's. As kids, we considered them delectable. Our standard diets were pretty bland. "Exotic" meant soggy egg rolls, chow mein, and chop suey. "Mexican" was tacos and tamales (how did we cope without chimichangas and chalupas?). "Thai" wasn't even part of our vocabulary. Now, city streets and suburban malls sport a United Nations of restaurants. We remember waiting for certain fruits and vegetables to be in season. Now everything is always available. When it's winter here, it's summer in New Zealand, after all. Yet we often feel deprived. Strawberries lose their flavor when you can have them all the time. More food choices and more diversity certainly aren't a bad thing, but they come at a cost. The exotic quickly becomes commonplace and boring, requiring ever newer and more expensive menus.

Eating out used to be a special occasion. Now we spend more money on restaurant food than on the food we cook ourselves. Swelling expectations. Swelling stomachs too, but that's another symptom.

INVENTION IS THE MOTHER OF NECESSITY

Consider, also, the kinds of goods that were deemed luxuries as recently as 1970 but are now found in well over half of US homes and thought of by a majority of Americans as necessities: dishwashers, clothes dryers, central heating and air conditioning, color and cable TV. Back in 1970, there were no microwave ovens, DVDs, cell phones, smartphones, fax machines, iPads, iPods, leaf blowers, Xboxes, or personal computers. Now, more than half of us take all of these goods for granted and would feel deprived without most of them. In the past ten years, the cost of using cell phones has more than doubled the amount that Americans spend on phone service. It takes a lot of energy to run all this stuff.

There always seems to be a "better" model that we've just got to have. Writing in 2000 about Compaq's then-new iPaq 3600 Pocket PC, *Seattle Times* technology reporter Paul Andrews warned that the iPaq, with its "sleek Porsche-like case and striking color screen," cost $500 more than an ordinary PalmPilot. "But without the color display, music, and photos of the iPaq, life seems pretty dull," he lamented.[13] Now, the iPaq is mostly forgotten, replaced by new "gotta have it" devices.

With the newest smartphones, we may never have to be patient again, except when they aren't loading properly, writes *Seattle Times* columnist Monica Guzman, in an article that is hopefully somewhat tongue-in-cheek.

> Smart phones are making things like long lines and late appointments more bearable. When I have to wait, though, even I'm surprised by how irritating it feels. Like during takeoff and landing. "Put away and stow all electronic devices." ... Beautiful views are just out the window, but I can't do exactly what I want to be doing.... No wait is too small for a smart phone to vanquish. When I work from home, the phone is never far. It's there, ready to go, when I need to not wait for food to warm up in the microwave or for the Keurig to pour a cup of tea.[14]

We expect the information to come faster and faster with each new device, and we grow anxious when it doesn't, another feverish expectation. In such a world, nature's pace becomes unbearable, "irritating," and worst of all, "boring."

We drive twice as much per capita as we did a half century ago and fly more than twenty-five times as much.[15] Middle-income Americans seldom ventured more than a few hundred miles from home then, even during two-week summer vacations. Now, many of us (not just the rich) expect to spend occasional long weekends in Puerto Vallarta or (in the case of New Yorkers) Paris. Everywhere, humble motels have been replaced by elegant "inns," humble resorts by Club Meds. Now, "I need a vacation" means I need to change continents for a few days.

THE CHANGING JONESES

It may be fear rather than greed that primarily drives our swelling expectations. Fear of not succeeding in the eyes of others. In one magazine ad from the '50s, readers are encouraged to "keep up with the Joneses" by driving what the Joneses were driving: a Chevy. A Chevy sedan at that, not even a Corvette. Just about the cheapest car around even then.

But the mythical Joneses don't drive Chevrolets anymore. And they're no longer your next-door neighbors either, folks who make roughly what you do. The economist Juliet Schor studied people's attitudes about consumption in a large corporation and found that most Americans now compare themselves with coworkers or television characters when they think about what they "need."

But corporations have become increasingly stratified economically in recent years. One frequently comes into contact with colleagues who are much better paid than oneself. Their cars, clothes, and travel plans reflect their higher incomes, yet set the standard for everyone else in the firm.

Likewise, says Schor, "TV shows a very inflated standard of living relative to what the true standard of living of the American public is. People on television tend to be upper-middle class or even rich, and people who watch a lot of TV have highly inflated views of what the average American has. For example, people who are heavy TV watchers vastly exaggerate the number of Americans with swimming pools, tennis courts, maids, and planes, and their own expectations of what they should have also become inflated, so they tend to spend more and save less."[16]

Schor says that as the gap between rich and poor grew during the 1980s, people with relatively high incomes began to feel deprived in comparison to those who were suddenly making even more. "They started to feel 'poor on $100,000 a year' as the well-known phrase puts it, because they were comparing themselves to the Donald Trumps and the other newly wealthy." It happened all the way down the income line, Schor says. "Everybody felt worse compared to the role models, those at the top."

Until the recent economic crisis began, Americans' feverish expectations had been reducing our personal savings rate steadily since the 1980s, from roughly 11 percent in 1982 to 1.5 percent in 2005. By contrast, the Princeton historian Sheldon Goran *(Beyond Our Means: Why*

America Spends While the World Saves), points out that savings rates in Germany, Italy, France, and some other western European nations have continued to exceed 10 percent, with the notable exception of the United Kingdom, where the savings rate has actually been negative.[17] Curiously, conservatives have often claimed that a strong social safety net would discourage savings because people would feel they didn't need to prepare for old age or emergencies. But in fact, a strong safety net, including free health care and education, seems to encourage savings, providing needed services at lower cost than the private marketplace.

THE EXAMPLE NOT TO FOLLOW: US

The Italian economist Stefano Bartolini calls the United States "the example not to follow."[18] He suggests that the American model of high spending and skimpy safety nets encourages greater consumption—and therefore longer work hours (see chapter 3). The pressures of work and consumption create stress and leave people little time for each other, increasing loneliness and unhappiness while at the same time creating a less inviting or sustainable natural and built common environment. We then try to restore social connections and environmental quality through private purchases. (Lonely? Buy a new car, and you will attract others. Living in an ugly world of strip malls? Visit a tropical paradise for a few days.) And so we spend more. It's the vicious cycle that affluenza encourages.

THE ADDICTIVE VIRUS

You suspect you may be a coffee addict when you're so hyped up that you start answering the front door *before* the doorbell rings! But when you can't resist buying a coffee mug with a picture of a coffee mug on it, it's official. You're hooked. For you and at least thirty-five million other javaholics (four to five cups a day), coffee is life; the rest is only waiting.

But coffee's not the worst of our addictions, not by a long shot. Fourteen million Americans use illegal drugs, twelve million Americans are heavy drinkers, and sixty million are hooked on tobacco. Five million Americans can't stop gambling away their income and savings. And at least ten million can't stop buying more and more stuff—an addiction that in the long run may be the most destructive of all.[19]

Lianne, a department store publicist in New York City, is a problem shopper. Every year, she uses her employee discount to rack up more than $20,000 in clothing and accessories. She finally suspected she might be addicted when she broke up with her boyfriend and moved her stuff out of his apartment. "Some women tend to shop a lot because they live out of two apartments, theirs and their boyfriend's," she explains. "You never look at your wardrobe as one wardrobe. But when I saw how many things I had that were identical, I began to see that maybe I did have a problem."[20]

Addiction to stuff is not easily understood. It's a bubbling cauldron of such emotional states as anxiety, loneliness, and low self-esteem. "I'd like to think I shop because I don't want to look like everybody else," Lianne confides anonymously, "but the real reason is because I don't want to look like myself. It's easier to buy something new and feel good about yourself than it is to change yourself."

Addicts need to go back for more in order to feel good again. The addictive substance or activity takes away the emotional discomfort of everyday life and also releases the built-up tensions of craving. The goal is to get back to a place of perceived power and carefree abandonment. The drinker suddenly becomes loose and uninhibited, certain he's the funniest man in the world. The gambler feels the elation of risk and possibility—putting it all on the line so Lady Luck can find him. The addicted shopper seeks the high she felt a few days earlier, when she bought a dress she still hasn't taken out of the box.

According to professor Ronald Faber, who has studied American advertising, compulsive buyers often report feeling heightened sensations when they shop. Colors and textures are more intense, and extreme levels of focus and concentration are often achieved—literally, altered states of consciousness. Some extreme shoppers compare their highs to drug experiences, while others have compared the moment of purchase to an orgasm.[21]

"I'm addicted to the smell of suede, the smooth texture of silk, and the rustle of tissue paper," admits one shopping addict. She also loves the captive attention she commands when she shops. And because her credit card is always ready for use, she can shop whenever she wants. Now, that's power.

NEVER ENOUGH

The thrill of shopping is only one aspect of the addiction to stuff. Many Americans are also hooked on building personal fortresses out of their purchases. Whether it's a new set of golf clubs or a walk-in closet full of sweaters and shoes, having the right stuff and sending the right signal somehow reassures addictive buyers. The problem is that the world's signals keep changing, so addicts never reach a point of having enough. The computer never has enough memory or virus protection and is never as fast as everyone else's. The SUV doesn't have a satellite-linked Global Positioning System, so how do we know where we are? The phone system is obsolete without Internet access, image messaging, and call waiting; the refrigerator doesn't dispense ice cubes, filter water, or have push-button, movable shelves (some even have flat-screen TVs on the door); and the big-screen TV is a good six feet narrower than the living room wall. Glaring deficiencies like these become unacceptable when affluenza sets in.

Economists call it the law of diminishing marginal utility, jargon that simply means we have to run faster just to stay in place. As the social psychologist David Myers phrases it, "The second piece of pie, or the second $100,000, never tastes as good as the first."[22]

Yet, despite diminishing returns that are plain to see, affluenza victims get stuck in the *more* mode, not knowing when or how to stop. If eating pie fails to satisfy, we think we need *more* pie to become satisfied. At this point, the affluenza virus has become an addiction. "Consuming becomes pathological because its importance grows larger and larger in direct proportion to our decreasing satisfaction," says the economist Herman Daly.

In terms of the social factors that trigger the addictive virus, our thanks go first to the pushers on the supply side. For example, when the highways to which we are addicted become clogged, dealers push *more* highways, which very soon become clogged as well. When we get used to a certain level of sexually explicit advertising, the pushers push it a step further, and then further, until preteens pose suggestively on network TV ads in their underwear.

It's the same in restaurants, fast-food outlets, and movie theaters, where portions get bigger, and then get huge. Plates of food become platters, Biggie Burgers become Dino Burgers, and boxes of popcorn become buckets. What's next, barrels requiring hand trucks? Our stomachs expand to accommodate the larger portions, which we soon regard as normal (sixty-four-ounce soft drinks and 1,400-calorie Monster burgers, normal?!).

Sometimes more and bigger are not enough. When we can't maintain our consumer highs with familiar products and activities, we search for new highs. Sports become extreme sports or fantasy sports in which thrill seekers bungee jump off skyscrapers or gamble in Internet fantasy sports leagues. Even real professional athletes, with fantasy salaries, can never get enough. When a bright young baseball prospect signs for $25 million a year, a veteran who makes only $12 million suddenly feels dissatisfied. This is the plight of the affluenza addict: even too much is not enough.

SHOPPING TO FILL THE VOID

Similarities among addictions are alarming. When the pathological becomes normal, an addict will do whatever is necessary to maintain the habit. Gamblers and overspenders alike bounce checks, borrow from friends, and go deep in debt to support their habit, often lying to loved ones about their actions. It's not hard to see the connection between addictive behavior and the huge craters in our culture and environment. Just as gamblers sell family heirlooms to continue gambling, so do addicted consumers sacrifice priceless natural areas, contentment, and tradition to maintain a steady stream of goods.

Psychologists tell us that pathological buying is typically related to a quest for greater recognition and acceptance, an expression of anger, or an escape through fantasy—all connected to shaky self-images. Writes Faber,

> One compulsive buyer bought predominantly expensive stereo and television equipment but demonstrated little interest when discussing the types of music or programs he liked. Eventually, it came out that his motivation for buying came mainly from the fact that neighbors recognized him as an expert in electronic equipment and came to him for advice when making their purchases.[23]

Faber reports that anger is often encoded in pathological buying. Debt becomes a mechanism for getting back at one's spouse or parent. Or in other cases, extreme shopping is a fleeting getaway from reality:

> Buying provides a way of escaping into a fantasy where the individual can be seen as important and respected. Some people indicated that the possession and use of a charge card made them feel powerful; others

found that the attention provided by sales personnel and being known by name at exclusive stores provided feelings of importance and status.[24]

In the years just after World War II the super-rich sought to conceal their profligacy, but since Ronald Reagan's first inaugural ball many have begun to flaunt it again. As the economist Robert Frank points out, there's been a rush on $15,000 purses, $10,000 watches, even $65 million private jets. Twenty million Americans now own big-screen TVs costing at least $2,000 each. Some buy their children $5,000 life-size reproductions of Darth Vader and $18,000 replicas of Range Rovers, $25,000 birthday parties and million-dollar bar mitzvahs. Yachts the size of mansions burst their berths in many a marina.[25]

Thus, from the hot zones of popular culture and stratified workplaces, our new Joneses—consciously or otherwise—spread the affluenza fever, swelling our expectations as never before. And stuffing us up.

CHAPTER 2

All Stuffed Up

> *A house is just a pile of stuff with a cover on it.*
>
> —GEORGE CARLIN

We're all stuffed up, literally! In our homes, workplaces, and streets, chronic congestion has settled into our daily lives—cultural clutter that demands constant maintenance, sorting, displaying, and replacement. For example, as affluenza infected the 1970s, the two-car garage became a standard feature of American homes, partly because all the newly acquired stuff wouldn't fit even into the expanding houses. By the late '80s many homes were being built with three-car garages—600 to 900 square feet of garage space alone. "That's almost as much square footage as an entire family lived in, in the early fifties," says the real estate agent La Nita Wacker. She takes us by a huge home with a four-car garage. Expensive cars and a boat are parked outside. The owner comes out wondering why La Nita is so interested in his place. "I own Dream House Realty," Wacker replies, "and yours is a dream house."[1]

"It was built to the specifications of my charming wife," the homeowner says with a laugh. "So why four garages?" asks La Nita. "It's probably because of storage," the man replies, explaining that the garages are filled with family possessions. "You never have enough storage, so you can never have enough garages," he adds cheerfully. La Nita asks if he has children. "They're gone now," he replies. "It's just me and the wife."

When Hurricane Sandy struck the East Coast in 2012, it exposed another dark symptom of affluenza. As fire and emergency support workers inspected the damage, they occasionally found households that resembled landfills occupied by hoarders. They found unopened soup cans fifteen and twenty years past their expiration date, and residents who couldn't remember how many dining room chairs lay hidden under bulging piles on the table. Hoarding, a psychiatric diagnosis in medical manuals, affects an estimated one in twenty Americans. "Compulsive savers often have difficulties in their personal relationships because of their excess stuff," says recovered hoarder Beth Johnson, who now operates the Clutter Workshop in West Hartford, Connecticut. She adds, "Interestingly, many 'savers' are creative, successful people in their exterior lives."[2]

Maybe we should feel lucky to have so many "halfway houses" available in a pinch if we just can't part with that record collection or file cabinet (with who knows what inside). With 2.3 billion square feet of self-storage space in the United States, every American could fit under the metal-roofed canopy of the U-Stuff-It universe. One in ten Americans currently rents space at a self-storage facility. Need affordable office space? Some facilities offer storage units complete with telephone service and Internet access. At other facilities, some low-income people actually live in their storage units—a stark illustration of how affluenza leaves so many behind.[3]

The question is, Do we have stuff, or does it have us? In a world filled with clutter, we too easily become overwhelmed, lose our way, and get swept along in a current that sweeps us to the mall or dot-com sites for more stuff, or to the car dealership for a new car, "nothing down."

CAR CLUTTER

Denver resident Alex Piersall, like many other Americans, could take his two midsize SUVs to the jagged peak of the mountain, as in the TV ads, but not into his own garage. Neither vehicle would fit in the fifty-year-old brick garage, so he ripped it down and built one suitable for a new millennium. Some of his neighbors in Denver's solid Washington Park haven't gotten around to that yet. Driving past the vintage neighborhood's homes, you see lots of expensive Escalades and Navigators grazing at curbside, desperate for exercise. But in a clogged-up metropolitan area like Denver, they aren't likely to get much.

What happened? America used to be a place where both a pizza delivery person and an ambulance driver could arrive before it was too late. In our brave new world of clutter, both are trapped in traffic. (Rule of thumb, circa 2014: The shortest distance between two points is always under construction.) In a South American short story, traffic is so hopeless that drivers abandon their cars and start foraging for food in neighboring villages. Eventually they start growing crops by the roadside. A baby is conceived and born before traffic begins to move again. While congestion hasn't yet reached quite that level in the United States (or South America), it may not be a bad idea to put a few packages of seeds in the glove compartment, just in case.

Get SATISFIED

Satis-fiction

METRO FOLLIES

The mother of all traffic jams is in Los Angeles, where Interstate 5 crosses highways 10, 60, and 101. More than half a million vehicles logjam through this stretch daily—not a pretty sight. According to the Texas A&M Transportation Institute, Los Angeles residents spend sixty-one hours a year stuck in traffic, compared with a national average of thirty-eight hours for other urban drivers. LA drivers waste twenty-seven gallons of gas per capita annually owing to congestion, and they're forced to breathe marginal air and listen to fast-talking traffic reports even though they're moving in slow motion.[4]

When it comes to traffic jams, we're all in it together, but some traffic engineers think only they hold the key to getting us back out. Rather than opting to reorganize our communities so less travel is necessary, the engineers are still road crazy after all these years. Having already paved over two-thirds of Los Angeles, their sights are set on places like Saint Louis, Tucson, and Colorado Springs.

With the highways clogged up, drivers increasingly "jump ship" into a neighborhood, cutting down alleyways and across vacant lots like Steve Martin's character in the movie *L.A. Story*. However, mechanical engineers think they have a more pragmatic, high-tech solution: "autonomous," or "self-driving," vehicles. At a recent conference sponsored by the *New York Times*, eggheads from Toyota, Google, Cisco, Stanford University, the California legislature, and the National Traffic Safety Administration discussed the imminent potential for cars to drive themselves, with humans as passengers.[5] "We used to think of the smartphone as a distraction while driving, but within ten years, the distraction may be an occasional interaction with our car," said one of them. (Think of the profits that are waiting for these companies and others if they convince us that autonomous cars are safer, more efficient, and mentally healthier.) They reported that in 2013, six million vehicles were already equipped with robotic intelligence for crash avoidance, automatic braking, parallel parking, and advanced navigation. The next step is cars that can drop you off at your destination, refuel, and neatly park themselves in stacked lots. Writes another proponent, "Once traveling in automated mode, the driver could relax until the turnoff. At this point, the system would need to check whether the driver could retake control, and take appropriate action if the driver were asleep, sick, or even dead." It's comforting to know that we may reach a destination even if we're DOA, but really, in a near-future world cluttered with misdirected robots bumping into each other on every street and every sector of our world, what's left to live for?

STUFF WARS AT THE AIRPORT

If American homes crammed with stuff are the metaphorical equivalent of congestion in the lungs, and highways are the plugged arteries, air travel must be the sneeze that propels affluenza carriers (that's us) through the air. Despite brief dips after 9/11 and during the early years of the Great Recession, total air travel continues to rise in the United States, from 295 million passengers in 1980 to 730 million in 2012.[6] But with increased security, higher baggage fees, and fewer snacks, some of the thrill is gone. The airlines' strategy is "More people, less stuff": cram in passengers with as little carry-on luggage as possible to reduce fuel costs. They didn't count on Americans gaining an average of twenty pounds since 1990, though, which has added an extra half a billion dollars in fuel costs since then. (Some airlines are beginning to charge by weight of both passenger and luggage.) Meanwhile, passengers have a different agenda—to keep their stuff with them so they don't have to wait for it at the baggage claim and can access laptop, cell phone, cosmetics, and emergency rations.

TRAINED TO BE ROBOTS

Did we Americans *choose* this consumptive way of life, or were we corralled into it with drumbeats of patriotism, social engineering, and economic fundamentalism? You already know what we think: that overconsumption has become the dominant trait of our culture. We Americans in particular try to meet individual needs like identity, expression, creativity, and belonging by owning and displaying our stuff. To find a mate, get a job, or be included in a certain circle of friends, we are expected to buy or have access to specific consumer goods—clothes, laptop computer, stylish car, magazines...

As Dave noted in the *The New Normal,* the individual is largely powerless to resist giving gifts during the holiday season. If his kids want to play sports at school, he and his partner need to buy the required equipment and also consume many tanks of gasoline to get the kids to practices and games. To avoid buying batteries, he may prefer to have a durable windup watch and alarm clock, but they aren't available anymore. Though he is skillful at repairing things, he has trouble getting into the workings of the typical appliance when it gets sick—after all, manufacturers and retailers want to sell *new* products.

It's not just advertising and public relations that stimulate consumption; it's our friends, our workplaces, and our policies. For example, since streets and traffic signals are paid for out of a city's general funds, residents pay for them (through sales taxes and property taxes) even if they bicycle or take public transit and use only one-tenth as much street space. It's the same theme with "free" parking. Even if we don't drive because we are too young, too old, too poor, or disabled, we still foot the bill because employers, property sellers, and businesses build the costs of mandated parking capacity into wages, mortgages, and price tags.

ANALYZING THE AMERICAN DREAM: WHERE THE CLUTTER COMES FROM

America's 114 million households—the authors' among them—contain and consume more stuff than all other households throughout history, put together. Behind closed doors, we churn through manufactured goods and piped-in entertainment as if life were a stuff-eating contest. Despite tangible indications of indigestion, we keep consuming, partly because we're convinced it's normal. Writes the columnist Ellen Goodman, "Normal is getting dressed in clothes that you buy for work, driving through traffic in a car that you are still paying for, in order to get to the job that you need so you can pay for the clothes, car and the house that you leave empty all day in order to afford to live in it."[7]

As in a monster movie, more stuff begins to take shape as we sit daydreaming about the perfect living room, the perfect body, or the neighborhood's sexiest lawn mower. Daydreams like these all require a steady stream of products that need to be hunted and gathered. On the vacation after next, maybe we'll hit the ski slopes in Colorado or hike in northern Italy, but before then we'll need to acquire some expensive equipment. In the book *High Tech/High Touch*, John Naisbitt and his coauthors describe some of the items necessary for "adventure" travel. "High-tech gear is available for every conceivable need, for every conceivable journey: digitally perfect-fit hiking boots, helmets with twenty-seven air vents, hydration packs, portable water purifiers, bike shorts with rubberized back-spray-repelling seats...."[8]

CHAPTER 3

Stressed to kill

We are a nation that shouts at a microwave oven to hurry up.
—JOAN RYAN, *San Francisco Chronicle*

"Affluenza is a major disease, there's no question about it," says Dr. Richard Swenson of Menomonie, Wisconsin, who practiced medicine for many years before changing his focus to writing and lecturing. Even in 1996, when John interviewed him for the Affluenza documentary, he was finding too many of his patients stretched to their limits and beyond, with no margin, no room in their lives for rest, relaxation, and reflection. They showed symptoms of acute stress.

POSSESSION OVERLOAD

Swenson observed that many of his patients suffered from what he calls possession overload, the problem of dealing with too much stuff. "Possession overload is the kind of problem where you have so many things, you find your life is being taken up by maintaining and caring for things instead of people," Swenson says. "Everything I own owns me. People feel sad, and what do they do? They go to the mall and they shop, and it makes them feel better, but only for a short time. There's an addictive quality in consumerism. But it simply doesn't work. They've gotten all these things, and they still find this emptiness, this hollowness. All they have is stress and exhaustion and burnout, and their relationships are vaporizing. They're surrounded by all kinds of fun toys, but the meaning is gone."

"Tragedy," observes Swenson, "is wanting something badly, getting it, and finding it empty. And I think that's what's happened."

The travel writer Rick Steves agrees. He spends a hundred days or so in Europe each year and notices a far more relaxed, less consumptive attitude toward life in contrast to that of the United States. "To me, it seems Americans have lost track of what life is about because we're pressured to constantly be growing, always more," Steves told John earlier this year. "It's like the hamster was going as fast as he could five years ago, and every year he's got to go faster. We need to get smart about what really matters—the well-being of our seniors, the health of our environment, the shaping of our children, the freedom to enjoy our lives without always having to pay for our financial well-being and constantly growing."

TIME FAMINE

American greetings over the past two decades have changed. Remember how, when you used to say "How are you?" to the friends you ran into at work or on the street, they'd reply, "Fine, and you?" Now, when we ask that question, the answer is often "Busy, and you?" (when they have time to say, "and you?"). "Me too," we admit. We used to talk of having time to smell the flowers. Now we barely find time to smell the coffee. "The pace of life has accelerated to the point where everyone is breathless," says Swenson. "You look at all the countries that have the most prosperity, and they're the same countries that have the most stress."

Tried to make a dinner date with a friend recently? Chances are the two of you have to look a month ahead in your appointment calendars. Even children carry them. Ask your coworkers what they'd like more of in their lives, and odds are they'll say "time." "This is an issue that cuts across race lines, class lines, and gender lines," says the African American novelist Barbara Neely. "Nobody has any time out there." We're all like the bespectacled bunny in Disney's *Alice in Wonderland*, who keeps looking at his watch and muttering, "No time to say hello, goodbye, I'm late! I'm late! I'm late!"

By the early 1990s, trend spotters were warning that a specter was haunting America: time famine. Advertisers noted that "time will be the luxury of the 1990s." A series of clever TV spots for US West showed time-pressed citizens trying to "buy time" at a bank called

Time R Us or in bargain basements. One store offered customers "the greatest sale of all TIME." A weary woman asked where she could buy "quality time." "Now you CAN buy time," the ads promised. "Extra *working* time with mobile phone service from US West."

More working time. Hmm.

We thought the opposite was supposed to be true: that advances in technology, automation, cybernetics, were supposed to give us more leisure time and *less* working time. We remember how all those futurists were predicting that by the end of the twentieth century we'd have more leisure time than we'd know what to do with? In 1965, a US Senate subcommittee heard testimony that estimated the workweek would run between fourteen and twenty-two hours by the year 2000.[1]

We got the technology, but we didn't get the time. We have computers, fax machines, cell phones, e-mail, robots, express mail, freeways, jetliners, microwaves, fast food, one-hour photos, digital cameras, frozen waffles, instant this, and instant that. But we have *less* free time than we did thirty years ago. And about those mobile phones: They do give you "extra working time" while driving but make you as likely to cause an accident as someone who's legally drunk. Progress? And then there are those leaf blowers...

Patience may be the ultimate victim of our hurried lives. David Shenk, the author of *The End of Patience*, says that such things as the speed of the Internet, e-mail, and on-line shopping mean that "we're packing more into our lives and losing patience in the process. We've managed to compress time to such an extent that we're now painfully aware of every second that we wait for anything." The elevators of a large Northeast hotel chain have Internet news monitors, and you can pedal and surf the Net at the same time at many fitness centers. Gas stations are considering putting in TV monitors on the islands to keep you amused while you're pumping.

THE HARRIED LEISURE CLASS

We should have paid attention to Staffan Linder. In 1970, the Swedish economist warned that all those predictions about more free time were a myth, that we'd soon be a "harried leisure class" starved for time. "Economic growth," wrote Linder, "entails a general increase in the scarcity of time." He continued, "As the volume of consumption goods increases, requirements for the care and maintenance of these goods also tends to increase, we get bigger houses to clean, a car to wash, a boat to put up for the winter, a television set to repair, and have to make more decisions on spending."[2]

It's as simple as this: increased susceptibility to affluenza means increasing headaches from time pressure.

Shopping itself, Linder pointed out, "is a very time-consuming activity." Indeed, on average, Americans now spend nearly three times as much time shopping as they do playing, talking, or reading with their kids. Even our celebrated freedom of choice only adds to the problem.

The psychologist Barry Schwartz, in his book *The Paradox of Choice*, warns that so many choices increase our anxiety and are likely to leave us less happy. He points out that many of us are regularly troubled by the sense that we may have made the wrong choice, that there was a better product or a lower price out there.

So many choices. So little time. Linder said this would happen, and he warned that when choices become overwhelming, "the emphasis in advertising will be placed on ersatz information," because "brand loyalty must be built up among people who have no possibility of deciding how to act on objective grounds." Ergo, if you're a marketer, hire a battery of psychologists to study which box colors are most associated by shoppers with pleasurable sex. Or something like that.

OVERWORKED AMERICANS

Linder argued that past a certain point, time pressure would increase with growing productivity. But he wasn't sure whether working hours would rise or fall. He certainly doubted they'd fall as much as the automation cheerleaders predicted. He was right. In fact, there seems to be some pretty strong evidence that Americans are working more than they did a generation ago.

Using Labor Department statistics, the Harvard economist Juliet Schor found that on average, American workers were toiling 160 hours—four full workweeks—*more* in 1991 than they did in 1969. "It's not only the people in the higher-income groups—who, by the way, have been working much longer hours," Schor said. "It's also the middle classes, the lower classes, and the poor. Everybody is working longer hours."[3] Indeed, according to the International Labor Organization, in October 1999 the United States passed Japan as the modern industrial country with the longest working hours. Forty-two percent of American workers say they feel "used up" by the end of the workday.

Sixty-nine percent say they'd like to slow down and live a more relaxed life.[4]

According to a 2013 Pew survey, more than half of all American mothers and fathers say they find it difficult to manage family and work responsibilities, and more than a third say they "always feel rushed." There are ironies to all of this. The same poll found that while mothers who work the fewest hours are the happiest, more mothers than ever before say they'd rather work full time.[5] Some of this irony results from the excessive material expectations of our affluenza-inflicted society, but much more seems to be the result of the increasing gap between rich and poor in America. For the median worker, jobs today pay less than they once did. Keeping up with the Joneses is far harder when moms work only part time. Where it used to take one full-time wage earner to support a four-member family in the 1960s at the median standard of living, it now takes two wage earners to support three people. We have managed to keep pace with new consumer expectations, but only by working longer and harder and, in many cases, going deep into debt, requiring even more work and stress to get back above water.

NO TIME TO CARE

Moreover, as Schor said, "The pace of work has increased quite dramatically. We are working much faster today than we were in the past.

And that contributes to our sense of being overworked and frenzied and harried and stressed out and burned out by our jobs." In the digital world, everybody wants that report yesterday.

Patience is so "yesterday." It wears thin rapidly when we get used to a new generation of computers. Karen Nussbaum, former director of the Women's Bureau at the Department of Labor, pointed out twenty years ago that "twenty-six million Americans are monitored by the machines they work on, and that number is growing. I had one woman tell me her computer would flash off and on: YOU'RE NOT WORKING AS FAST AS THE PERSON NEXT TO YOU!" Doesn't just thinking about that make your blood pressure rise?[6]

Americans are feeling this big-time. A 2013 Harris Interactive Poll found that 83 percent of American workers say they are stressed out on the job. Seventy-five percent of workers report physical symptoms of stress, and workplace stress costs our economy more than $300 billion a year.[7]

Meanwhile, we have less time to recuperate from the work frenzy. A survey by Expedia found that Americans gave back an average of three vacation days to their employers in 2003, a gift to corporations of $20 billion. By 2011, the gift had risen to four days per worker and $67 billion. Only 38 percent of American workers use all their vacation days, and 72 percent say they regularly check in with the office and do work while on holiday.[8] As for their reason for doing so, most said they didn't want to be seen as slackers when the next round of layoffs came. Others said they simply couldn't take time off and keep up with the demands of their job.

NO-VACATION NATION

Of course, that's when they get vacations at all. A new report from the Center for Economic and Policy Research called "No-Vacation Nation" makes it clear that at least a quarter of American workers receive no paid vacation time at all. A 2008 poll by the Opinion Research Corporation found that the *median* vacation time taken by Americans was a little over a week, while a study by Jody Heymann and Alison Earle of Canada's McGill University found that the United States was one of only five nations in the world with no legal guarantee of paid vacation time. The others? Suriname, Guyana, Nepal, and that paragon of human rights, Burma. That's it.[9]

Dr. Sarah Speck, who runs the Cardio-Vascular Wellness Program at Seattle's Swedish Hospital, reminds us that vacations are an essential break from stress, which she calls "the new tobacco." One of her presentations shows how our cardiovascular system looks under stress and how it looks after a life of smoking; you can't tell the difference.

"Stress is ubiquitous." says Speck. "It can do great harm to us. The way we work is all out.

We basically work too much, and we have too many demands on our time. Stress causes us to constrict our blood vessels just like nicotine and tobacco does. It is as important in developing heart disease as having uncontrolled blood pressure or being medically obese; that's the biochemical power of being overworked and overburdened and feeling stressed."

Speck points out that "men who don't take vacations are 30 percent more likely to have a heart attack than men who do take vacations," and for women the number is even higher, at 50 percent.[10] A study done by Wisconsin's Marshfield Clinic also found that women who don't take regular vacations are far more likely to suffer from depression—up to eight times as likely in fact.[11]

All of this takes a physical toll that is far higher than that generated by stress in other rich countries less afflicted by affluenza. "We don't spend enough time on our health portfolios. We spend too much time on our financial portfolios," says Speck. "We've got to have our replenishing time. So what I'm now seeing is instead of people having heart attacks in their sixties and seventies, like when I first became a cardiologist, I'm now seeing it in their forties and fifties."

A cheerful woman with a wry sense of humor, Speck has some advice for patients: slow down and stop chasing the chimera of more stuff. "I have patients that come in and tell me they can't get control of their stress, that they're not sleeping, that they don't know what to do, and I tell them, 'Take two weeks and call me in the morning.'"

But many Americans can't do that; they don't even get two weeks. So in 2009, Representative Alan Grayson of Florida introduced a bill in Congress that would have guaranteed a modest vacation—one to two weeks—for American workers. It would have been seen as laughably weak in most countries, but here in America where stuff is prized and time is not, it was viewed almost as a threat to Western civilization itself, at least our version of it. One of us, John, joined Grayson in a press conference supporting the bill. John was accused on Fox News of wanting to turn America into a land of slackers and (OMG!), a "twenty-first century France!" Perhaps the bill would have forced Americans to appreciate good food and wine. It never got out of committee. Grayson reintroduced the bill in 2013, but its prospects seemed even bleaker since the Republicans, who won control of the House of Representatives in 2010, opposed any mandates for business. They forget that it was a conservative Republican president, William Howard Taft, who, a hundred years ago, suggested that American workers should get two or three *months* off each year to improve their health, productivity, and family bonds.[12]

WHAT DO WE DO WITH PROGRESS?

Juliet Schor reminds us that the United States has seen more than a doubling of productivity since World War II. "So the issue is: What do we do with that progress? We could cut back on working hours. We could produce the old amount in half as much time and take half the time off. Or we could work just as much and produce twice as much." And, says Schor, "we've put all our economic progress into producing more things. Our consumption has doubled, and working hours have not fallen at all. In fact, working hours have risen."[13]

Europeans made a different decision. In 1970, worker productivity per hour in the countries that make up the European Union was 65 percent that of Americans. Their GDP per capita was about 70 percent of ours because they worked longer than we did back then. By 2005, EU productivity stood at 91 percent of ours, and several European economies were more productive per worker-hour than we are. But real per capita GDP in those countries is still only about 72 percent that of the United States. They have a lot less stuff than we do. So what happened? It's simple: The Europeans traded a good part of their productivity gains for time instead of money. So instead of working more than we do, they now work much less—nearly nine weeks less per year.

As a result, they live longer and are healthier, despite spending far, far less per capita on health care. In fact, the United States is stressed to kill. We rank dead last (or "dead first" as the physician Stephen Bezruchka puts it) in health among rich nations, with the shortest life expectancy, and we are now expected to spend 19 percent of our total GDP on health care by the year 2014.[14] Can you say "Mr. Yuk"?

Affluenza is certainly not the only cause of time stress in America, but it is a major cause. Swelling expectations lead to a constant effort to keep up with the latest products and compete in the consumption arena. That in turn, forces us to work more so we can afford the stuff. With so many things to buy, and the need to work harder to obtain them, our lives grow more harried and more pressured. As one activist put it, "If you win the rat race, you're still a rat," and you may be a dead one.

In recent years, many scientists have come to believe that viruses and other infections make us more susceptible to heart attacks. Their conclusions have come from studying influenza viruses. But they should look more closely at affluenza as well.

CHAPTER 4

Family fractures

Affluenza is a family problem. In a variety of ways, the disease is like a termite, undermining American family life, sometimes to the breaking point. We have already mentioned time pressures. Then, too, the pressure to keep up with the Joneses leads many families into debt and simmering conflicts over money matters that frequently result in divorce. Indeed, the American divorce rate, despite reaching a plateau in the 1980s and declining a bit since then, is still double what it was in the '50s, and family counselors report that arguments about money are precipitating factors in 90 percent of divorce cases.[1]

But modern life in the Age of Affluenza affects marriage in more complex ways, spelled out clearly by the psychiatrists Jacqueline Olds and Richard Schwartz in their book *The Lonely American*. Longer working hours and the demands of caring for stuff require that parents find something to cut in their frenetically busy lives. What goes is time spent with friends and community members. Parents spend more time with their children today than a generation ago, though much of it consists of chauffeuring their children from one event to another, as Dr. William Doherty points out.

Doherty, a family therapist and professor at the University of Minnesota, warns that today's kids are terribly overscheduled, as "market values have invaded the family." Parents often see family life as about instilling competitive values in their children so they can achieve the best résumés to get into the best colleges to get the best jobs to earn the most money. Meanwhile, even though parents sacrifice a lot of personal time, including time for each other, to be with their kids, Doherty says the number of families that regularly eat dinner together or take vacations together has dropped by at least a third since 1970.[2]

Olds and Schwartz argue that, much of the time, only one parent is spending time with a child, leaving children with less chance to see how couples can effectively manage a marriage. And a greater focus on their children leaves most parents with less time to be alone together. Olds and Schwartz write that "even the most loving of couples can start to feel slightly estranged when they use up all their leisure time pursuing child-centered activities."[3] But by the same token, expectations of marriage are higher now, with spouses more likely to make greater demands on each other.

Worn out by work and childcare, parents depend more on each other to satisfy emotional needs, often spending more time at home, a process futurist Faith Popcorn called cocooning. Much of this time is spent in front of the TV—long-work-hour countries like the United

States, Japan, and Korea have the highest rates of TV viewing; short-work-hour countries like the Netherlands and Norway have the least—because parents are more exhausted when they return home, and TV is the perfect activity for burned-out people since there is nothing to do but press the remote and be entertained.[4] But the more TV viewing, the more people are exposed to television advertising and the hot zones of affluenza. "Chief among the obstacles" to a good family life, write Olds and Schwartz, is "the frenetic pace of the twenty-first-century workplace, and the length of the workday and workweek. It deprives people of time for social lives and it drains them of the energy to make those lives happen."[5]

Olds and Schwartz say the time that gets squeezed in this arrangement is community time, which puts more strain on marriages. "Most couples now socialize less with family and friends and, consequently, receive less support from a wider social network," they point out. A leading authority on the history of American families, Stephanie Coontz, agrees, arguing that the expectations couples place on each other threatens the institution of marriage and our social fabric as a whole. Until the modern era, Coontz reminds us, "most societies agreed that it was dangerously antisocial, even pathologically self-absorbed, to elevate marital affection and nuclear family ties above commitments to neighbors, extended kin, civic duty and religion."[6]

While the American divorce rate has flattened in recent years, that is due in large part to fewer people being willing to make the commitment in the first place. Between 1950 and 2011, the marriage rate fell by two-thirds. In 2006, for the first time ever, more Americans households (50.3 percent) were headed by unmarried adults than married ones. Moreover, as Olds and Schwartz point out, more Americans are living alone than ever before. They suggest that this has led to elevated consumerism, as a single-occupancy household (unless part of a cohousing or other arrangement) must have its own set of appliances. This creates unintended environmental effects: single-person households use twice as many resources per capita as four-person households and 77 percent more energy per capita.[7]

But the trend toward solitary living has also resulted in an increase in loneliness. A Time magazine/AARP report in 2010 showed a near-doubling (from 20 to 35 percent) in the percentage of Americans over age forty-five that could be categorized as "chronically lonely" in the previous decade alone.[8] These loners often consume more, as defensive purchases to mask their loneliness (or of pills—more than 60 percent of the world's antidepressants are sold in the United States), but they are increasingly both unhappy and unhealthy.

Compared with other rich countries, the United States is a lousy place for families (with far fewer social supports), but perhaps it's even worse for children. A 2013 UNICEF study, "The Welfare of Children in Rich Countries," ranked the United States twenty-six out of twenty-nine nations surveyed, using criteria including child poverty, education levels, safety, risky behaviors, health, housing, and the environment.[9] Only Latvia, Lithuania, and Romania fared worse. The top countries were all in Europe, led by the Netherlands, which ranked number one in several categories, followed by Sweden and other Nordic countries. Dutch children also ranked themselves as happiest, with US children coming in twenty-third in their assessment of their lives. What Dutch moms and dads—also rated as the world's most satisfied parents—have is time for their kids and themselves. A majority work less than full time, yet their economic system allows them to live comfortably and securely, though more modestly than the average American.

We must concede that no system has been as effective as America's generally unfettered free market in delivering the most goods at the lowest prices to consumers (think Wal-Mart). And in the Age of Affluenza, such success has become the supreme measure of value. But human beings are more than consumers, more than stomachs craving to be filled. We are producers as well, looking to express ourselves through stable, meaningful work. We are members of families and communities, moral beings with an interest in fairness and justice, living organisms dependent on a healthy and beautiful environment. We are parents and children.

Our affluenza-driven quest for maximum consumer access undermines these other values. To produce goods at the lowest prices, we are willing to lay off thousands of workers and transfer their workplaces from country to country in search of cheap labor. We shatter the dreams of those workers who are discarded, and often shatter their families as well. The security of whole communities is considered expendable. Lives are disrupted without a second thought. And as we shall see, children are pitted against parents, undermining family life even further.

CHILDHOOD AFFLUENZA

In 1969, when John was twenty-three, he taught briefly at a Navajo Indian boarding school in Shiprock, New Mexico. His third-grade students were among the poorest children in America, possessing little more than the clothes on their backs. The school had few toys or other sources of entertainment. Yet John never heard the children say they were bored. They were continually making up their own games. And though racism and alcoholism would likely scar their lives a few years later, they were, at the age of ten, happy and well-adjusted children.

That Christmas, John went home to visit his family. He remembers the scene, a floor full of packages under the tree. His own ten-year-old brother opened a dozen or so of them, quickly moving from one to the next. A few days later, John found his brother and a friend watching TV, the Christmas toys tossed aside in his brother's bedroom. Both boys complained to John that they had nothing to do. "We're bored," they proclaimed. For John, it was a clear indication that children's happiness doesn't come from stuff. But powerful forces keep trying to convince America's parents that it does.

THE CHILDREN'S MARKETING EXPLOSION

Spending by—and influenced by—American children recently began growing a torrid 20 percent a year and is expected to reach $1 trillion annually in the next few years. In 1984, kids four to twelve spent about $4 billion of their own money. By 2005, they spent $35 billion. Marketing to children has become the hottest trend in the advertising world.[10]

"Corporations are recognizing that the consumer lifestyle starts younger and younger," explains Joan Chiaramonte, who does market research for the Roper Starch polling firm. "If you wait to reach children with your product until they're eighteen years of age, you probably won't capture them."[11]

From 1980 to 2004 the amount spent on children's advertising in America rose from $100 million to $15 billion a year, a staggering 15,000 percent! In her book, *Born to Buy*, Juliet Schor points out that children are now also used effectively by marketers to influence their parents' purchases of big-ticket items, from luxury automobiles to resort vacations and even homes. One hotel chain sends promotional brochures to children who've stayed at its hotels, so the kids will pester their parents into returning. Schor points out that many American kids recognize logos by the age of eighteen months and ask for brand-name products at the age of two. The average child gets about seventy toys a year. For the first time in human history, children are getting most of their information from entities whose goal is to sell them something rather than from family, school, or religious groups. The average twelve-year-old in the United States spends forty-eight hours a week exposed to commercial messages. Yet American children spend only about forty minutes per week in meaningful conversation with their parents and less than thirty minutes of unstructured time outdoors. Susan Linn, the author of *Consuming Kids*, writes, "Comparing the advertising of two or three decades ago to the commercialism that permeates our children's world is like comparing a BB gun to a smart bomb."[12]

Children under seven are especially vulnerable to marketing messages. Research shows that they are unable to distinguish commercial motives from benign or benevolent motives. One '70s study found that when asked who they would believe if their parents told them something was true and a TV character (even an animated one like Tony the Tiger) told them the opposite was true, most young children said they'd believe what the TV character told them. Both the American Psychological Association and the American Academy of Pediatrics say advertising targeting children is inherently deceptive.

What psychological, social, and cultural impacts are these trends having on children? A 1995 poll found that 95 percent of American adults worry that our children are becoming "too focused on buying and consuming things." Two-thirds say their own children measure their self-worth by their possessions and are "spoiled."[13]

VALUES IN CONFLICT

In Minneapolis, the psychologist David Walsh, author of *Selling Out America's Children*, teaches parents ways to protect their offspring from falling captive to commercialism. After years spent treating so-called problem children, Walsh worries that childhood affluenza is reaching epidemic levels. He sees a fundamental collision of values between children's needs and advertising.

"Market-created values of selfishness, instant gratification, perpetual discontentment, and constant consumption have become diametrically opposed to the values most Americans want to teach their children," says the grandfatherly Walsh, presenting his concerns with gentle passion.[14]

Today's children are exposed to far more TV advertising than their parents were. The average child sees nearly 40,000 commercials a year, about 110 a day. In 1984, deregulation of children's television by the Federal Trade Commission allowed TV shows and products to be marketed together as a package. Within a year, nine of the top ten best-selling toys were tied to TV shows.

But more importantly, perhaps, there's a big difference between today's ads and those of a generation ago. In the old ads, parents were portrayed as pillars of wisdom who both knew and wanted what was best for their children. Children, on the other hand, were full of wonder and innocence, and eager to please Mom and Dad. There was gender stereotyping—girls wanted dolls, and boys wanted cowboys and Indians—but rebelling against one's parents wasn't part of the message.

KIDS AS CATTLE

Now the message has changed. Marketers openly refer to parents as "gatekeepers," whose efforts to protect their children from commercial pressures must be circumvented so that those children, in the rather chilling terms used by the marketers, can be "captured, owned, and branded." At a 1996 marketing conference called Kid Power, held appropriately at Disney World, the keynote address, "Softening the Parental Veto," was presented by the marketing director of McDonald's.

Speaker after speaker revealed the strategy: Portray parents as fuddy-duddies who aren't smart enough to realize their children's need for the products being sold. It's a proven technique for neutralizing parental influence in the marketer-child relationship.

Presenters at Kid Power '96 further revealed how marketers now use children to design effective advertising campaigns. Kids are given cameras to photograph themselves and their friends to see how they dress and spend their time. They are observed at home, at school, in stores, and at public events. Their spending habits are carefully tracked. They are gathered into focus groups and asked to respond to commercials, separating the "cool" from the "uncool."

The "coolest" contemporary ads frequently carry the message delivered by Kid Power '96 speaker Paul Kurnit, a prominent marketing consultant, as seen in the *Affluenza* documentary. "Antisocial behavior in pursuit of a product is a good thing," Kurnit stated calmly, suggesting that advertisers could best reach children by encouraging rude, often aggressive behavior and faux rebellion against the strictures of family discipline. There is, some critics say, a serious danger in this: If rude, aggressive behavior becomes the norm for children as they emulate advertising models, to what level will children have to escalate their aggressive activities to really feel they are rebelling?

BETTER THAN STRAIGHT A'S

In the Age of Affluenza, voters demand tax cuts and reductions in public spending as their personal spending habits leave them with growing credit debt. Then, too, more and more affluent families are sending their children to private schools, further reducing voter support for public school systems.

As funding for education tightens, school boards all across America have turned to corporations for financial help. In exchange for cash, companies are allowed to advertise their products on school rooftops, hallways, readerboards, book covers, uniforms, and buses.

"Children in our society are seen as cash crops to be harvested," explains Alex Molnar, a professor of education at the University of Colorado who has been investigating commercialism in the schools for many years. Angry and passionate, Molnar readily displays his collection of "curriculum materials" created by corporations for use in the public schools.

In one, students find out about self-esteem by discussing "Good and Bad Hair Days" with materials provided by Revlon. In others, they learn to "wipe out that germ" with Lysol, and they study geothermal energy by eating "Gusher's Fruit Snacks" (the "teachers' guide" suggests that each student should get a gusher, bite into it, and compare the sensation to a volcanic eruption!). They also learn the history of Tootsie Rolls, make shoes for Nike as an environmental lesson, count Lay's potato chips in math class, and find out why the Exxon Valdez oil spill wasn't really harmful at all (materials courtesy of—you guessed it—Exxon) and why clear-cutting is beneficial—with a little help from Georgia-Pacific.

Fortunately, a parent-teacher backlash is emerging in a few communities. In late 2001, the Seattle School Board voted to create an anticommercial policy, but Molnar points out that today, many more states allowing advertising on the sides of school buses, a revenue generator first pioneered in Colorado Springs in the early 1990s.[15]

CAPTIVE KIDS

As affluenza becomes an airwave-borne childhood epidemic, America's children pay a high price. Not only does their lifestyle undermine our children's physical health, but their mental health seems to suffer too. Psychologists report constantly rising rates of teenage depression and thoughts about suicide, and a tripling of actual child suicide rates since the 1960s.[16]

Some of this stems from the overscheduling of children to prepare them for our adult world of consumerism, workaholism, and intense competition. This can reach truly ridiculous levels. Since the passage of the No Child Left Behind Act, nearly 20 percent of American school districts have banned recess for elementary school children. The idea, as one Tacoma, Washington, school administrator put it, is to "maximize instruction time to prepare the children to compete in the global economy." This is nuts. We're talking second graders here.

Kate Cashman, a humor columnist, wondered if we didn't have it backward. At a time of rising childhood obesity, we're getting rid of recess while inviting junk food into our schools. She suggested we reverse that—more recess, less junk food. She'd call her policy the "No Child Left with a Fat Behind Act." Sign us up to lobby in favor of the act. Let's try to get it passed in every state! It may sound silly, but it makes far more sense than most of the legislation that's out there these days.

What kind of values do our children learn from their exposure to affluenza? In a recent poll, 93 percent of teenage girls cited shopping as their favorite activity. Fewer than 5 percent listed "helping others." In 1967, two-thirds of American college students said "developing a meaningful philosophy of life" was very important to them, while fewer than one-third said the same about "making a lot of money." By 1997, those figures were reversed.[17] A 2004 poll at UCLA found that entering freshman ranked becoming "very well off financially" ahead of all other goals. Juliet Schor surveyed children aged ten to thirteen for their responses to the statement, "I want to make a lot of money when I grow up." Of those children, 63 percent agreed; only 7 percent thought otherwise.

Jacqueline Olds and Richard Schwartz point out that a questionnaire called the Narcissistic Personality Inventory finds a 30 percent increase in self-centeredness among students, with more than two-thirds now scoring above what the average was in 1982, when the survey began. "There is no other example in empirical psychology research of personality changing as rapidly and dramatically," they warn.[18] What does this bode for our future?

FAMILY VALUES OR MARKET VALUES?

Concerns about the impact of market values and affluenza on family life have come primarily from the liberal end of the American political spectrum. But some conservatives have also begun to look carefully at what they see as an inherent tension between market values and family values. Edward Luttwak, a former Reagan administration adviser and the author of the critically acclaimed book *Turbo-Capitalism*, expressed his concerns about the issue rather bluntly: "The contradiction between wanting rapid economic growth and dynamic economic change and at the same time wanting family values, community values, and stability is a contradiction so huge that it can only last because of an aggressive refusal to think about it."[19]

Calling himself "a real conservative, not a phony conservative," Luttwak says, "I want to conserve family, community, nature. Conservatism should not be about the market, about money.

It should be about conserving things, not burning them up in the name of greed."

Too often, he says, so-called conservatives make speeches lauding the unrestricted market (as the best mechanism for rapidly increasing America's wealth), while at the same time saying "we have to go back to old family values; we have to maintain communities." "It's a complete non sequitur, a complete contradiction; the two of course are completely in collision. It's the funniest after-dinner speech in America. And the fact that this is listened to without peals of laughter is a real problem."

"America," Luttwak contends, "is relatively rich. Even Americans that are not doing that well are relatively rich, but America is very short of social tranquillity; it's very short of stability. It's like somebody who has seventeen ties and no shoes buying himself another tie. The US has no shoes as far as tranquillity and the security of people's lives is concerned. But it has a lot of money. We have gone over to being a complete consumer society, a 100 percent consumer society. And the consequences are just as one would predict them: mainly lots of consumption, lots of goodies and cheap things, cheap flights, and a lot of dissatisfaction."[20]

CHAPTER 5

Community chills

That which is not good for the beehive cannot be good for the bee.
—MARCUS AURELIUS

People are so fascinating that I love to sit at my computer and learn about them.
—TIME COLUMNIST JOEL STEIN

You may have seen the ad for an SUV, picturing a suburban street of expensive, identical ranch-style houses with perfect lawns. The SUV being advertised is parked in the driveway of one of them. But in every other driveway is ... a tank. A big, deadly Army tank. It's a stark, ironic ad, reminding us how chilling our communities have become as our war of all-against-all consumer competition continues. How much our sense of community has changed since the 1950s! Back then, Dave used to walk with his grandfather four or five blocks to the town square in Crown Point, Indiana. Everyone knew his grandfather, even the guy carrying a sack of salvaged goods. Half a century later Dave still remembers the names of his grandparents' neighbors and the summer backyard parties they threw.

In the fifties, Americans sat together with their neighbors, cracking up at Red Skelton's antics. In 1985, we still watched *Family Ties* as a family, but by 2013, each member of a family often watched his or her own TV—while also texting messages or talking with Siri, the iPhone robo-genie. Isolation and passive participation became a way of life. What began as a quest for the good life in the suburbs degenerated into private consumption splurges that separated one neighbor from another. We began to feel like strangers in our own neighborhoods—it wasn't just the "Mad Men" who were ill at ease. Huge retailers took advantage of our confusion, expanding to meet our new "needs." The more we chased bargains and the paychecks that bought them, the more vitality slipped away from our towns. Now, if we want to experience Main Street—the way it was in the good old days—we create a virtual identity on a website like Second Life or we travel to Disney World to visit faux communities where smiling shopkeepers, the slow pace, and the quaintness remind us that our real communities were once close-knit and friendly. How will Disney portray the good old days of the suburbs, in future exhibits? Will it orchestrate background ambience—highway traffic, jackhammers, and beeping garbage trucks—to make it more realistic? Will it re-create gridlock with bumper-to-bumper cars, complete with smartphones to tell our families we'll be late for the next ride? Will our tour of the "gated community" require more tickets than rides through the "inner city" do? Will Disney hire extras to play the roles of suburbanites who can't drive—elderly, disabled, and low-income residents, peeking out from behind living room curtains?

ALONE TOGETHER

Where can America's stranded nondrivers go, in today's world? There are at least twenty million Americans of voting age who don't drive. There are fewer colorful cafés down the block, or bowling alleys or taverns, where neighbors can "be apart together, and mutually withdraw from the world," in the words of writer Ray Oldenburg. Such "great good places" or "third places," apart from both home and work environments, are disappearing or moving to the fake "neighborhoods" in megamalls.

"We've mutated from citizens to consumers in the last sixty years," says James Kuntsler, the author of *The Geography of Nowhere*. "The trouble with being consumers is that they have no duties or responsibilities or obligations to their fellow consumers. Citizens do. They have the obligation to care about their fellow citizens and about the integrity of the town's environment and history."[1]

The Harvard political scientist Robert Putnam has devoted his career to the study of "social capital," the connections among people that bind a community together. He observed that the quality of governance varies with the level of involvement in such things as voter turnout, newspaper readership, and membership in choral societies. He concluded that far too many Americans are "bowling alone." (More people are bowling now than a generation ago, but fewer of them bowl in leagues.) Once a nation of joiners, we've now become a nation of loners. Only about half of the nation's voters typically vote in presidential elections. Fewer are attending public meetings on town or school affairs, PTA participation has fallen dramatically since 1970, and fraternal organizations like the Elks and Lions are becoming endangered species.[2]

"We are not talking simply about nostalgia for the 1950s," said Putnam in an *Atlantic* interview. "School performance, public health, crime rates, clinical depression, tax compliance, philanthropy, race relations, community development, census returns, teen suicide, economic productivity, campaign finance, even simple human happiness—all are demonstrably affected by how (and whether) we connect with our family and friends and neighbors and co-workers."[3] In other words, when consumption and profit are the guiding lights of a local culture, its best qualities are guaranteed to decline.

The jury's out on whether the digital romance that's swept us off our feet will make our communities and lives more satisfying in the long run. In the book *Alone Together*, Sherry Turkle observes a troubling irony: as a society, we settle for a digital illusion of companionship without the demands of friendship. "It used to be 'I have a feeling, I want to make a call.' Now it's 'I want to have a feeling, I need to make a call.'" Turkle quotes a twenty-six-year-old lawyer whose cell phone has become the center of her universe. "When there is an event on my phone," says the young woman, "there's a brightening of the screen. Even if the phone is in my purse ... I see it, I sense it. I always know what is happening on my phone." Venturing deeper into a digital forest, we see employees in staff meetings trying to text while still somehow making eye contact, and teenagers risking their lives (and ours) to check messages while driving (and in some cases, while dying). In recent news: the tragic and all-too-common story of sixteen-year-old Savannah Nash, on her first solo drive to the grocery store. She turned left off the highway without seeing an oncoming semitrailer truck. "There was a text message found on her phone that hadn't been sent yet," said the highway patrolman responding to the accident, adding that up to one-fourth of traffic accidents in the United States are now related to texting.[4]

AMERICA IN CHAINS

Another symptom of civic degeneration is the disappearance of traditional civic leaders of community organizations. Bank presidents and business owners with long-standing ties to the community are bounced from positions of community leadership when US Bank, Wal-Mart, Office Max, and Home Depot come to town to put them out of business. What do we get when the chains take over? Lower prices, cheaper stuff. But what we lose is a sense of belonging and a sense of cultural identity. At a locally owned coffee shop, you might see artwork by a friend who lives down the street. The shop is *your* coffee shop, and you stand a better chance there of coaxing neighbors to look up from their laptops to talk. At your independent bookseller, you'll find books from small presses that publish a wider variety of books than mainstream publishers, and shopkeepers who actually know something about the books' contents.

By using economies of scale in purchasing and distribution, and being able to stay in the market even at a loss, these monolithic retailers can drive out competition within a year and in some cases sooner. And we go along with it, for the lower prices—forgetting about the overall costs. In search of better buys and higher tax revenue, consumers and city council members typically first sacrifice Strip Avenue, then downtown, to the franchise developers, forgetting that much of a franchise dollar is electronically transferred to corporate headquarters, while a dollar spent at the local hardware stays put in towns or neighborhoods, as small businesses hire architects, designers, woodworkers, sign makers, local accountants, insurance brokers, computer consultants, attorneys, advertising agencies—all services that the big retailers contract out nationally. Local retailers and distributors also carry a higher percentage of locally made goods than the chains, creating more jobs for local producers. When we buy from the chains, instead of a multiplier effect, we get a "divider effect." In virtually every economic sector, the franchises have divided and conquered the community-based, independent stores. Together, Home Depot and Lowe's control 36 percent of the home improvement market. Starbucks and Dunkin' Donuts have together knocked about half of the coffee shops out of business, and when it comes to books, Amazon and Barnes & Noble rule the roost, with 49 percent of the market share.[5] With e-books making up almost a fourth of publisher sales in the United States, browsing in comfortable little bookstores is becoming a lost pastime. There's only one location in America—a barren plain in South Dakota—that isn't within a hundred miles of McDonald's, and the top ten chain restaurants collectively grossed about $100 billion in 2012. Impressive, but compared to Wal-Mart, still small change. When your company's annual revenue ($469 billion in 2012) equals about as much as America's Medicare expenditures, that's the big time.[6] In a world where more than half of the world's largest economies are corporations, Wal-Mart wields more power than most of the world's countries. Fortunately, many US towns and cities are challenging that power.

AL NORMAN, SPRAWL BUSTER

Twenty years ago, Al Norman spearheaded a Wal-Mart resistance campaign in his hometown—Greenfield, Massachusetts—and won. After his story appeared in *Time, Newsweek*, the *New York Times*, and *60 Minutes*, "My phone started ringing and hasn't stopped," he says. "I've been to most of the states now, teaching hometown activists what tools are available."[7] He's still on the Wal-Mart beat, and his Sprawl Busters website lists success stories from 440 towns and cities that have prevented unwanted invasions of big-box stores. Norman has personally coached many of these to victory, but he's also very familiar with the defeats and the impacts that can follow. "A classic example is the small town of Ticonderoga, New York," he says. "The local newspaper documented that in the first eight months of Wal-Mart occupancy, business fell by at least 20 percent at the drugstore, jeweler, and auto parts stores. But the game was totally over at the Great American Market, the town's only downtown grocery store. First they cut their operating hours, then dropped the payroll from twenty-seven people to seventeen. It wasn't long before the grocery closed completely. Many of the people who shopped at the GAM were the elderly, low-income people without access to a car."[8]

"I've been here twenty-five years," a downtown Sunoco station owner told Norman. "On the week before Christmas in prior years, you couldn't find a parking space on this street. This year, you could have landed a plane on it." Says Norman with no lack of candor, "Instead of being a shot in the arm to the economy, Wal-Mart has been like a shot in the head." He compares Wal-Mart with Publix Supermarkets, owned by its 152,000 employees. Publix operates an employee stock ownership plan that programmatically distributes company stock at no cost. It also has a group health, dental, and vision plan as well as company-paid life insurance. "Unlike Wal-Mart," says Norman, "Publix has been listed for the past fifteen years in Fortune magazine's 100 best companies to work for. You won't find Wal-Mart on that list, because Wal-Mart has more employee-based lawsuits than men's suits. At every link in the chain, someone is being exploited, from Shenzhen, China, to Sheboygan, Wisconsin."[9]

In 2013 our social defenses were down. Distracted by material things and out of touch with social health, we watch community life from the sidelines. Hurrying to work, we see a fleet of bulldozers leveling a familiar open area next to the river, but we haven't heard yet what's going in there. Chances are good it's a Wal-Mart, McDonald's, or Starbucks.

SOCIAL SECESSION

What happens when affluenza causes communities to be pulled apart (for example, when a company leaves town and lays off hundreds of people), or crippled by bad design? We "cocoon," retreating further inward and closing the gate behind us. Across the United States, at least 10 percent of this country's homes are in gated communities, according to Census Bureau data. (Including secured apartment dwellers, prison inmates, and residential security-system zealots, at least one in five Americans now lives behind bars.)

"We are a society whose purported goal is to bring people of all income levels and races together, but gated communities are the direct opposite of that," the sociologist Edward Blakely writes in the book *Fortress America*. "How can the nation have a social contract without having social contact?"[10] Robert Reich observes, "Across the nation, the most affluent Americans have been seceding from the rest of the nation into their own separate geographical communities with tax bases (or fees) that can underwrite much higher levels of services. They have relied increasingly on private security guards instead of public police, private spas and clubs rather than public parks and pools, and private schools. Being rich now means having enough money that you don't have to encounter anyone who isn't."[11]

In 1958, trust was sky high. Seventy-three percent of Americans surveyed by Gallup said they trusted the federal government to do what is right either "most of the time" or "just about always," a number that plummeted to just 19 percent in 2013. The slogan of the popular 1990s TV series, *The X-Files*, was "trust no one," and Americans have taken that cold advice to heart. Yet, as Putnam writes, "When we can't trust our employees or other market players, we end up squandering our wealth on surveillance equipment, compliance structures, insurance, legal services, and enforcement of government regulations."[12]

QUEASY

If an eight-year-old girl can walk safely to the public library six blocks away, that's one good indicator of a healthy community. For starters, you have a public library worth walking to and a sidewalk to walk on. But more important, you have neighbors who watch out for each other. You have social capital in the neighborhood—relationships, commitments, and networks that create an underlying sense of trust. Yet in many American neighborhoods, trust is becoming a nostalgic memory. Seeing children at play is becoming as rare as sighting an endangered songbird. After a horrifying string of mass shootings in US schools, 62 percent of parents of school-aged children now want to hire armed guards at schools. Meanwhile, the $34-billion-a-year gun industry is on a roll: annual background checks by firearms vendors have doubled since 2006.[13]

Here's one bizarre yet fairly common indicator of our queasiness: a high percentage of recently deceased people request to remain in touch with their cell phones, for all of eternity. Funeral directors report that in effect, dying doesn't have to mean hanging it up. Says Noelle Potvin, a funeral home counselor for Hollywood Forever, "It seems that everyone under 40 who dies takes their cell phones with them. A lot of people say the phone represents the person, that it's an extension of them, like their class ring."[14]

COOPERATION VERSUS CORPORATION

Local buying and investing has become a very potent antidote to affluenza and the profiteering it spawns. Like acupuncture or a herbal remedy, the localization movement is precise, preventive, and in tune with changing times. Corporations are often ill-equipped to customize their products and services to meet regional needs. For example, local banks can better assess the risk of a loan, and local independent groceries can better meet specific ethnic demands. Small businesses can be more personable and responsive as the economy continues to shift toward services and experiential spending. Take the food industry, a great example of localization. Although 70 percent of the American diet is processed food, and the American landscape is dotted with 100,000 McDonald's and other top-ten fast-food restaurants in the United States, companies like Whole Foods Market and Organic Valley (a farmer-owned cooperative) are leading the charge back to food that keeps us healthy. A champion of local food, Alice Waters, writes, "When we eat fast-food meals alone in our cars, we swallow the values and assumptions of the corporations that manufacture them. According to those values, eating is no more important than fueling up, and should be done quickly and anonymously." Yet food is far more than that; throughout human history, it was a way to come together, to express our identity, and to be rooted in the earth. Food delivers not just physical health, but also social health. "At the table, we learn moderation, conversation, tolerance, generosity and conviviality; these are civic virtues," says Waters.[15]

A GEOGRAPHY OF NOWHERE?

Have we become a nation too distracted to care? Like the medium-size fish that eat small fish, we consume franchise products in the privacy of our homes, then watch helplessly as the big-fish franchise companies bite huge chunks out of our public places, swallowing jobs, traditions, and open space. We assume that someone else is taking care of things—we pay them to take care of things so we can concentrate on working and spending. But to our horror, we discover that many of the service providers, merchandise retailers, and caretakers are not really taking care of us anymore. It might be more appropriate to say they're *consuming* us.

CHAPTER 6

Heart failure

We are the hollow men. We are the stuffed men.
—T.S. ELIOT

CINCINNATI—The blank, oppressive void facing the American consumer populace remains unfilled despite the recent launch of the revolutionary Swiffer dust-elimination system, sources reported Monday. The lightweight, easy-to-use Swiffer is the 275,894,973rd amazing new product to fail to fill the void—a vast, soul-crushing spiritual vacuum Americans of all ages face on a daily basis, with nowhere to turn and no way to escape.... Despite high hopes, the Swiffer has failed to imbue a sense of meaning and purpose in the lives of its users.
—FROM THE HUMOR NEWSPAPER *THE ONION*

The road switchbacks up, down, and around precipitous canyons, crosses raging streams, and winds by glassy lakes offering mirror images of an immense snow-covered volcano, the main attraction in Washington State's Mount Rainier National Park.

Each year, two million people drive the road. More than a few stop to admire the beautiful stone masonry, so perfectly in harmony with the natural setting, that forms the guardrails for the road or the graceful arches of its many bridges. This is quality work, built to last, built for beauty as well as utility. Built by the Civilian Conservation Corps (CCC).

In the 1930s, during the depths of the Great Depression, hundreds of young men came to Mount Rainier—ordinary, unemployed working men, mostly from cities back east. Living in tent camps or barracks, they built many of the marvelous facilities that visitors to the park now take for granted. At a time when the dominant notion is that the government never does anything well, the work of the CCC at Mount Rainier and many other national parks provides something of a corrective.

The men's work was laborious, performed in snow, sleet, or blazing sun, and their wages barely provided subsistence. Their accommodations were anything but plush, and they had little to entertain them except storytelling and card games. Most could carry all the possessions they owned in a single suitcase. Yet when the author Harry Boyte interviewed veterans of the CCC, he found that many looked back on those days as the best of their lives.

They'd forgotten the dirt, the strained muscles, the mosquito bites. But they remembered with deep fondness the camaraderie and the feeling they had that they were "building

America," creating work of true and lasting value that would be enjoyed by generations yet unborn. The sense of pride in their CCC accomplishments was still palpable sixty years later.[1]

What the men of the CCC, and the countless other people who give to their communities have in common is the understanding that meaningful activity matters more than money and that, indeed, it is better to give than receive. They've learned that fulfillment comes from such efforts. But in our consumer society they are becoming an exception.

The more Americans fill their lives with things, the more they tell psychiatrists, pastors, friends, and family members that they feel empty inside. The more toys our kids have to play with, the more they complain of boredom. Two thousand years ago, Jesus Christ predicted they would feel that way. "You cannot serve both God and mammon [money]," Christ warned. What profit would it bring a person, he asked his followers (Matthew 16:26), were that person to gain the whole world but lose his soul? In the Age of Affluenza, that question is seldom asked, at least not publicly. It should be.

POVERTY OF THE SOUL

When Mother Teresa came to the United States to receive an honorary degree, she said, "This is the poorest place I've ever been in my life," recounts Robert Seiple, the former director of World Vision, a Christian charity organization. "She wasn't talking about economics, mutual funds, Wall Street, the ability to consume," he adds. "She was talking about poverty of the soul."[2]

Shortly before he died of a brain tumor, the Republican campaign strategist Lee Atwater made a confession. "The '80s," he said, "were about acquiring—acquiring wealth, power, prestige. I know. I acquired more wealth, power, and prestige than most. But you can acquire all you want and still feel empty." He warned that there was "a spiritual vacuum at the heart of American society, a tumor of the soul."[3]

Ironically, many contemporary "conservatives," some of whom loudly profess their religious values, are devotees of the philosophy of an atheist, the Russian-born philosopher Ayn Rand, who in contrast to Mother Teresa (and Atwater at the end of his life), preached a doctrine of economic survival of the fittest, idolizing the self-made entrepreneur who crushes his rivals but from whom all blessings for workers ultimately flow. Rand, a near-deity for many Tea Party followers and for public figures as influential as Paul Ryan and Alan Greenspan, proclaimed "the virtue of selfishness" and argued that government supports of any kind lead to sloth and weakness—and ultimately, the loss of freedom.

By contrast, Francis, the new Roman Catholic pope, finds such a philosophy of self-centeredness abhorrent. According to the pope, unfettered greed and consumerism of the type advocated by Rand has led people to believe that money is more important than anything else. "Unbridled capitalism has taught the logic of profit at any cost, of giving in order to receive, of exploitation without looking at the person," said Francis. "The results of such attitudes can be seen in the crisis we are now living through."[4] The Dalai Lama recently expressed similar feelings.

Indeed, in all our great religious traditions, human beings are seen as having a purpose in life. Stripped to its essentials, it is to serve God by caring for God's creations and our fellow human beings. Happy is the man or woman whose work and life energies serve that end, who finds a "calling" or "right livelihood" that allows his or her talents to serve the common good. In none of those traditions is purpose to be found in simply accumulating things, or power, or pleasure—or in "looking out for number one."

One seldom hears work described as a calling anymore. Work may be "interesting" and "creative" or dull and boring. It may bring status or indifference—and not in any sense in relation to its real value. Our lives are disrupted far more severely when garbage collectors stop working than when ballplayers do. Work may bring great monetary rewards or bare subsistence. But we almost never ask what it means and what it serves. For most, though certainly not all, of us, if it makes money, that's reason enough. Why do it? Simple. It pays.

UNDER THE SMILE BUTTONS

But millions of Americans do hunger for meaning. That's what Michael Lerner, a rabbi and writer, found when he worked in a "stress clinic" for working families in Oakland, California. Along with his coworkers, Lerner originally "imagined that most Americans are motivated primarily by material self-interest. So we were surprised that these middle-class Americans often experience more stress from feeling that they are wasting their lives doing meaningless work than from feeling that they are not making enough money."[5]

Lerner and his colleagues brought groups of working people from various occupations together to talk with each other about their lives. "At first, most of the people we talked to wanted to reassure us, as they assured their coworkers and friends, that everything was fine, that they were handling things well, that they never let stress get to them, and that their lives were good." It was, he says, the kind of response that pollsters usually get when they ask people superficial questions about life satisfaction. But in time, as participants in the groups felt more comfortable being honest about their emotions, a different pattern of responses emerged.

"We found middle-income people deeply unhappy because they hunger to serve the common good and to contribute something with their talents and energies, yet find that their actual work gives them little opportunity to do so," Lerner writes. "They often turn to demands for more money as a compensation for a life that otherwise feels frustrating and empty."

"It is perhaps this fear of no longer being needed in a world of needless things that most clearly spells out the unnaturalness, the surreality, of much that is called work today," wrote Studs Terkel in his best-seller *Working*. Perhaps it's feelings such as those described by Lerner and Terkel that have led to one of the most disturbing of contemporary American statistics: The rate of clinical depression in the United States today is *ten* times what it was before

1945.[6] Over any given year, nearly half of American adults suffer from clinical depression, anxiety disorders, or other mental illnesses. As Americans increasingly fall victim to affluenza, feelings of depression, anxiety, and lowered self-esteem are likely to become even more prevalent. Such a prediction finds scientific support in a series of recent studies carried out by two professors of psychology, Tim Kasser and Richard Ryan. They compared individuals whose primary aspirations were financial with others who were oriented toward lives of community service and strong relationships with other people.[7]

Their conclusions were unequivocal: Those individuals for whom accumulating wealth was a primary aspiration "were associated with less self-actualization, less vitality, more depression and more anxiety." Their studies, they wrote, "demonstrated the deleterious consequences of having money as an important guiding principle in life."

CHANGING STUDENT VALUES

Kasser and Ryan's studies confirm the wisdom of religious traditions that warn about the dangers of preoccupation with wealth. But such wisdom has been falling on deaf ears for quite some time now. In 1962, when Tom Hayden penned the Port Huron Statement, the founding manifesto of Students for a Democratic

Society (SDS), he declared, "The main and transcending concern of the university must be the unfolding and refinement of the moral, aesthetic and logical capacities" to help students find "a moral meaning in life."[8]

"Loneliness, estrangement and isolation describe the vast distance between man and man today," Hayden wrote. "These dominant tendencies cannot be overcome by better personnel management, nor by improved gadgets, but only when a love of man overcomes the idolatrous worship of things by man." During the '60s, calls such as Hayden's for a meaningful life of service to the world—responding in part to John F. Kennedy's inaugural admonition to "ask not what your country can do for you; ask, rather, what you can do for your country"—inspired tens of thousands of students.

WHEN LEFT AND RIGHT AGREED

As with affluenza's impact on families and children, critics of the psychic emptiness of the consumer lifestyle come most often from the political Left these days. But that wasn't always so. Before Reagan, many conservatives hadn't yet hitched their star completely to Ayn Rand–style free-market worship. Prominent conservative philosophers and economists were often as critical of consumerism as were leftists like Erich

Fromm or Herbert Marcuse, suggesting that it leads to lives without meaning.

Wilhelm Röpke was one of the giants of traditional conservative economic thought. "*Homo sapiens consumens* loses sight of everything that goes to make up human happiness apart from money income and its transformation into goods," Röpke wrote in 1957. Those who fall into the "keeping up with the Joneses" lifestyle, he argued, "lack the genuine and essentially nonmaterial conditions of simple human happiness. Their existence is empty, and they try to fill this emptiness somehow."[9]

Long before Enron, WorldCom, and other scandals involving corporate greed, Röpke posed powerful questions about the moral direction of consumer society:

> Are we not living in an economic world, or as R.H. Tawney says, in an "acquisitive society" which unleashes naked greed, fosters Machiavellian business methods and, indeed allows them to become the rule, drowns all higher motives in the "icy water of egotistical calculation" (to borrow from the *Communist Manifesto*), and lets people gain the world but lose their souls? Is there any more certain way of dessicating the soul of man than the habit of constantly thinking about money and what it can buy? Is there a more potent

poison than our economic system's all-pervasive commercialism?[10]

Can you imagine a conservative writing something like that today?

In his book *A Humane Economy: The Social Framework of the Free Market*, Röpke pointed out (following Adam Smith) that in a capitalist society—which, as a conservative, he strongly supported—it is all the more important for each individual to ask questions about the moral value of his or her activities and not merely be carried along by market currents. Without such vigilance, he suggested, life would become hollow. "Life is not worth living," he wrote, "if we exercise our profession only for the sake of material success and do not find in our calling an inner necessity and a meaning that transcends the mere earning of money, a meaning which gives our life dignity and strength."[11]

STANDARDIZED PEOPLE

Perhaps the best explanation of how the overblown pursuit of material aims leads to meaningless, perpetually bored lives was provided by another conservative, the philosopher Ernest van den Haag. First, he pointed out, mass production, which makes the universal consumer lifestyle possible, drives large numbers of people out of more varied occupations as artisans and small farmers and instead agglomerates them in factories, where the division of labor reduces the scope of their activities to a few repetitive motions. Their work offers neither variety nor control.

In time, their output is sufficient enough, and their organized demands effective enough, that they begin to share in the material fruits of their labor. But to provide the quantity of goods that makes that possible, they must accept mass-produced, and therefore standardized, products. "The benefits of mass production," van den Haag wrote, "are reaped only by matching de-individualizing work with equally deindividualizing consumption." Therefore, he argued, "failure to repress individual personality in or after working hours is costly; in the end, *the production of standardized things by persons also demands the production of standardized persons*" [emphasis ours].[12]

De-individualization, the result of material progress itself, cannot help but strip life of both meaning and inherent interest. The worker-consumer is vaguely dissatisfied, restless, and bored, and these feelings are reinforced and enhanced by advertising, which deliberately attempts to exploit them by offering new products as a way out. Consumer products and the mass media—itself made possible only by ads for consumer products—"drown the shriek of unused capacities, of repressed individuality," leaving us either "listless or perpetually restless," declared van den Haag. The products and the media distract us from the soul's cry for truly meaningful activities.

The individual who finds no opportunity for self-chosen, meaningful expression of inner resources and personality suffers, said van den Haag, "an insatiable longing for things to happen. The external world is to supply these events to fill the emptiness. The popular demand for 'inside' stories, for vicarious sharing of the private lives of 'personalities' rests on the craving for private life—even someone else's—of those who are dimly aware of having none whatever, or at least no life that holds their interest."[13]

What the bored person really craves is a meaningful, authentic life. The ads suggest that such a life comes in products or packaged commercial experiences. But religion *and* the science of psychology say it's more likely to be found in such things as service to others, relationships with friends and family, connection with nature, and work of intrinsic moral value.

AFTER AFFLUENZA

Our technologically advanced culture offers opportunities for much more meaningful and creative lives than most of us lead. Our amazingly productive technologies could allow all of us to spend less time doing repetitive, standardized work, or work whose products bring us little pride, by allowing us to trade higher wages for reduced working hours.

Such choices would allow more time for freely chosen, voluntary, often unpaid work that enhances our relationships and communities and/or allows us to express more fully our talents and creativity. And such choices would allow us more time to find meaning and joy in the beauty and wonders of nature, in the delightful play of children, or in the restoration of our damaged environment. They would give us time to think about what really matters to us, and how we really want to use the remaining years of our lives.

CHAPTER 7

Social scars

America's affluenza casts an enormous shadow over the rest of the world. While even poor Americans live with luxuries unimagined by the rich a century ago, the worldwide gap between rich and poor continues to grow. Two billion of the world's people still live in a state of destitution, on income equivalents of less than two dollars a day. Many of them make the apparel and other consumer products we buy. Try an experiment: walk through Wal-Mart (or any other big-box store) and check out where the products are from. Chances are what you can buy so cheap is made in a place where the conditions of labor are no better than they were in the United States a hundred years ago.

In 1993, a Thai toy factory burned to the ground. Unable to escape, hundreds of female workers perished. Their charred bodies lay among the ruins of the building, a firetrap similar to many throughout the developing world where millions of plastic toys are made for American children. Here and there amid the blackened rubble were the toys themselves.

Many of the women were mothers whose meager incomes would not allow them to buy for their own children the toys they were making for export. More recently, the collapse of a

Bangladesh textile factory in 2013 resulted in 1,127 deaths, while a fire in another killed 112 workers. Safety conditions in these plants are like those that prevailed in the United States before the infamous Triangle Shirtwaist Factory Fire of 1911, which killed 146 female textile workers.[1]

According to the Associated Press, "Bangladesh is the third-biggest exporter of clothes in the world, after China and Italy. There are 5,000 factories in the country and 3.6 million garment workers. But working conditions in the $20 billion industry are grim, a result of government corruption, desperation for jobs, and industry indifference. Minimum wages for garment workers are among the lowest in the world at 3,000 takas ($38) a month."[2]

At least 1,800 workers have died in factory fires and building collapses in Bangladesh since 2005, many of them while producing cheap clothes for the American market. The grisly images from those disasters, and the facts that lie behind them, speak volumes about the widening canyon that separates the haves and have-nots in the Age of Affluenza.

As we mentioned earlier, no economic system produces consumer goods as cheap as the unfettered, deregulated free market. It can, for example (especially with the help of regimes that allow workers little freedom to organize), produce children's toys so cheap that they can be shipped halfway around the world and still be given away with two-dollar meals at fast-food restaurants like McDonald's and Burger King.

Americans have long considered their country—unlike those in the developing world—a "classless" one, with few citizens who are either very rich or very poor. But this notion of a classless America has always been suspect. Even in 1981, when all political efforts to counteract or quarantine affluenza were abruptly abandoned, the United States ranked thirteenth among twenty-two leading industrial nations in income equality.

Today, we're dead last.[3]

THE OTHER AMERICA

The rising tide of American affluence hasn't lifted all boats, but it has drowned a lot of dreams. A titanic gulf now separates rich and poor in America. Indeed, during the '80s, three-quarters of the increase in pretax real income went to the wealthiest 1 percent of families, who gained an average of 77 percent. Medianincome families saw only a 4 percent gain, while the bottom 40 percent of families actually lost ground. Lower-income workers did better during Clinton's second term, keeping the gap from widening, but during the first decade of the twenty-first century, the news was even worse: *most* Americans saw their incomes fall, while the "1 percent" continued to capture two-thirds of the income gains.[4]

As the super-rich increased their share of national income during the '80s, they also became stingier. They gave a far smaller share of their incomes to charity than was previously the case. In 1979, people who earned an income of more than $1 million (in 1991 dollars) gave away 7 percent of their after-tax income. Twelve years later, that figure had dropped to less than 4 percent.[5] This, at a time when advocates of sharp cuts in government welfare programs suggested that private charity would make up much of the difference. Instead, not surprisingly, the percentages of families in poverty, which had been declining, began once again to rise. The number of people who were working (and not on welfare) but earning below-poverty wages nearly doubled during the '80s.[6]

In spite of America's image as a cornucopia of plenty, where the shelves of supermarkets are always fully stocked, more than ten million Americans go hungry each day; 40 percent of them are children, and the majority, members of working families. Millions of other Americans keep hunger from the door by turning frequently to programs such as food banks and soup kitchens. By 2010, the US Department of Agriculture categorized one American family in seven as "food insecure," the highest percentage ever recorded. Before 2006, we called that "hunger," but the name was changed during the Bush administration to allow us to look away more easily. Shockingly, Republicans in Congress now want to strip billions from the food stamp budget and hand the money to the rich in the form of even deeper tax cuts.[7]

In 1980, the top 1 percent of Americans earned about 9 percent of our national income; by 2008, they were earning 23 percent, more than the bottom 50 percent of Americans put together.[8]

The distribution of wealth is even more skewed. By 1999, 92 percent of all financial wealth (stocks, bonds, and commercial real estate) in America was owned by the top 20 percent of families (and 83 percent of stock was owned by the top 10 percent). Many of the richest Americans find ways to pay little or nothing in the way of taxes. In 2004, for example, the tax share paid by the wealthiest 1 percent of Americans fell by 19 percent, while that paid by median-income Americans rose by 1 percent. Overall, despite conservative claims of mushrooming government, tax rates have been falling since 1980; the rate for the richest 1 percent has dropped by a third, from 35 percent to 22 percent.[9]

Meanwhile, nearly fifty million Americans were living in poverty by 2010 (about the same number as those without health insurance), up from thirty-seven million in 2007 and, in absolute terms, the largest number of poor since the poverty rate was established half a century earlier. Sixteen percent of Americans fall below the poverty line, and twenty million of them live in families that earn less than $10,000 a year.[10]

THE BIG WINNERS...

At one point, before a drop in Microsoft stock prices halved his net worth, Bill Gates held assets worth about $90 billion, nearly as much as the bottom half of the American population (and greater than the gross national products of

119 of the world's 156 nations). By contrast, 40 percent of all Americans own no assets at all.

Nothing better illustrates the extent to which affluenza has been embraced in America than the compensation awarded senior executives of large companies. Average CEO pay has continued to increase at double-digit rates. Nike CEO Mark Parker earned $35.2 million in 2012, up 219 percent from just a year earlier. By 2012, CEOs earned 354 times what their average workers made, up from 42 times as much in 1982 and 84 times as much in 1990.[11] By contrast, until recently, when they began to feel a need to keep up with their American counterparts, Japanese and German CEOs earned only about 20 times as much as average workers.

AND THE LOSERS

In 2000, the columnist David Broder reported that the people who clean the bathrooms and offices of "the masters of the universe" (as he calls high-tech millionaires) in Los Angeles were earning poverty-level wages. He found janitors picketing for a pay raise that would bring them $21,000 a year by 2003. Even at that pay scale, it would have taken 27,380 such janitors to earn as much as a single Los Angeles CEO, Michael Eisner of Disney, made in 1998 ($575 million).[12]

To the affluent, the poor have become invisible. "There are millions of people whose work makes our life easier, from busboys in the restaurants we patronize to orderlies in the hospitals we visit, but whose own lives are lived on the ragged edge of poverty," Broder wrote. "Most of us never exchange a sentence with these workers." In sight, but out of mind.

One fact Americans used to point to as evidence of a "classless" society was that (compared to the wealthy of Latin America, for example) few American families employed servants to do cleaning and housework. But as we become increasingly a two-tiered class society, that's changing. Upper-middle-income Americans are turning to domestic servants in a big way. In 1999, between 14 and 18 percent of American households employed an outsider to do their cleaning, a 53 percent increase from 1995. America's 900,000 house cleaners and servants earned an average of $8.06 an hour in 2003, below the poverty line for three-person families. "This sudden emergence of a servant class is consistent with what some economists call the 'Brazilianization' of the American economy," wrote Barbara Ehrenreich in *Harpers*. "In line with growing class polarization, the classic posture of submission is making a stealthy comeback," charges Ehrenreich, who worked as a maid for $6.63 an hour to research the story. She points out that one franchise, Merry Maids, even advertises its maid services with a brochure boasting that "we scrub your floors the old fashioned way—on our hands and knees."[13]

Doing research for her best-seller *Nickel and Dimed,* Ehrenreich went a-scrubbing from McMansion to McMansion in Portland, Maine, working under rules that even prohibited her from taking a drink of water while cleaning a house. She discovered that some homes had hidden video cameras to be sure she stayed on track. She was amazed at the messes that people left for her, especially the children, one of whom exclaimed "Look, Mommy, a white maid!" upon seeing Ehrenreich.

Having "cleaned the rooms of many overly privileged teenagers," as she worked as a maid, Ehrenreich concluded that "the American overclass is raising a generation of young people who will, without constant assistance, suffocate in their own detritus."

Whether or not they are literate enough to know what that means.

THE POOR PAY TWICE—AND THEN SOME

Affluenza affects Americans across all income barriers, but its impacts are more destructive for the poor. In the first place, the poor are often the original victims of the environmental consequences of cost-cutting production strategies. They live disproportionately in areas where environmental contaminants and patterns of pollution are most severe—for example, in

Louisiana's notorious "Cancer Alley," petrochemical companies unleash a frightening barrage of carcinogens into the air and water.

At the same time, vastly inflated wage scales paid to winners in the new "information economy" lead to competitive bidding on housing stock that drives the cost of shelter beyond reach of even average earners. Many are forced to leave the communities where they and their families have spent their entire lives.

Finally, the poor are taunted by television programs and commercials that flash before them images of consumption standards that are considered typical of the average American, but which they have no possibility of achieving—except perhaps by robbing a bank or winning the lottery.

In our poorest communities, the sense of deprivation has been intense for years. In the *Affluenza* documentary, the trend spotter Gerald Celente tells of a conversation he had with a man who works with youthful gang members. "I asked him, 'What's the one thing that you see that's causing a lot of these problems?'" Celente says. "Without skipping a beat, he said, 'Greed and materialism. These kids don't feel like their lives would be worth anything unless they have the hottest product that's being sold in the marketplace.'"

Margaret Norris, co-director of the Omega Boys Club in San Francisco, agrees. She says the ethic among the low-income youths she works with is "Thou Shalt Get Thy Money On," and by any means necessary. Such desperation often leads to crime.

"Never mind, just lock 'em up" seems to be our social response to this situation. Overall crime rates have been falling in the past two decades, a trend that the British economist Richard Layard convincingly argues is due, sadly, in large part to the availability of abortion. Another reason is that the United States already has locked more than two million of its people behind prison bars, the largest percentage of any nation in the world, and ten times the rate in most industrial countries.[14]

California alone has more inmates than France, Germany, Great Britain, Japan, Singapore, and Holland combined. In some dying Rust Belt industrial cities, like Youngstown, Ohio, prisons have become the biggest source of jobs. Private companies like the Corrections Corporation of America make millions running lockup facilities. Smart Wall Street brokers play "dungeons for dollars," investing heavily in the new privatized prison industry.

INEQUALITY HURTS EVERYONE

In their powerful book, *The Spirit Level*, the British epidemiologists Richard Wilkinson and Kate Pickett show that highly unequal countries have poorer outcomes in more than two dozen indicators of well-being, from health to happiness to crime. While in every country, the rich are healthier and happier than the poor, even the rich in unequal countries are not as healthy or happy as those in more egalitarian ones. Wealthy Americans live only about as long as poor Europeans.[15]

Nonetheless, America's obsession with wealth continues unabated as we continue to pursue the chimera that freedom means no limits on the right to get as rich as possible. Europeans see freedom differently. A Danish student told John that she felt free because she had health care and free education and an economic safety net, and so would her children, giving her the freedom to choose a job she loved rather than the one that paid the most.

GLOBAL INFECTION

The social scars left by affluenza are being replicated throughout the entire world, as more and more cultures copy the American lifestyle. Each day, television exposes millions of people in the developing world to the Western consumer lifestyle (without showing them its warts), and they are eager to be included. David Korten, the author of *When Corporations Rule the World*, once believed they could and should be included. Korten taught business management at Stanford and Harvard, then worked in Africa, Asia, and Central America for the Harvard

Business School, the Ford Foundation, and the US Agency for International Development.

"My career was focused on training business executives to create the equivalent of our high-consumption economy in countries throughout the world," Korten says. "The whole corporate system in the course of globalization is increasingly geared up to bring every country into the consumer society. And there is a very strong emphasis on trying to reach children, to reshape their values from the very beginning to convince them that progress is defined by what they consume."

Korten believes that, by pushing consumer values in developing countries, he was spreading the affluenza virus. As he continued to work in the "development" field, the symptoms of that virus became increasingly apparent. He gradually realized that his efforts were causing more harm than good. "I came to see that what I was promoting didn't work and couldn't work," he reflects. "Many people's lives were actually worse off. We were seeing the environment trashed, and we were seeing the breakdown of cultures and the social fabric."[16]

As affluenza, the disease of unbridled consumerism, spreads throughout the world, the gap between rich and poor grows ever wider, and the social scars that still remain somewhat hidden in the United States fester as open sores elsewhere. The grim shantytowns of Rio tumble to the golden sands of Copacabana and Ipanema.

The luxurious malls of Manila stand alongside the Smoky Mountain, a massive garbage dump where thousands of people live right in the refuse, dependent for their survival on what they can scavenge.

In some ways, a cactus-like plant that grows in the Kalahari Desert of southern Africa may be the metaphor for today's divided world. The razor-thin Bushmen of the Kalahari eat the bitter hoodia plant because it takes away the pangs of hunger. But now pharmaceutical companies have patented the hoodia's appetite-suppressant properties. They have created hoodia plantations and market a diet product containing hoodia to obese Americans and Europeans. The diet product, which hit the world in 2008, stands as a symbol for a divided world where some have too much food, and millions more, far too little. One-fifth of the world's people—1.2 billion human beings—live in "extreme poverty," on incomes of $1.25 day or less, slowly dying of hunger and disease.[17] Three billion others also desperately need more material goods. Yet, were they to begin consuming as we do, the result, as we learn in the next two chapters, would be an environmental catastrophe.

It is critical that we begin to set another example for the world, and quickly.

CHAPTER 8

Resource exhaustion

We buy a wastebasket and take it home in a plastic bag. Then we take the wastebasket out of the bag, and put the bag in the wastebasket.
—LILY TOMLIN, COMEDIAN

Since the earth is finite, and we will have to stop expanding sometime, should we do it before or after nature's diversity is gone?
—DONELLA MEADOWS

In case our society needs one more recipe for disaster, the Daily Grist writer Jim Meyer thinks he has a winner. "Ever wonder about the future of energy?" he asks, as if earnestly. "Will it be wind? Solar? Geothermal? No wait, I got it, tar sands! ... They've got everything oil does, but they're harder to get, crappier when you get them, and leave a much bigger mark on the climate.... Tar sands are deposits of about 90 percent sand, water, and clay mixed with only about 10 percent high-sulfur bitumen, a viscous black petroleum sludge containing hydrocarbons, also known as 'natural asphalt.'" Referencing the proposed Keystone XL Pipeline (which, if built, would originate in tar-sands-stricken

Alberta, Canada), Meyer says, "It would pump 1.1 million barrels of bitumen sludge a day, crisscrossing much of the continent's freshwater supply, all the way to the Gulf of Mexico."[1]

The first step, he instructs, is to clear-cut the unsightly boreal forest in Canada—and many of its indigenous plants and animals. Then, "get yourself some massive excavators, the biggest moveable objects on the planet, each capable of gouging out 16,000 cubic meters of earth an hour, and ripping pits into the planet fifteen stories deep." After crushing the sand boulders with gigantic machines and adding solvents to make the final slurry transportable, you're ready to start cooking up a batch of tar sands. But there's a glitch: "Somebody added solvents to our tar," Meyer notes, "so here comes the hydro-treating that removes the solvents, nitrogen, sulfur, and various metals. The process uses a lot of water and energy in the form of natural gas and oil. (Hey, what are we trying to make again?) Next, heat it again to remove carbon and add hydrogen, then it's off in another pipeline to an oil refinery, though most of the old refineries aren't up to the task of handling the filthy bitumen, so you'll need to build new refineries or upgrade old ones. Presto! You're cooking with gas!"

It takes about four tons of sand and four barrels of fresh water to make a barrel of synthetic oil, which is good for about forty-two gallons of gas, or one fill-up of a respectable-size

SUV. "The good news is about 10 percent of that water is recycled!" says Meyer. "On the downside, the other 90 percent is dumped into toxic tailing ponds, which currently cover about 19 square miles along the Athabasca River, and are leaking into the ecosystem at a rate of perhaps eleven million liters a day."[2]

WARNINGS FROM THE PAST

Our thanks to the tireless researchers and writers at *Grist*, who, even while covering environmental disasters day after day, can maintain a (caustic) sense of humor. Meyer's point, of course, is that we'll never again inherit a 150-year portfolio of easily accessible petroleum and that we'd better stop pretending we're somehow *entitled* to buy and sell cheap energy. As participants in a global economy, we're writing checks that have a high probability of bouncing very soon. Our overconsuming way of life is drawing down natural capital—the *real* principal in our account—consisting not only of petroleum and metals but also water, farmland, trees, climatic stability—at rates never seen before on this side of the universe. We've hit a tipping point: until we change our lifestyle to one that's culturally richer but materially more efficient and moderate, we'll risk cardiac arrest at a civilizational scale. (Not a pretty thought ... we're talking about hurricanes like Katrina and Sandy every year, up and down the world's coastlines.)

Historians have observed a handful of recurring symptoms in civilizations whose practices, beliefs, and habits eventually proved lethal. No surprise that they look all too familiar:
- Resource stocks fall; wastes and pollution accumulate.
- Exploitation is undertaken of scarcer, more distant, deeper, or more dilute resources (which are invariably more expensive).
- Natural services like water purification, fisheries, and flood control become less effective, requiring artificial substitutes like fish farms, bottled water, and engineered levees and barrier walls.
- Chaos in natural systems grows: more natural disasters, less biological resilience.
- Demands grow for military or corporate access to more remote, increasingly hostile regions.[3]

Why is our global economy resorting to environmentally and socially destructive technologies like fracking to get at natural gas, removing mountaintops to mine coal, and drilling from mile-deep, risky offshore rigs to slurp ancient oil deposits? *Because easily mined resources are rapidly becoming a thing of the past. There are measurable limits to growth, and we are bumping up against them.* Why has fish farming become a sizable, biologically unstable industry in the last decade? *Because we've overfished many of the world's oceans and lakes.* (Pacific bluefin tuna is now so scarce that sushi restaurateurs recently bid $1.7 million for a single, jumbo-size fish in Tokyo's Tsukiji fish market!) Why is the insurance industry so spooked by the stark realities of climate change? *Because there's growing chaos in natural systems*—in 2012, the hottest year on record, damages in the United States from natural disasters like floods on the East Coast, forest fires in the Rockies, and deep drought in Texas came to $139 billion. (About a fourth of this was covered by private insurance; the rest was covered by the federal government, which effectively cost each American taxpayer about $1,100).[4]

Here's a major part of the problem: "Industry moves, mines, extracts, shovels, burns, wastes, pumps, and disposes of *four million pounds* of material in order to provide one average middle-class family's needs for a year," write the coauthors of *Natural Capitalism*. Americans spend more for trash bags, golf balls, and bottled water than many of the world's countries spend for everything. In an average lifetime, each American consumes a reservoir of water (forty million gallons, including water for personal, industrial, and agricultural use) and a small tanker of oil (2,500 barrels).[5]

Because few of us supply our own materials for daily life, almost everything we consume, from potatoes to petroleum to pencils, comes from somewhere else. "The problem is that we're running out of 'somewhere elses,' especially as developing countries try to achieve a Western style of life," says the Swiss engineer Mathis Wackernagel. Dividing the planet's biologically productive land and sea by the number of humans, Wackernagel and his Canadian colleague William Rees come up with 5.5 acres per person. That's if we put *nothing* aside for all the other species. "In contrast," says Wackernagel, "the average world citizen uses more than 7 acres—what we call his or her 'ecological footprint.'

"That's over 30 percent more than what nature can regenerate. In other words, it would take 1.3 years to regenerate what humanity uses in one year." He continues, "If all people lived like the average American (with *thirty*-acre footprints, we'd need five more planets." (To find out the size of your own ecological footprint, take the quiz at the Redefining Progress website: www.myfootprint.org.)

Wackernagel observes, "We can't use all the planet's resources, because we're only one species out of ten million or more. Yet if we leave half of the biological capacity for other species (or if the human population doubles in size), human needs must come from less than three acres per capita, only about *one-tenth* of the capacity now used by Americans."[6] The solution? No sweat, we'll use the market, right? We'll just go out and buy five more planets.

Let's use more stuff!

SCRAPING THE BOTTOM OF THE BARREL

Vince Matthews, a former state geologist of Colorado, talks about *resource pyramids* a lot these days. What he means by this term is that when a mineral is first exploited, it's highly concentrated, cheap, and easy to extract. For example, when copper was first mined, its concentration at or near the surface was 7 percent—a *much* higher quality than anything we now mine. As we move down the conceptual pyramid, the ore or mineral becomes more expensive to extract, partly because more energy is used to extract it. It's a lower-quality resource, and even if there are thousands of such deposits, each one will be less profitable per dollar invested than what we're used to. In many cases, it will also cause more environmental damage, as we rediscovered with the 2010 Deepwater Horizon oil spill.[7]

Matthews gives the example of Bingham Canyon Mine, also known as Kennecott Copper Mine, near Salt Lake City. This huge open pit mine, about three-fifths of a mile deep and two and a half miles wide, has been extremely lucrative in its 107 years of operation: more than 17 million tons of copper and 23 million ounces of gold have graced the global economy so far. But in April 2013, nature tried to fill the pit back up: a landslide dumped 165 million tons of rock, dirt, and low-grade ore into the hole, a volume which, by one estimate, would bury a chunk of land the size of New York City's Central Park 65 feet deep. At Bingham Canyon, it buried its fair share of mining equipment, including a small fleet of monster dump trucks each valued at more than $3 million. Though early warnings with seismic equipment prevented fatalities, this largest human-caused slide in history has resulted in hundreds of employee layoffs.[8] Says Matthews, "It seems likely that the market price of copper will go up as a result." He stresses that when resources are too low on the resource pyramid and too expensive, they're not worth extracting. "We're seeing this effect throughout the mining, drilling, and fracking industry," he says. "The best way to keep remaining minerals affordable is to consume less of them."

Because of its diverse properties, copper is of one humanity's most strategic metals, used not only in electrical infrastructure, construction, and electronic circuitry but also in renewable energy technologies like wind generators and solar technology. For example, a single large wind generator (2.4mW) requires more than eight tons of copper. If both the United States and China meet 2020 wind energy targets, where will *1.5 million tons* of inexpensive copper come from? More than half of the copper ever used—in the last ten millennia—was extracted in the past twenty-four years, and by some estimates, this metal will be too low on the resource pyramid to mine within forty or fifty years.[9]

Similarly, if the world's overdeveloped nations bring millions more hybrid and electric vehicles into the global fleet, the demand for rare earth elements like neodymium, lanthanum, and cerium (with unique luminescent, catalytic, and magnetic properties) will skyrocket. The United States has a slight problem here: China has been very busy making deals. While the US snoozed, it signed supply contracts all over the world on these high-tech metals, and 97 percent of the rare earth reserves are now controlled by this new superpower, whose leaders plan to use their near-monopoly strategically.[10] In a recent skirmish with Japan over territorial waters, China threatened to cut off Japan's supply of rare earth elements, a hammerlock that prompted the Japanese to immediately release the Chinese ship captain they held in custody.

The picture is not rosy for petroleum, either, despite low-pyramid discoveries in North Dakota, offshore Brazil, and elsewhere. "In fifty-four of the world's sixty-five oil-producing countries, oil production is declining," Matthews reports. "So we'd have to discover new reserves every day to make up for an overall 5 percent decline annually in production. And the top of the petroleum pyramid will never be seen again." Matthews is most concerned not about minerals, but fertilizer, the price of which is on a steadily upward trend. Again, China's consumption of fertilizer has increased 800 percent since 1990, causing many farmers around the world to rethink the way they grow their crops.[11]

Says Lester Brown of Earth Policy Institute, "We still talk about the gold rushes of the nineteenth century, but in today's world, land is the new gold."[12] Countries such as China, Saudi Arabia, and South Korea are leading a neocolonial charge to acquire farmable land. Why the land grabbing? Because the most valuable commodity of all, grain, is also becoming scarce on the market. In 2007, world grain production fell behind demand, largely because of drought. Leading grain exporters like Russia and Argentina began to lower their exports to keep domestic food prices down, and Vietnam, the world's second-largest rice exporter, banned exports altogether for a few months. A 2011 World Bank analysis reported that at least 140 million acres have been leased or purchased, mostly in Africa—"an area that exceeds the cropland devoted to corn and wheat combined in the United States."[13]

We don't hear these kinds of reports on popular news programs, partly because advertisers indirectly or directly control what gets reported, but data like this leaves us wondering, what will happen? Are we headed back to the Stone Age? No, but since we can't change the shapes of these various resource pyramids, we have to change ourselves instead. We'll have to make it immoral and even illegal not to recycle all resources. The European Union has experimented successfully with "extended producer responsibility," which requires manufacturers to take back products at the end of their useful lives, so the materials can be recycled. Certainly, if consumer expectations come back down from the stratosphere, resource demand will fall, and so will prices, as they did during the Great Recession. Although the United Nations has recently released reports about the "underutilized" protein content of insects, not many Americans would step up to *that* plate. Yet there is a growing sector of the American population that already practices "meatless Mondays" to reduce both the amount of grain inefficiently fed to livestock and the health risks to themselves. More efficient vehicles, more durable products, more decentralized and renewable energy production, the restoration of naturally productive ecosystems, an increase in renting and sharing rather than buying—all these are pieces of a sustainable, culturally abundant economy.

"CAN'T WE KEEP PLUNDERING, FOR JUST A LITTLE WHILE LONGER?"

What must the world's animal species think of us? Surely they wonder why we are so industriously disassembling the habitats that mutually support us. For example, because of disease, rising ocean temperatures, pollution, and other stressors, huge coral reefs that were here when Columbus sailed in the Caribbean have died off in this decade. As glaciers and icebergs melt, and prairies disappear under suburban developments, species scramble to make a living. The changes are too fast for maple trees and coffee plantations to move north or for polar bears to swim twice as far to hunt seals (their hunting bases—the icebergs—have melted). Before nature's health began to slide, we rarely thought about how a product got to us; we just consumed it and threw the leftovers away. We didn't think about the plants, animals, and even human cultures that were displaced or destroyed when the materials were mined. Now, when biologists like Norman Myers and E.O. Wilson tell us we may be in the middle of the most severe extinction since the fall of the dinosaur sixty-five million years ago, many are slowly moving beyond denial.[14] We are losing species a thousand times faster than the natural rate of extinction.

Depressed yet? Facts like these hit us like urgent, middle-of-the-night phone calls, don't they? They leave us with two distinct choices: either stay informed, get involved, and help create the values shift we so desperately need, or on the contrary, do nothing. Sit on the sidelines with our digital devices, pretending everything is fine. People like Tim DeChristopher and Bill McKibben have opted, heroically, to get busy, to become culture changers. DeChristopher just served twenty-one months in federal custody for a single act of civil disobedience: the Bureau of Land Management was auctioning off leases to drill for oil and gas on public lands, and although DeChristopher didn't have the capital, his winning bids for 22,500 acres came to $1.8 million (which he later raised from donations). This nonviolent, confrontational act helped shift the environmental movement into a different gear. At the 2011 Power Shift conference in Washington, DC, he inspired listeners to honor their convictions: "We hold the power right here to create our vision of a healthy and just world, if we are willing to make the sacrifices to make it happen," he said. "Climate Change and the injustices we are experiencing are not being driven solely by the coal industry, lobbyists, or politicians. They're also happening because of the cowardice of the environmental movement."[15]

Sentiments like these helped inspire acts of nonviolent civil disobedience, as in the arrest of 1,253 protesters of the Keystone XL pipeline. At the Forward on Climate rally in Washington, DC, McKibben was arrested, along with Sierra Club's executive director, Michael Brune, who broke with the organization's 120-year tradition barring civil disobedience. McKibben, whose 1989 book *The End of Nature* pioneered public awareness of climate change, has become a reluctant hero on the environmental front, founding the influential 350.org in 2008 to educate and advocate about climate change. More than five thousand demonstrations in 181 countries made the 350.org International Day of Climate Action in 2009 a rousing success, and an estimated fifty thousand people showed up at the Forward on Climate rally in 2013, where McKibben praised the large crowd for being "antibodies kicking in as the planet tries to fight its fever."

McKibben's most effective messaging so far may be the organization's 2012 "Do the Math" lecture series, in which he and his team traveled across the United States in a bus, stopping in twenty-one cities to present the urgent nature of climate change. The lectures spotlighted the number *2 degrees Celsius*—a limit accepted by most global leaders as the official "line in the sand" that must not be crossed. To keep the planet's average temperature below this target (and preserve life as we know it) we'll have to release no more than 565 gigatons of carbon dioxide. Yet, the fossil fuel industry already has five times that amount (2,795 gigatons) of carbon in their reserves. Reporting that the huge energy companies (Exxon, Shell, BP, Chevron, Conoco Phillips) receive $6.6 million a day in federal subsidies, McKibben concludes, "We're paying them to keep polluting."[16] These companies also spend a combined $100 million a day to explore the furthest reaches of the planet for more profitable oil, and $440,000 a day to lobby Congress. Rex Tillerson, CEO of Exxon, receives about $100,000 a day and has recently acknowledged that human-caused climate change is indeed a reality, yet with a shrug, he assumes that "people will adapt."[17] The question is, can he sleep at night?

DeChristopher's passionate final statement at his jail sentencing in 2011 is a harbinger of the outrage that is finally stirring in the ranks of citizen activists. Referring to environmental activism, he said, "At this point of unimaginable threats on the horizon, this is what hope looks like. In these times of a morally bankrupt government that has sold out its principles, this is what patriotism looks like. With countless lives on the line, this is what love looks like, and it will only grow."[18]

ON THE PAPER TRAIL

On a sixty-mile hike on Vancouver Island's West Coast Trail, Dave's then sixteen-year-old son, Colin, and he *got* the value inherent in unmarketed, pristine nature—in their lungs, and in their senses—especially the sense of being alive. They realized, *You don't need as much stuff when you genuinely appreciate the value of what's already here.* As their heads cleared, other forms of wealth besides money came into focus: the biological brilliance of the rain forest and ocean around them, the social and cultural wealth of the indigenous inhabitants of Vancouver Island, and health, surely the most valuable wealth of all.

Originally constructed as a survival route for shipwrecked sailors, the West Coast Trail provides spectacular vistas of bright blue ocean and white, pounding surf, often through dark silhouettes of shady rain forest. Tide pools filled with starfish and crabs, families of bald eagles soaring silently overhead, and the breathing spouts of hundreds of humpback whales all speak of nature's abundance.

Yet the beaches were littered with the trunks of dead spruce and fir trees, river-borne escapees from a logging industry that has transformed much of the island's natural capital into barren terrain. One photograph from that trip shows Colin standing on a sawed-off trunk the size of a small stage. He and his father were graphically reminded that many of the products they consumed back home had their beginnings in this particular bioregion, where 10 percent of the world's newsprint comes from.

If asked that week what Vancouver Island was good for, the father and son probably would have said in exhilaration, "Wilderness. Let it regenerate." If the logger whose flatbed-semi can transport three 80-foot tree trunks had been asked the same question, he'd have said, "Timber. Let me harvest it." The issue isn't a simple one, especially since Americans consume a third of the world's wood. Yet, after returning home from their travels in Canada, Dave resumed his higher-than-average consumption of paper, being a writer, while the logger probably looked for a nearby pristine place to take his kids for a hike, being also a father.

The fact is, logging practices like these force society to work harder. Though difficult to track directly, water utility bills go up when logging sediments pollute rivers that supply drinking water. Taxes go up when roads and bridges are washed out by floodwaters that run off clear-cut land. The price of lumber and paper goes up as companies feel compelled to advertise how "green" their practices are. In short, we each write checks and work extra hours to smooth over our collective "out of sight, out of mind" sloppiness.

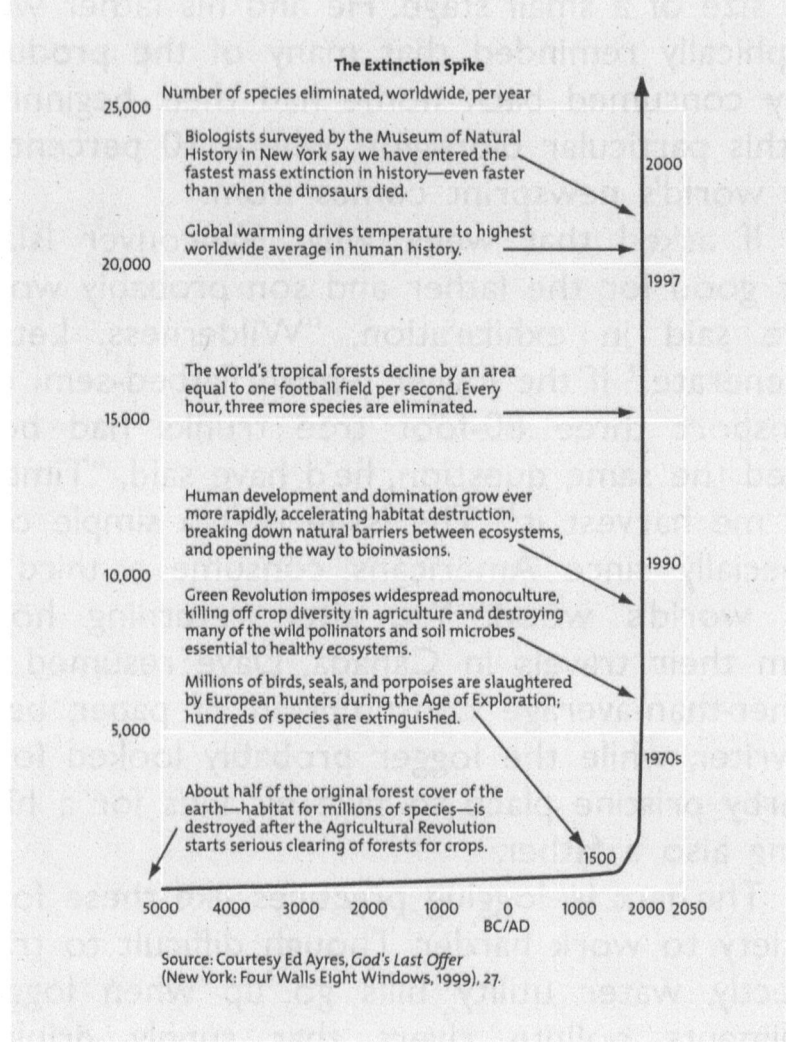

Source: Courtesy Ed Ayres, *God's Last Offer* (New York: Four Walls Eight Windows, 1999), 27.

WHAT HAPPENED?

What will civilizations of the far future say about our careless consumer era? Will they somehow deduce the causes of the calamitous decline in species diversity? Or will they shrug their shoulders (if they have shoulders to shrug), the way our scientists do when they ponder extinctions and collapses of the past? "It was climate change," the future scientists might conclude. "Inefficient use of land," others will hypothesize. But for the sake of our civilization's dignity, let's hope that none of them uncovers humiliating evidence of our obsessive, oblivious need for cheap processed snacks, gasoline, digital games, and underwear.

CHAPTER 9

Industrial diarrhea

DDT is good for me!
— 1950S JINGLE

The chemical age has created products, institutions, and cultural attitudes that require synthetic chemicals to sustain them.
—THEO COLBURN ET AL., *Our Stolen Future*

Imagine spotting them through binoculars at a baseball game—icons of advertising's hall of fame, lounging in front-row seats behind home plate. Look, there's the Marlboro Man and Joe Camel, signing autographs and passing out smokes to the kids. The Energizer Bunny flings handfuls of batteries into the crowd like Tootsie Rolls, while Ronald McDonald argues defensively with an environmentalist about hormones, antibiotics, and pesticide residues detected in the Big Mac. The plump Pillsbury Doughboy giggles as the Jolly Green Giant looks down on the game from the parking lot, ho-ho-hoing every time the home team scores. No one messes with a guy that size, even though chunks of pesticide slough off his green body like gigantic flakes of dry skin.

They seem so innocent, so endearing, don't they? So American. Many of us grew up with these guys, and we love their entrepreneurial optimism, their goofiness, their cool. Our demand for products like theirs has kept the US economy in the growth mode, overall, for more than half a century, and it really can't be denied that America's dazzling products make life seem bright, shiny, and convenient. But at what cost to our health, and the planet?

A GENERATION OVERFLOWING WITH SURPRISES

"Americans have a tradition of trusting manufacturers," says Suzanne Wuerthele, a toxicologist in the Environmental Protection Agency's Denver office. "Ever since the days of the flour mill, the small leather-tanning company, and the blacksmith, products have been assumed innocent until proven guilty—just the opposite of the way it should be. We've worked within an 'acceptable risk' strategy. Industry's stance is, 'Show me the dead bodies, or else let me make my product the way I want to.' When a disaster happens, industry begins to respond, and sometimes not even then."[1]

As Wuerthele points out, the track record for synthetic chemicals is laced with unpleasant surprises. "From nuclear radiation and CFCs to the various chlorinated hydrocarbon pesticides, we're always playing catch-up, finding out about health and ecological effects after it's too late. The most recent surprise is that genetically engineered organisms can migrate into the environment, even when they're engineered into the cells of plants. For example, pollen from genetically engineered corn plants migrates to plants like milkweed, where it has been shown to kill the Bambis of the insect world—Monarch butterflies. That shouldn't have caught the corporate and government scientists by surprise—with hundreds of thousands of acres of genetically engineered corn already planted—but it did."

We typically assume that somebody else is minding the shop, making sure all these chemicals are nontoxic. Yet the truth is that out of 84,000 chemicals in common commercial use, only about 1,500 to 2,000 have been tested for carcinogenicity. In fact, of the 3,000 chemicals produced at the highest volume, roughly two-fifths have no testing data on basic toxicity.[2] Writes Sandra Steingraber in *Living Downstream,* "The vast majority of commercially used chemicals were brought to market before 1979, when federal legislation mandated the review of new chemicals. Thus many carcinogenic environmental contaminants likely remain unidentified, unmonitored, and unregulated."[3] Steingraber, herself a victim of bladder cancer, recalls the advertising blitz for DDT, a product that returned home victorious from World War II after protecting American soldiers from malaria and other diseases overseas. "In one ad," writes Steingraber, "children splash in a swimming pool while DDT is sprayed above the water. In another, an aproned housewife in stiletto heels and a pith helmet aims a spray gun at two giant cockroaches standing on her kitchen counter. They raise their front legs in surrender. The caption reads, 'Super Ammunition for the Continued Battle on the Home Front.'"

That battle continues, though we're not always in agreement about who the enemy is. If we had microscopic vision, the horrors we'd see in our own houses would send us running for the door: microscopic bits of plastics, carpet fibers, and pesticides disappear into the nostrils of family members and never come out! Of chemicals commonly found in homes, 150 have been linked to allergies, birth defects, cancer, and psychological abnormalities, according to the Consumer Product Safety Commission.[4]

TOXIC DREAM HOUSE

David and Mary Pinkerton were trusting souls. They were buying their dream house in Missouri, and they liked to walk through the construction site after work, to see the house taking shape. On one visit just before moving in, David noticed a health warning printed on the subflooring. Irritation of the eyes and upper respiratory system could result from exposure to the chemicals in the plywood. But David trusted the builder. "He makes a living building houses. He wouldn't put anything in there that would hurt anybody."

"Within a month," write the authors of *Toxic Deception*, "the three girls and their parents had grown quite ill. David would sit in an old overstuffed chair until supper was ready; after dinner he would usually go right to bed.... One night Mary tried to make dinner and David found her leaning against the wall with the skillet in her hand.... All five had bouts of vomiting and diarrhea that would wake them up, almost nightly. Brenda no longer wanted to go to dance classes, even though ballet had been 'her big thing in life,' Mary later recalled."[5]

After the family was forced to evacuate the house within six months of moving in, a state environmental inspector found ten parts per million of formaldehyde in the house, many times higher than the standard. As many as forty million Americans may be allergic to their own homes, according to the American Lung Association, and twenty-five million Americans—about one in twelve—have already been diagnosed with asthma. This chronic disease—typically caused by allergic reactions that create inflammation—accounts for millions of sick days from work and school every year (more than $50 billion annually) as we continue to bombard ourselves with chemicals in paint fumes, cleaning products, air "fresheners," particleboard, plastics, glues, wallpaper, cosmetics, and a hundred other standard products of the twenty-first century. Here's a macabre formaldehyde footnote: only half as much formaldehyde is needed to embalm a deceased American today than was needed twenty years ago, because our bodies are already partially "embalmed" with high levels of formaldehyde in our blood, organs, and tissue.[6]

A new chemical substance is discovered every nine seconds of the working day, as the "invisible hand of the market" demands new miracles such as squeezable plastic containers or more enjoyable "mouth feel" in our snack foods. There is no place on earth that does not contain runaway molecules. "Tree bark sampled from more than 90 sites ... found that DDT, chlordane, and dieldrin were present no matter how remote the area," writes the environmental writer Anne Platt McGinn.[7] Scientists at the Mount Sinai School of Medicine found an average of fifty or more toxic chemicals in the bloodstreams and urine samples of nine volunteers, most of whom led normal or even environmentally conscious lives.[8]

Get SATISFIED

Spill baby, spill

DEAD ZONES

Among the most exotic of the chemicals being found in waterways are orphan molecules from the American lifestyle: trace amounts of pain relievers, antibiotics, birth control pills, perfumes, codeine, antacids, cholesterol-lowering agents, antidepressants, estrogen-replacement drugs, chemotherapy agents, sunscreen lotions, and hormones from animal feed lots. These compounds survive the assault of sewage treatment's microbes, aeration, and chlorination and eventually show up unannounced in drinking water. "In the past we looked for the really toxic actors that have immediate effects like death or cancer," says Edward Furlong, a chemist with the US Geological Survey. "Now we're starting to look more closely at compounds whose effects are subtle." To his surprise, Furlong discovered what he calls "the Starbucks effect," an indicator that caffeine may be giving aquatic life an unsolicited buzz. In addition to being a basic fuel of the American lifestyle (twenty-six gallons a year per capita), caffeine is a persistent and detectable compound. Just as it often persists in our bodies when we try to sleep, it also lingers in our rivers and streams. These findings are only the most recent in a series of aquatic conundrums presented by our affluence-seeking, no-effort-required civilization.[9]

Per capita consumption of bottled water increased by more than 1,000 percent between 1997 and 2013, becoming a $27 billion a year industry with annual sales of more than nine billion gallons—twenty-four gallons per capita—according to the American Beverage Association.[10] Yet the Natural Resources Defense Council advises that bottled water, at up to a thousand times the cost of tap water, is not only expensive but also somewhat suspect. At least a third of the bottled water on the market is just packaged tap water, and another 25 percent contains traces of chemical contaminants.[11]

A decade or so ago, fishermen began reporting a "dead zone" in the Gulf of Mexico, where their nets always come up empty and their lines never record a strike. By the time the Mississippi River reaches the Gulf of Mexico, it contains enough pesticides, wasted nutrients (from eroded farm soil), and petrochemicals to poison a body of water the size of New Jersey. Luxury cruise ships in the Gulf add insult to critical injury by dumping raw sewage and other waste into open waters. Because of regulatory loopholes, cruise ships can legally discharge "graywater" (used water that doesn't contain human waste) anywhere and can dump human waste and ground-up food when they're more than three miles from shore. Scuba diving, anyone?

No more appealing are the huge islands of waste caught in continent-size oceanic whirlpools in the North Pacific and elsewhere. Mostly composed of tiny bits of eroded plastic, these "gyres" threaten aquatic life that ingests mouthfuls of this toxic minestrone soup. We're literally littering them to death.

DEADLY MIMICRY

The surprises just keep coming, don't they, some of them involving other dead zones in the Great Lakes, the Arctic, and, potentially, even the human womb. Like evidence in a gruesome criminal case, the mounting data tell us more than we really want to know. In *Our Stolen Future,* the scientist and author Theo Colburn, along with her colleagues, compiled thousands of data sets spanning three decades. The data report chaos and dysfunction in the natural world: male alligators with stunted sex organs, roosters that can't crow, eagles that don't build nests to take care of their young, "gay" female seagulls that nest together because males aren't interested, whales with both male and female sex organs, and other cases of "sexual confusion."

The key finding was that these persistent chemicals fake their way into the endocrine system, masquerading as hormones like estrogen and androgen in a deadly case of miscommunication. When hormones, our chemical messengers, are released or suppressed at the wrong time in the wrong amounts, life gets bent out of shape. One experiment studied the health of children whose mothers had eaten fish contaminated with polychlorinated biphenyls (PCBs) during pregnancy. Compared with a control population, the two hundred exposed children, on average, were born sooner, weighed less, and had lower IQs.[12]

GENETIC ROULETTE

About thirty years ago, scientists perfected technology that can insert genes with certain traits into organisms. If you want a strawberry that tolerates cold temperatures, why not insert trout genes into the berry's genetic structure? If you want to protect corn from agricultural pests, why not put a pesticide gene right into the corn seed, so pests die when they eat the corn? Or what if you're a scientist at Monsanto who wants corn or soybeans to be Roundup Ready—resistant to the company's flagship herbicide, Roundup—so that farmers can spray as much Roundup as they want and sales of the herbicide skyrocket? Why not use existing laws that enable genetically engineered organisms (GMOs) to be *patented?* Why not force farmers to sign a contract that forbids them from saving seeds from the crop, and sue farmers whose cornfields accidentally contain GMOs because pollen from the engineered seeds drifted onto their farms? If these actions reduce pesticide use, increase yields, result in healthier corn and higher profits, aren't they justified?

The problem is, pesticide use is *increasing* on crops planted with GM (genetically modified) seeds as pests and weeds become resistant.[13] Roundup Ready crops now account for 94 percent of the soybean crops and upward of 70 percent for soy and cotton, USDA figures show. Between 1996 (when the first herbicide-resistant crops became available) and 2011, GMOs have led to a net increase in pesticide use of 404 million pounds, a 7 percent gain overall. Yields are essentially just holding steady when compared with non-GMO seeds (and in some cases are decreasing); and the health effects of foods containing GMOs are increasingly coming into question, as presented in Jeffrey M. Smith's eye-opening documentary *Genetic Roulette* and exhaustively researched book with the same title. Both present hard evidence that when livestock and wildlife have a choice between GM food and non-GM, they invariably choose the seeds developed with natural selection. In one of many examples, Smith writes, "The cows came to the first trough containing GM corn, sniffed it and withdrew. They then walked over to the next trough and finished off the non-GM corn. This same scenario was repeated over and over again using both cows and pigs on six or seven farms."[14]

What are their instincts telling these animals? Even without access to countless lab studies, their immune systems apparently sense potential problems. Already documented in lab tests are disruptions in endocrine systems; the transfer of genes into beneficial bacteria in stomachs; antibiotic-resistant diseases; kidney damage; allergies; and significantly increased mortality.

More evidence comes from India, where cotton growers who signed contracts with Monsanto seed vendors find themselves on a treadmill: the Indian government has issued warnings that cotton crop yields can decline after the first five years of production with GM seeds because of "growing parasite and pest infestations and the need for greater pesticide use, higher costs tied to both the GM seeds and the greater pesticide use, [and] Bt cotton's heavy water demands which are twice those of traditional cotton crops." According to one news account, this has led to a staggering number of suicides among Indian farmers; according to the Indian Ministry of Agriculture, a thousand or more small Indian farmers commit suicide every month, largely because of GM-generated crop failures and debts.[15]

The company that brought us Agent Orange, dioxin, PCBs, and the bovine growth hormone is coming under increasing scrutiny by agricultural experts and the general public. National polls show that more than 90 percent of Americans are in favor of mandatory product labeling for GMOs, and companies like Whole Foods have announced that labeling will be required on the products they sell.

So far, about a dozen state legislatures have taken up the issue, and federal legislators have introduced a bill to require labeling, but largely due to massive industry spending to prevent labeling requirements, these bills haven't passed. Unfortunately, H.R. 933 did pass, including a provision that "prohibits federal courts from banning the sale and planting of genetically modified organisms, even if they are proven to be dangerous to human health." The law has been dubbed the "Monsanto Protection Act" by food and health activists.

If there's nothing wrong with what some call Frankenfood, what are the manufacturers and vendors afraid of? Just label what's in the foods, and let us make the decision whether or not to buy them. One way to avoid GMOs is to buy USDA-certified organic food, which is not allowed to contain GMOs. A new "ethical shopping" app called Buycott can be used at the supermarket to find out where your groceries come from and how to participate in consumer campaigns.

A SMELL FROM HELL

The products that cause industrial diarrhea often seem remote and out of our control: plastic packaging, processed food, toys, cars, and computer circuit boards. But when we track hazardous chemicals from their sources to their points of use, we see they are not really remote at all: even the familiar bacon on our plates literally results in industrial diarrhea, as the writer Donovan Webster describes:

> Raising hogs used to be a family business, until one enterprising North Carolina farmer made it big business. But this booming national industry is churning out at least one unwelcome by-product—millions of gallons of pig waste that soil the water and foul the air.
>
> The smell is what hits you first. Like a hammer, it clamps against the nerve endings of your nose, then works its way inside your head and rattles your brain. Imagine a filthy dog run on a humid day; a long-unwashed diaper in a sealed plastic bag; a puffed roadkill beneath the hottest

summer sun. This is that smell: equal parts outhouse and musk, with a jaw-tightening jolt of ammonia tossed in.

In recent years, this potent mix of acrid ammonia, rotting-meat ketones, and spoiled-egg hydrogen sulfide has invaded tens of thousands of houses—and millions of acres—across rural America. The vapor billows invisibly, occasionally lifting off and disappearing for hours or weeks, only to return while the neighbors are raking leaves, scraping the ice off their windshield, or setting the table for a family cookout.[16]

Isn't it time to say good-bye to the obsolete Industrial Revolution—plagued from the start with industrial diarrhea—and bring in a new era of civic oversight and ecological design?

CHAPTER 10

A cancerous culture

> *The only chance of satisfaction we can imagine is getting more of what we have now. But what we have now makes everybody dissatisfied. So what will more of it do—make us more satisfied, or more dissatisfied?*
> —A CLIENT OF PSYCHOLOGIST JEREMY SEABROOK

Maybe the proof is in the pillow: the fact that more than thirty million Americans have chronic insomnia is one convincing indicator that all is not perfect in Camelot. We spend about $25 billion a year on sleep products, from pills to white-noise apps to comfort-zoned beds, but sleep researchers tell us that on average, humans in overdeveloped countries like ours sleep a full hour and a half less than we did a hundred years ago. In addition to peddling the pills that summon creepy luminescent green moths to our bedrooms in the TV ads, pharmaceutical companies in 2012 hustled Americans for $325 billion in prescription drugs. Among many other prescriptions (with, on average, seventy potential side effects apiece) we swallow half the world's antidepressants.[1]

The US Food and Drug Administration estimates that more than a hundred thousand Americans die from "properly" prescribed drugs each year[2] (compared with about ten thousand deaths from illegal drugs), making prescription drugs the fourth-leading cause of death in the United States. What's the problem? Well, in a word, *delirium*. Over the last generation, the United States became ground zero for an all-consuming epidemic that has become a global frenzy. Price tags and bar codes began to coat the surfaces of our lives, as every single activity became a transaction. Eating, entertainment, socializing, health, even religion—all became market commodities. To jump-start sex, take a pill. To eat, grab a couple of pizzas or, if the stock is doing well, order a three-course dinner (complete with a floral arrangement) from a store-to-door caterer. To exercise, join a health club. For fun, buy a crate-load of products on the Internet. To quit smoking, buy a nicotine patch, or ask your doctor for clinical doses of laughing gas! (No joke.)

In recent years our household budgets have expanded to include day care, dog care, elder care, health care, lawn care, house care—in direct proportion to our quest to be "care-free." But this way of life is not sustainable, nor is it genuinely satisfying. Our consumption habits demand more debt and longer work hours, reducing our social connections, a central foundation of happiness. To compensate for the feelings of loneliness, we then buy more stuff, seeking friendship through products. This way of life tries to meet nonmaterial needs with material goods, a losing strategy.

The 2013 OECD Factbook—which compares data from the twenty-seven member countries of the Organisation for Economic Co-operation and Development (many of the Factbook's tables also include others such as China, India, Brazil, Russia, Indonesia, and South Africa)—doesn't paint a pretty picture of *real* wealth in the United States. In traditional measurements of wealth, such as GDP per capita, the Stars and Stripes scores in the top five; and in disposable household income, the top fifteen. But look at some of the other categories: for example, only sixteenth best in household debt. Other rankings are twenty-first in suicide rate; twenty-fourth in renewable energy as a percentage of total energy; twenty-fifth in both hours worked and part-time employment; twenty-sixth in doctors per thousand adults; twenty-eighth in life expectancy; thirty-third in municipal waste per capita; thirty-eighth in water consumption per capita; thirty-ninth in obesity; thirty-eighth in total carbon dioxide emissions; forty-first in health care expenditures as a percentage of GDP.[3]

The results of a 2013 National Institutes of Health–commissioned study are no less shameful for Americans.[4] Compared with sixteen other developed countries (Australia, Austria, Canada, Denmark, Finland, France, Germany, Italy, Japan,

Norway, Portugal, Spain, Sweden, Switzerland, the Netherlands, and the United Kingdom) the United States scored at or near the bottom in infant mortality, traffic deaths, adolescent pregnancy, AIDS, obesity, heart disease, lung disease, and activity-limiting diseases like arthritis. It doesn't stop there, either: The United States spends more on its military than the next twelve nations on the list combined; it's the best in the world at imprisoning people; it has the highest divorce rate and the highest rate of both illicit and prescription drug use.

The progressive economist David Korten points to other indicators of decline in human capital—"skills, knowledge, psychological health, capacity for critical thought and moral responsibility"—as well as social capital, "the enduring relationships of mutual trust that are the foundation of healthy families, communities and societies."[5] Simply put, Korten believes our economic crisis is about a broken paradigm that consistently places financial values ahead of life values. Something needs to be done, quickly, partly to model a healthier lifestyle to those in other countries who would (catastrophically) follow us on our wild goose chase. If money can't buy better results, what can? We believe the answer is fundamentally simple: our culture needs different priorities guided by a different definition of success.

The psychologist Richard Ryan points to scores of studies—his own among them—showing why material wealth does not create happiness. "We keep looking outside ourselves for satisfactions that can only come from within," he explains. In the human species, happiness comes from achieving intrinsic goals like giving and receiving love. Extrinsic goals like monetary wealth, fame, and appearance are surrogate goals, often pursued as people try to fill themselves up with "outside-in" rewards. "People with extrinsic goals sharpen their egos to conquer outer space, but they don't have a clue how to navigate inner space," Ryan says.

"We've documented that unhappiness and insecurity often initiate the quest for wealth," he continues. In three studies with 140 adolescents, Ryan and colleague Tim Kasser showed that those with aspirations for wealth and fame were more depressed and had lower self-esteem than other adolescents whose aspirations centered on self-acceptance, family and friends, and community feeling.[6]

"The wealth seekers also had a higher incidence of headaches, stomachaches, and runny noses," Ryan says. He believes that while people are born with intrinsic curiosity, self-motivation, and playfulness, too often these qualities are squelched by "deadlines, regulations, threats, directives, pressured evaluations, and imposed goals" that come from external sources of control rather than self-motivated choices and goals. Their findings do not prove that rich people are always unhappy (some are, some aren't, depending on how they use their money). But they do point out that seeking extrinsic goals can dislodge us from vital connections with people, nature, and community—and that can make us unhappy.

Dysfunctions and disconnects seem to disrupt everyone's life these days, rich and poor alike. Donella Meadows cuts to the heart of it in *Beyond the Limits:*

> People don't need enormous cars; they need respect. They don't need closets full of clothes; they need to feel attractive and they need excitement and variety and beauty. People don't need electronic equipment; they need something worthwhile to do with their lives. People need identity, community, challenge, acknowledgment, love, and joy. To try to fill these needs with

material things is to set up an unquenchable appetite for false solutions to real and never-satisfied problems. The resulting psychological emptiness is one of the major forces behind the desire for material growth.[7]

Opinion polls reveal that Americans crave reconnection with the real sources of satisfaction, but we can't find our way back through all the jingles, static, and credit card bills.

FINDING REAL WEALTH

The more *real* wealth we have—such as friends, skills, libraries, wilderness, and afternoon naps—the less money we need in order to be happy. Throughout history, many civilizations have already discovered this truth, for example as the cedars of Lebanon and the topsoil of northern Africa were used up, cultures finally wised up, learning to substitute knowledge, playfulness, ritual, and community for material goods. During resource-scarce periods such as the eighteenth century, the Japanese culture developed a national ethic that centered on moderation and efficiency. An attachment to the material things in life was seen as demeaning, while the advancement of crafts and human knowledge were seen as lofty goals, as were cultural refinements such as *kenjutsu* (fencing), *jiujitsu* (martial arts), *saka* (tea ceremony and flower arrangement), and *go* (Japanese "chess"). The culture became so highly refined that the firearm was banned as too crude and destructive a method of settling differences. In this "culture of contraction," an emphasis on quality became ingrained in a culture that eventually produced world-class solar cells and Toyota Priuses. The Japanese ethical goal, *mottainai*, which loosely translates as "Don't waste resources; be grateful and respectful," is evidence of a culture that aspires to quality.

CULTURE SHIFT

If asked what we each want out of life, most would probably say we want less stress than we have now, and more laughter. We want a greater sense of control over how we spend our time, including fewer everyday details like security codes, telephone calls to be made, and endless consumer choices (which health insurance? which sunscreen? which mutual fund?). We want more energy and vitality and fewer "worn-out" days. We want the people in our lives to really understand and care about us—people whom we love and respect in return; activities and passions that foster creativity and self-expression; a sense that our lives have meaning and purpose; a feeling of being safe in our neighborhoods and having the respect of our peers. These are the kinds of things that make us happy.

When we're lucky enough to have these important things in our lives, we are less likely to beg doctors for antidepressants and more likely to sleep soundly on a cushion of well-being. We're less likely to be dependent on the approval of others and more likely to know in our own hearts that we're on the right track. We spend less time at the mall hunting and gathering what we hope are the latest fashions and hippest products, and more time completely absorbed in activities that make the time fly past. When we understand who we are and what we want, we have a greater sense of clarity and direction. Rather than feel that something is wrong or insufficient, we feel content. We know instinctively that we have "enough," and those nagging, insecure voices go silent at last.[8]

LOWER ON THE HIERARCHY?

Many of us know a few unique individuals—often elderly—who are healthy, wise, playful, relaxed, spontaneous, generous, open-minded, and loving: people who focus on problems outside themselves and have a clear sense of what's authentic and what's not. They are people for whom life gets in the way of work, on purpose. In fact, work is play, because they choose work they love. The sociologist Abraham Maslow called these people "self-actualized." Maslow concluded that most Americans had met the basic physical needs (the only ones that are primarily material) and security needs and had progressed to at least the "love and belongingness" rung of the hierarchy. Many individuals were higher than that.

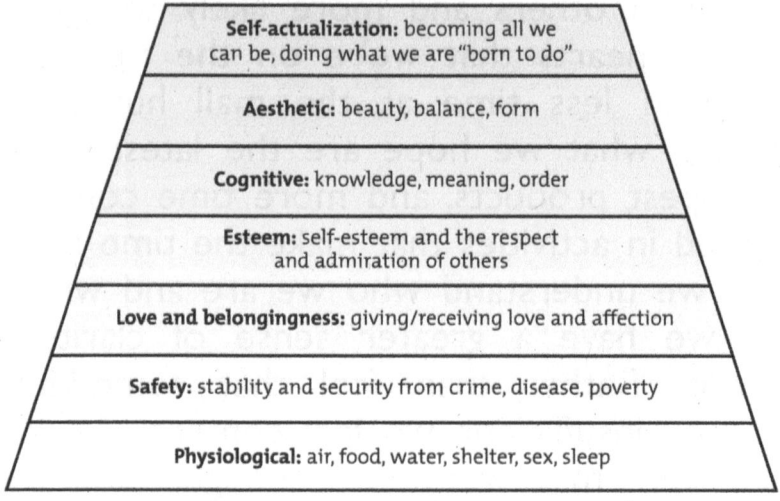

MASLOW'S HIERARCHY OF NEEDS

The question is, has America—weakened by the fever of affluenza—slipped down the hierarchy in the last thirty years? It seems the rungs of Maslow's ladder have become coated with slippery oil, as in a cartoon. According to polls, we're more fearful now. We're more insecure about crime, the possible loss of our jobs, and catastrophic illness. How can we meet innate needs for community when sprawl creates distance between people? How can we feel a sense of beauty, security, and balance if beautiful open spaces in our communities are being smothered by new shopping malls and rows of identical houses? How can we have self-respect in our work if it contributes to environmental destruction, social inequity, and isolation from living things? (The highest incidence of heart attacks is on Monday morning; apparently some would rather die than go back to work.)

IN THE FLOW

The work of the psychologist and author Mihaly Csikszentmihalyi provides valuable insights about where we need to go from here. In his classic book, *Flow*, he observes, "In normal life we keep interrupting what we do with doubts and questions. 'Why am I doing this? Should I perhaps be doing something else?' Repeatedly we question the necessity of our actions, and evaluate critically the reasons for carrying them out."[9]

After decades of interactive interviews with people from all walks of life—elderly Korean women and Japanese teenage motorcycle gang members; assembly line workers in Chicago; artists, athletes, surgeons—Csikszentmihalyi identified a universal human goal: "optimal experience," or *flow*, in which "the ego falls away and time flies. Every action, movement, and thought follows inevitably from the previous one, like playing jazz. Your whole being is involved, and you're using your skills to the utmost." The psychologist's interviewees consistently reported that flow occurs when they are challenged and yet feel that they are, or could become, equal to the challenge, when they have a sense that they are improving their skills, and when there are clear goals. To be genuinely happy, he concluded, we need to *actively* create our experiences and our lives, rather than passively let the media and marketers create it for us.

Writes Csikszentmihalyi, "What we found was that when people were pursuing leisure activities that were expensive in terms of the outside resources required—activities that demanded expensive equipment, or electricity, or other forms of energy measured in BTUs, such as power boating, driving, or watching television—they were significantly *less* happy than when involved in inexpensive leisure. People were happiest when they were just talking to one another, when they gardened, knitted, or were involved in a hobby; all of these activities require few material resources, but they demand a relatively high investment of psychic energy."[10]

For the ancients, happiness was a function of rational development; a reward for leading a virtuous, balanced life. Aristotle, for example, believed that happiness must be evaluated over a lifetime (not just in the lick of an ice cream cone, as in our world of instant gratification). Happiness, he believed, consists of a blend of moderation, gentleness, modesty, friendliness, and self-expression: harmony and balance in which desire is tempered through rational restraint. Try finding these qualities on sale in a typical American megamall.

The author and activist Alan Durning lyrically reminds us where we belong and where we can feel truly grounded: "In the final analysis, accepting and living by sufficiency rather than excess offers a return to what is, culturally speaking, the human home: to the ancient order of family, community, good work and good life; to a reverence for skill, creativity, and creation; to a daily cadence slow enough to let us watch the sunset and stroll by the water's edge; to communities worth spending a lifetime in; and to local places pregnant with the memories of generations."[11]

ARE WE CHEATING ON OUR GENES?

What kind of a deal have we arranged as a national culture? In exchange for some hundred thousand hours per lifetime of commuting and jobs that often fail to inspire us, we often settle for houses too big to maintain, superficial connections with people, easily broken gadgets, and nutrition-free processed food: counterfeit rewards that can't possibly meet our needs. So why do we cling to them? Apparently because that's the way our culture is programmed and because we are physically, psychologically, and socially addicted.

In an ancient bundle of the human brain, the nucleus accumbens—aka the "reward center"—continuously dispenses chemical substances like dopamine when our actions register "hits" of pleasure. A kind of chemical pinball machine, the reward center's underlying purpose is to seek out and score survival needs like food, water, leisure, energy, sex, and social connection.

The problem is, the reward center isn't evolving as fast as technology. For example, sugar is chemically rewarded by the reward center because of its apparent energy potential, but the human body has never experienced anything as concentrated as a box of Dunkin' Donuts or Pop-Tarts. We behave as if we've discovered a blueberry bog when really it's just another mood swing and a pound of weight we'll have to carry around. Sex seems to spell survival to the reward center, despite the anthropologically unfamiliar specter of overpopulation. Fast-moving images on television seem to be related to survival, so we surf these images to score chemical rewards. (Laboratory rats are so addicted to self-induced stimulation of the reward center that they lose 40 percent of their body weight, and die.)[12] Why bother to "save the planet," learn to handcraft a table, or make a new friend when our reward centers feast on calculated hits and bits of images, tastes, memories, emotional cocktails that promise pleasure, security, vitality, and social conquest?

ADDICTED TO GENEROSITY

The good news is that our collective intuition remains fundamentally intact. We still have a decent shot at creating a healthy new identity—a different way of living. We just need to collectively embrace the "click" of culture shift. In other words, demand a more sensible direction. It's time for a cultural revolution, a social tsunami, using proven interventions like nonviolent civil disobedience, focused social media and mentoring, and strategies Dave calls anthropolicy (policies aligned with what we truly need) and biologic (designing with nature rather than against it).

Here's why we're beginning to pull our civilization back to its set point: our primordial bonds with generosity and altruism are even stronger than our cultural affair with stimulation, speed, and gratification. By examining human responses to various images with MRI technology, neurologists observe that altruism and cooperation outcompete even virulent addictions like gambling, drugs, war, shopping, and superficial sex. One of the very strongest, most satisfying stimulants is the universal bond of love between mother and child. Healthy hormones flow like a mountain stream in response to images of nursing and developmental playing.

Can we tap into the power of generosity and trust to override the momentum of a quick-hit culture? Of course we can; we've already returned to our anthropological set point many times before. By trashing counterfeit rewards and culturally destructive behavior, we can make new agreements about what it means to be unselfish and truly successful. Instead of deadlines and dying species, we'll choose lifelines and living wealth.

WANTING WHAT WE HAVE

An old story about a native Pacific Islander rings true in the Age of Affluenza. A healthy, self-motivated native relaxes in a hammock that swings gently in front of his seaside hut as he plays a wooden flute for his family and himself. For dinner, he picks exotic fruits and spears fresh sunfish. He feels glad, and lucky to be alive. (Think of it—he's on "vacation" most of the time!) Suddenly, without warning, affluenza invades the island. Writes Jerry Mander, "A businessman arrives, buys all the land, cuts down the trees and builds a factory. He hires the native to work in it for money so that someday the native can afford canned fruit and fish from the mainland, a nice cinderblock house near the beach with a view of the water, and weekends off to enjoy it."[13] Like Pacific Islanders, we've been cajoled into meeting most of our needs with products brought to us courtesy of multinational corporations—what you might call takeout satisfaction. (From the maternity ward at a franchise Columbia/HCA hospital to an embalming room owned by the Houston-based Service Corporation International—which today handles the final remains of one of every eight Americans—we are wards of the Corporation.) As we consent to identify ourselves with the social species "consumer," our sense of confidence becomes dependent on things largely out of our control. For example, we suffer mood swings with the rising and falling of economic tides. If overtime work hasn't gotten us that BMW yet, maybe *more* overtime will, along with another refinance of our house.... Are we *still*, somehow, convinced we'll find peer approval, self-esteem, and meaning in material things if we just keep looking?

PART TWO

Causes

CHAPTER 11

Early infections

Now that you've been introduced to affluenza and its multiple symptoms, you may be asking yourself how we got to where we are today. What was the genesis of affluenza? Is it a bug that's always been there, just part of human nature? Is it culturally conditioned? Could it result from both nature and nurture? Those are the questions we'll attempt to answer in the next section of this book. We'll examine early efforts to contain or quarantine the disease, and attempt to understand how the virus mutated and grew more virulent over time in response to the forward march of history.

We believe it's necessary to understand the epidmiology of affluenza in order to begin to fight it effectively. As we researched this aspect of the issue, we became convinced that affluenza is not a new disease. But during the last half century, it has been spreading faster than ever before, as cultural values that once kept it in check have eroded under modern commercial pressures and technological changes.

THE SEARCH FOR PATIENT ZERO

When epidemiologists trace the evolution of a disease, they look for the first individual known to have contracted it, who is given the inglorious label "Patient Zero." For example, the official Patient Zero for the AIDS epidemic was a South African man who died in 1959 (though it is suspected that the disease originated as early as the 1920s).

So who was affluenza's Patient Zero? In the Judeo-Christian-Islamic tradition, there were two of them: Adam and Eve. While they had everything they needed in the Garden of Eden, they transgressed God's limits to eat the forbidden apple. So the first lesson in the Bible is an admonishment against coveting more than we need. Greed was, in fact, the original sin.

Some evolutionary biologists suggest that the uncertainties of primitive life meant that a hoarding orientation became part of human nature. Those folks who stored food in good times had it to sustain them in lean times. They survived and passed their hoarding genes on to their offspring.

Ergo, amassing stuff is as human as apple pie.

But on the other hand, for 99 percent of the time we *Homo sapiens* have existed on earth, we were hunter-gatherers. Our problem was that our food-seeking activities quickly depleted the areas we lived in of fruits, nuts, animals, and other edibles. So we often had to move on to allow those areas to rebound. Mobility was the name of the primitive game. And mobility didn't allow one to carry a whole lot of cargo. Hence a simpler, stuff-free life was a requirement for survival. A genetic propensity toward hoarding would have been downright deadly.

ORIGINAL AFFLUENCE

Life for hunter-gatherers was fraught with danger—from wild animals, accidents, disease, and an occasional enemy. Infant mortality was high, as were infirmities. Broken bones didn't heal well. Modern medicine might have been a godsend.

But the Stone Age wasn't as miserable as most of us believe. Some anthropologists who have observed contemporary "Stone Age" cultures call them "the original affluent societies."[1] Studies of such groups as the !Kung Bushmen of the Kalahari Desert indicate that before modernization confined them in smaller regions and destroyed the biological habitats from which they found subsistence, these hunter-gatherers were able to provide for their basic needs on as little as three or four hours of work a day. So-called Stone Age life apparently included more leisure time than does our own.

The UCLA anthropologist Allen Johnson and his family spent two years living with a Stone

Age tribe called the Machiguenga, hunter-gatherers who also practice some subsistence agriculture and inhabit the upper regions of the Amazon rain forest in Peru. He says he came to Machiguenga country loaded down with a huge footlocker full of possessions. "One of the lessons we learned over a period of just a few months, actually, was to dispense with most of our possessions," Johnson recalls. "This kind of minimalist existence became quite comfortable to us after a while and we began to feel that all these other possessions were completely superfluous. I learned from the Machiguenga that we could be comfortable living a much simpler life."

Johnson found the Machiguenga not quite affluent enough to get by on a four-hour workday. "Anthropologists," he says "may have gone a little bit overboard in describing how easy it is to be a hunter-gatherer, but the Machiguenga are certainly able to meet all their needs with six to eight hours of work. And that leaves a lot of time. The Machiguenga struck me as people who always have enough time. They're never in a hurry."

He came to admire their gentle ways and kind interactions with each other, the pleasure they found in quiet observation of their surroundings, the fact that they never seemed to get bored.

"There seems to be a kind of general satisfaction in the things that they do," Johnson says. "It's just a pleasure to be around the Machiguenga when they're working. They're calm, they're physically comfortable. They're sewing or weaving, or making a box or a bow and arrow. And there's a sense of them enjoying it as we might enjoy a hobby or a craft. No time pressure."

"One of the things they do in the evening," he observed, "is sit around telling stories. And as you go by a Machiguenga house in the evening, you'll see through the slats of the walls of the house. You'll see the fire glowing and hear people's voices softly telling stories. If a man went hunting, he'll tell the story with the sights and the sounds and the smells. They also tell folktales. I've translated a lot of them, and they're absolutely beautiful, a real literature."[2]

BACK IN THE USA

Like many other travelers who return from time spent with so-called underdeveloped or primitive cultures, Johnson had trouble returning to the fast-paced, possession-laden life in the United States. Culture shocked, he walked through a supermarket aisle entirely filled with cake mixes and wondered, "Is this really progress?"

Life in Los Angeles seemed surreal. His children complained regularly of boredom despite a plethora of toys and activities. People he met seemed constantly busy but unsatisfied with their lives, working and consuming frantically as if to fill "some kind of hole or emptiness," an emotional state he never encountered among the Machiguenga.

Johnson doesn't romanticize the Machiguenga's existence. Their life expectancy was short, as they often fell victim to jungle diseases. But they hadn't a hint of affluenza.

So it's not "human nature." But it's easy to find evidence of early infection among societies that achieved agricultural surpluses sufficient to allow long-term settlements, class divisions, and the beginnings of city life. In such cultures, political and economic hierarchies flourished, and as they strove for greater riches, members of the upper echelon began to oppress the poor and subjugate their neighbors. Without naming it as such, prophetic traditions in all civilizations, East and West, challenged their lordly brethren who had been infected by affluenza. "Beware an act of avarice; it is a bad and incurable disease," warned an ancient Egyptian proverb.[3]

The Buddha taught that the way to happiness and enlightenment lies in reducing desire, which he thought to be the cause of suffering.

MORAL ANTIDOTES

The Hebrew prophets railed against those who amassed riches by oppressing the poor and the weak. Moderation was the key: "Give me neither poverty nor riches, but only enough," reads the book of Proverbs. One day each week, the Sabbath, was to be kept completely free of moneymaking and to thereby remain holy. Of the Sabbath, the great Jewish scholar Rabbi Abraham Heschel writes, "He who wants to enter the holiness of the day must first lay down the profanity of chattering commerce ... and fury of acquisitiveness."[4] The book of Deuteronomy, written about 700 BC, admonishes against wasting things, the natural corollary to a life of material desire. As Rabbi Daniel Schwarz puts it, "When you waste creation, it's like spitting at God."

The ancient Greeks, too, warned against affluenza. David Shi, the author of *The Simple Life* and president emeritus of Furman University, told viewers of the *Affluenza* documentary that "simplicity is an ancient, even a primordial, ideal," explaining that the Greeks spoke of the 'middle way,' that midpoint between luxury and deprivation." Aristotle warned against those "who have managed to acquire more external goods than they can possibly use, and are lacking in the goods of the soul." By contrast he suggested that happiness would come to "those who have cultivated their character and mind to the uppermost and kept acquisition of external goods within moderate limits." "Aristotle was the first to maintain the diminishing marginal utility of money," writes the philosopher Jerome Segal. "His belief was that each additional increment of money is of progressively less benefit to its possessor, and beyond a certain point, having more is of no value and may even be harmful."[5]

"Unlimited wealth," Aristotle wrote, "is great poverty." Two groups of Greek nonconformists, the Stoics and the Cynics, were even more critical of materialism. By the time of the birth of Christ, their ideas were widespread. The Roman philosopher Seneca, a Stoic, challenged his own culture: "A thatched roof once covered free men; under marble and gold dwells slavery."

According to the New Testament scholar Burton Mack, early Christian teachings bore a strong resemblance to those championed by Epictetus, Diogenes, and other followers of the Cynic tradition in Greece. Living simply, the Cynics mocked the conventional culture of their affluent peers. Their ideas were widely known throughout the Mediterranean region two millennia ago.

But perhaps the strongest rebuke to incipient affluenza came from Jesus himself. He continually warned of the dangers of wealth, declaring it the major impediment to entry into the kingdom of heaven. It would be easier for a camel to pass through a needle's eye than for a rich man to enter heaven, he told his followers. The rich man who wished to follow Jesus was told he would first have to sell his possessions and give the money to the poor. "He went away unhappy, for he had great wealth."[6]

Don't store up treasures on earth, Christ commanded. Rather be like the birds and flowers, who possess nothing. God takes care of them, and their beauty is not matched by Solomon in all his glory. The earliest of Jesus's disciples and believers lived in simple communities where they shared all things in common and preached that "the love of money is the root of all evil."

"I think one of the most riveting passages in the New Testament is where Christ warns about mammon, which is the power of wealth, the power of money," says Richard Swenson, a physician who lectures widely in evangelical churches. "Christ says you cannot serve both God and mammon. He didn't say it's hard, it's difficult, it's tricky. He said it's impossible."

In fact, one of Jesus's final public acts was a stinging rebuke to the affluenza that had begun to permeate his society. By chasing the money lenders from the temple and overturning their tables, he challenged physically (one might even say violently) a profane commercialism that had crept into even the holiest of places.

The Christian theologian and environmental scientist Calvin DeWitt says our modern consumer philosophy turns scriptural teachings on their head: "Consume more, then you'll be happy. Remain discontented with everything so that you'll continue to strive for more and more. That's the message we hear. But the biblical teaching is to be content with what you have, honor God, take care of creation, give your bread to the hungry. Then joy comes as a by-product of service. If you take those teachings and just write their antithesis, you find yourself describing our current consumer society."

A CLASH OF CULTURES

In the spring of 1877, the famous leader of a tribe of hunter-gatherers addressed a council of his people, gathered around him on the windswept plains of South Dakota. The Lakota Sioux chief Tatanka Yotanka (Sitting Bull) gave thanks for the change of seasons and the bounty that the earth freely provided. But he warned his people about "another race, small and feeble when our fathers first met them, but now great and overbearing." He described the pale-faced men and women who had come to mine and till the earth, carrying with them (and seeking to convert the Indians to) the words of a man who preached brotherhood, peace, and goodwill among all, a preference for the poor, and a life free from the encumbrances of worldly possessions.

Something, apparently, had gotten lost in the translation, because as Sitting Bull observed, "These people have made many rules which the rich may break but the poor may not. They take tithes from the poor and weak to support the rich who rule. They claim this mother of ours, the earth, for their own and fence their neighbors away; they deface her with their buildings and their refuse. Their nation is like a spring freshet that overruns its banks and destroys all who are in its path. We cannot dwell side by side."[7]

Of the white invaders, Sitting Bull said, one thing was certain: *"The love of possession is a disease with them."* Today he might have called that disease "affluenza." Back then, he would have found that even among the whites, there were many who shared his fears of the virus in their midst.

CHAPTER 12

An ounce of prevention

The fear of affluenza, though never identified as such, has been part of the American tradition since colonists arrived here from Europe. It was a mixed bunch that risked life and livelihood to cross the Atlantic on small wooden ships. The first came seeking riches. The Spanish wanted gold; the French, furs. The Dutch sought new trade routes to the fabled Indies.

But among the early arrivals from England were refugees seeking to escape what they had come to view as a godless materialism rapidly taking root in Europe. "When the Puritans arrived in the New World, one of their major premises was their desire to try to create a Christian commonwealth that practiced simple living," explains the historian David Shi.

In the Massachusetts Bay Colony, the Puritans adopted what were known as sumptuary laws, forbidding conspicuous displays of wealth. They required colonists to wear simple clothing, for example. But because they were never applied fairly, the laws failed to stem a growing trade in luxury goods arriving in the New World from Europe. Wealthier, politically powerful Puritans could effectively ignore the laws and wear whatever they chose, while their poorer brethren were punished for transgressions of the dress code. In effect, the sumptuary laws exacerbated visible class differences.

In Pennsylvania the Quakers, under the leadership of John Woolman, were more successful in their efforts to keep affluenza at bay. "My dear friends," Woolman preached, "follow that exercise of simplicity, that plainness and frugality which true wisdom leads to."[1] "Among Quakers," writes the philosopher Jerome Segal, "the restrictions on display and consumption became more widely applicable. Most important, the pursuit of luxurious consumption was linked to a broad range of injustices and social problems, including alcoholism, poverty, slavery, and ill treatment of the Indians."[2]

YANKEE DOODLE DANDIES—NOT!

In some respects, the American Revolution itself was a revolt against affluenza. The British colonial masters bled their American colonies in order to support a lifestyle of luxury approaching decadence. The English lords often spent half the day dressing, much of it on their ever-more-elaborate headpieces (this is the origin of the term *bigwigs*). Then they stuffed themselves on dinners that took hours to consume.

The American colonists, meanwhile, grew angry at the taxes imposed on them to keep British coffers full. But at the same time, colonial leaders were troubled by the unbridled pursuit of wealth on the part of some of their own countrymen. "Frugality, my dear, must be our refuge," wrote John Adams to his wife, Abigail, during the revolution. "I hope the ladies are everyday diminishing their ornaments, and the gentlemen, too. Let us drink water and eat potatoes rather than submit to unrighteous domination."[3]

At the end of the eighteenth century, as the world changed politically with the triumph of the American and French revolutions, it was also changing economically. The Industrial Revolution's "dark, satanic mills" (in William Blake's words) brought steam power and assembly-line techniques, making possible the production of textiles and other goods in a fraction of the time previously required. Benjamin Franklin argued that with such productive tools at humanity's disposal, it was possible to reduce the labor time needed to produce all the "necessaries and comforts" of life to three or four hours a day.

But in fact, the opposite occurred. During the early Industrial Revolution, working hours were roughly doubled, rather than reduced. The medieval workday, scholars now estimate, averaged about nine hours; more in summer, fewer in winter.[4] Moreover, the pace of work was quite slow, with frequent breaks for rest.

And in some parts of Europe, workers enjoyed nearly 150 religious holidays, when they didn't work at all. Pieter Breughel's sixteenth-century paintings of peasants dancing, feasting, or napping in their wheat fields in the afternoon were accurate portrayals of the life he witnessed.

THE SPIRIT OF SAINT MONDAY

But with the Industrial Revolution, factory workers—driven into desolate, Dickensian industrial cities as the land they once farmed was enclosed for sheep raising—were working fourteen, sixteen, even eighteen hours a day. In 1812, one factory owner in Leeds, England, was described as humane and progressive because he wouldn't hire children under ten years of age and limited children's working hours to sixteen a day.

But factory workers did not readily comply with the new industrial discipline. Stripped of their old religious holidays, they invented a new one: Saint Monday. Hung over from Sunday nights at the tavern, they slept in late, or failed to show up to work at all. Workers were paid on a piece-rate basis, and at first only worked as long as they needed to subsist. If an employer paid them more as an incentive to work more, he soon found that his strategy backfired. As Max Weber put it, "The opportunity of earning more was less attractive than that of working less."[5]

This was obviously a pre-affluenza situation.

Consequently, as Karl Marx repeatedly pointed out, employers sought to pay the lowest wages possible so that workers would have to keep working long hours simply to survive. But while such miserliness was rational behavior for individual employers, it undermined capitalist industry as a whole. Workers' lack of purchasing power led to overproduction crises that periodically destroyed entire industries.

"In these crises," Marx and Engels wrote in *The Communist Manifesto* (1848), "a great part not only of the existing products but also of the previously created productive forces are periodically destroyed.... Society suddenly finds itself put back into a state of momentary barbarism.... And how does the bourgeoisie get over these crises? On the one hand, by enforced destruction of a mass of productive forces; on the other, by the conquest of new markets, and by the more thorough exploitation of old ones."[6]

MARX ON AFFLUENZA

So just how is this "more thorough exploitation" accomplished? In effect, by exposing one's potential customers to affluenza. Of course, Marx never used the term, but in a brilliant passage from *The Economic and Philosophical Manuscripts of 1844*, worth quoting from at length, he describes the process. "Excess and immoderation" become the economy's "true standard," Marx wrote, as

> the expansion of production and of needs becomes an ingenious and always calculating subservience to inhuman, depraved, unnatural, and *imaginary* appetites ... Every product is a bait by means of which the individual tries to entice the essence of the other person, his money. Every real or potential need is a weakness which will draw the bird into the lime.... The entrepreneur accedes to the most depraved fancies of his neighbor, plays the role of pander between him and his needs, awakens unhealthy appetites in him, and watches for every weakness in order, later, to claim the remuneration for this labor of love.[7]

That passage, written 169 years ago, accurately describes much of modern advertising, which, indeed, stimulates "imaginary appetites," and consistently uses sex, fear, and personal anxieties to sell products. Ultimately, though, Marx believed that market expansion would always be inadequate and that overproduction crises could only be prevented if the workers themselves gained ownership of the factories and used the machinery for the benefit of all. That didn't mean an ever-growing pie of material production simply shared more equitably. Marx's goal was never a materialistic one. Indeed, he stressed that to simply increase the purchasing power of workers "would be nothing more than a better remuneration of slaves and would not restore, either to the worker or to the work, their human significance and worth."[8]

WEALTH AS DISPOSABLE TIME

Neither would "an enforced equality of wages," made law by a socialist government, lead to happiness, which, Marx believed, was to be found instead in our relationships with other people and in the development of our capacities for creative expression. "The wealthy man," he wrote, "is one who needs a complex of human manifestations of life and whose own self-realization exists as an inner necessity." He further suggested that "too many useful goods create too many useless people."[9]

Of course, Marx understood that human beings must have enough wholesome food, decent shelter, and protective clothing. Mass production, he believed, made it possible for everyone to achieve these ends. And to do so each person would have to perform a certain minimum amount of repetitive, noncreative labor. Marx called this time, which he and Engels estimated could be reduced (even in the mid-1800s) to as little as four hours a day, "the realm of necessity."

*Get*SATISFIED

The Satisfaction of Enough in a nutshell

The work time necessary to satisfy real material needs could be reduced further by increases in productivity, "but it always remains a realm of necessity. Beyond it begins that development of human power, which is its own end, the true realm of freedom," when self-chosen activity prevails. Of this realm of freedom, Marx added, "the shortening of the working day is its basic prerequisite." "A nation is really rich if the working day is six hours rather than twelve," Marx wrote, quoting approvingly the anonymous author of a British article written in 1821: "Wealth is liberty—liberty to seek recreation, liberty to enjoy life, liberty to improve the mind: it is disposable time and nothing more."[10]

In 1819, the Swiss economist Jean Charles de Sismondi expressed similar ideas, arguing that political and economic leaders focused too much on making humans rich and too little on making them happy. "The objective of government", he wrote, "is, or ought to be, the happiness of men united in society." One way to achieve this, he suggested, was to allow all workers, sharing as equally as possible in the fruits of their labor, "to have more leisure with less labor."[11]

SIMPLY THOREAU

Meanwhile, across the Atlantic, an American movement offered a similar critique of industrialization and the acquisitiveness it engendered. The transcendentalists, as they called themselves, idealized the simple life, close to nature, and started intentional communities (none destined to last very long) such as Brook Farm and Fruitlands, based on their principles.

Better remembered, if similarly short-lived, was Henry David Thoreau's 1845 sojourn to a one-room cabin he built on the shore of Walden Pond, near Boston. "Simplicity, simplicity, simplicity," wrote Thoreau in *Walden*. "Most of the luxuries, and many of the so-called comforts of life, are not only not indispensable, but positive hindrances to the elevation of mankind."[12]

In *Life without Principle,* Thoreau was even more damning of the acquisitive industrial personality, already in need of antibodies for affluenza. Like Marx, Thoreau believed that true wealth meant sufficient leisure for self-chosen creative activity, suggesting that half a day's labor should be enough to procure real material necessities. "If I should sell both my forenoons and my afternoons to society as most appear to do, I am sure that for me there would be nothing left worth living for," Thoreau wrote.

> Let us consider the way in which we spend our lives. The world is a place of business. What an infinite bustle.... There is no sabbath. It would be glorious to see mankind at leisure for once. It is nothing but work, work, work. I cannot easily buy a blank book to write thoughts in; they are commonly ruled for dollars and cents.... I think there is nothing, not even crime, more opposed to poetry, to philosophy, ay, to life itself than this incessant business.[13]

"If a man should walk in the woods for love of them half of each day, he is in danger of being regarded as a loafer, but if he spends his whole day as a speculator, shearing off those woods and making earth bald before her time, he is esteemed an industrious and enterprising citizen,"[14] Thoreau wrote, in words all the more relevant today, when corporate speculators shear off entire forests of old-growth redwoods to pay for junk bonds.

For Marx, Thoreau, and many other oft-quoted, but more often ignored, philosophers of the mid-nineteenth century, industrial development could only be justified because, potentially, it shortened the time spent in drudgery, thereby giving people leisure time for self-chosen activity.

Given a choice between more time and more money, these philosophers chose the former. For precisely a century following Thoreau's retreat to Walden, that choice, as our next chapter suggests, would engage Americans in a broad and energetic debate. Then, suddenly, it would be resolved—in favor of more money. But it would not be forgotten.

CHAPTER 13

The road not taken

Our lives shall not be sweated
From birth until life closes
Hearts starve as well as bodies
Give us bread, but give us roses...

Small art and love and beauty
Their drudging spirits knew
Yes, it is bread we fight for
But we fight for roses too.

—JAMES OPPENHEIM, DECEMBER 1911

After the horrors of the Civil War, a new, quieter conflict, ultimately more powerful in its impact, emerged in the United States. Two roads, as Robert Frost put it in his lovely poem "The Road Not Taken," presented themselves to Americans, and after a period of indecision that lasted nearly a century, we chose one of them, "and that has made all the difference."

Nineteenth-century Americans still had more respect for thrift than for spendthrifts, and the word *consumption* meant something different then. As Jeremy Rifkin explained in the *Affluenza* documentary, "If you go back to Samuel Johnson's dictionary of the English language, to *consume* meant to exhaust, to pillage, to lay waste, to destroy. In fact, even in our grandparents' generation, when somebody had tuberculosis, they called it 'consumption.' So up until this century, to be a consumer was not to be a good thing, it was considered a bad thing."

Yet the factory system had made possible a tremendous efficiency in the time required to produce products. And herein lie the roots of the new conflict: what to do with all that time? One side suggested that we make more stuff; the other believed we should work less. Luxury or simplicity. Money or time. Bread or roses.... Or perhaps a balance of both?

THE RIGHT TO BE LAZY

Across the Atlantic, a similar argument was brewing. In 1883, while in a French prison, Paul Lafargue, a son-in-law of Karl Marx, wrote a provocative essay called "The Right to Be Lazy," challenging the make more, have more ethic. Lafargue mocked industrialists who "go among the happy nations who are loafing in the sun" and "lay down railroads, erect factories, and import the curse of work."[1]

Lafargue deemed laziness "the mother of arts and noble virtues" and suggested that even then, factories were so productive that only three hours a day of labor should be required to meet real needs. Like Marx, he pointed out that

Catholic Church law had given workers many feast days honoring the saints when work was forbidden. It was no surprise, he suggested, that industrialists favored Protestantism (with its work ethic), which "dethroned the saints in heaven in order to abolish their feast days on earth."

At the same time in England, William Morris, a poet, artist, and essayist (and designer of the Morris chair), claimed that under the factory system, "the huge mass of men are compelled by folly and greed to make harmful and useless things."[2] "An immensity of work," wrote Morris, was expended in making "everything in the shop windows which is embarrassing or superfluous."

"I beg of you," he pleaded,

> to think of the enormous mass of men who are occupied with this miserable trumpery, from the engineers who have had to make the machines for making them, down to the hapless clerks who sit day-long year after year in the horrible dens wherein the wholesale exchange of them is transacted, and the shopmen, who not daring to call their souls their own, retail them ... to the idle public which doesn't want them but buys them to be bored by them and sick to death of them.[3]

"The good life of the future," said Morris, would be totally unlike the life of the rich of his day. "Free men," he maintained, "must live simple lives and have simple pleasures." Morris defined a decent, wealthy life as requiring "a healthy body, an active mind, occupation fit for a healthy body and active mind, and a beautiful world to live in."

THE SIMPLE LIFE

Back in the United States, new institutions like the department store helped promote a life of conspicuous consumption. "Urban department stores came in during the 1880s," says the historian Susan Strasser, "basically to create the sort of place where people go and lose themselves and meanwhile spend their money." By the 1890s, wealthy Americans proudly displayed the material signs of their success, wearing affluenza on their sleeves, you might say. But not everyone was impressed.

"In the late nineteenth century, there was a major revival of American interest in simple living," says the historian David Shi. "Theodore Roosevelt was one of the foremost proponents of a simpler life for Americans during that period. Roosevelt was quite candid in saying that for all his support for American capitalism, he feared that if it were allowed to develop unleashed it would eventually create a corrupt civilization." Shi provides other examples of this turn-of-the-century interest in simplicity in his wonderful book *The Simple Life*. Even America's best-selling magazine, *The Ladies' Home Journal*, promoted simplicity during that era.

THE ORIGINAL OCCUPY

When the Occupy Wall Street protesters took over New York City's Zucotti Park in September 2011 to champion the cause of "the 99 percent," they had no idea that exactly a hundred years earlier, their theme was anticipated in a beautiful novel by James Oppenheim, a former Greenwich Village teacher and settlement house worker. Harper Brothers published *The Nine-Tenths* in New York in September 1911. Its title anticipates the 99 percent of Occupy fame. But the novel provides a far more nuanced understanding of human need and political organizing than that of the angry but unfocused later movement.[4]

The novel fictionalizes two real events while changing their order. The first of these events was the Triangle Shirtwaist Fire, a well-known disaster that resulted in the death of 146 young women on March 24, 1911. In the novel, the Triangle Fire becomes "the East Eighty-First Street Fire." It starts with a carelessly tossed cigarette in a print shop and results in the death of dozens of very young women, who work making hats one floor higher in the same building. Overcome with guilt, the owner of the print shop, Joe Blaine, learns of the plight of poor women workers in New York and, in an effort to redeem himself, sells his shop and uses the money to start a paper, *The Nine Tenths,* which helps the women workers organize a major strike. The real strike on which the story is based took place more than a year before the Triangle Fire.

In the fall and winter of 1909 and 1910, in what was deemed "the Uprising of the Thirty Thousand," masses of factory workers shut down their machines and took to the streets, supported by the Women's Trade Union League. Their demands centered on safe working conditions, an increase in pay, and shorter working hours. The fictional *Nine-Tenths* is the organ of solidarity that holds them together and publicizes their cause when the mainstream press will not. This was the original Occupy.

After a few months, in the novel as in reality, the Uprising of the Thirty Thousand ends with a measure of success, as many employers give in to the women's key demands. The most prominent of the real holdouts was the Triangle Shirtwaist Company, which refused to improve safety conditions. A year later, its belligerence produced tragedy.

After the strike, Joe marries and goes on a honeymoon. On his return to New York, he describes his hopes for their city, "the city of five million comrades":

> They toil all day with one another; they create all of beauty and use that men may need; they exchange these things with each other; they go home at night to gardens and *simple* houses, they find happy women

there and sunburnt, laughing children. Their evenings are given over to the best play.... They have time for study, time for art, yet time for one another.[5]

Oppenheim's vision of the good life, while still infused by the gender bias of his day, is an enlightened one of modest homes, modest comfort, and most of all, *time* to appreciate the things that are not things but are the best things in life. Oppenheim understood that poor as these women were, they could not live on money alone. They needed the nonmaterial joys of life—art, beauty, nature, play, learning, friendship, and love, and for all of these things, they needed time.

In December of that same year, 1911, Oppenheim published the work for which he is most famous, a poem called "Bread and Roses," which became a popular song by Judy Collins in 1976. "Hearts starve as well as bodies," a line from the poem reads. "Give us bread, but give us roses." The poem describes the women of the Uprising of the Thirty Thousand, marching through New York, watched from "a million darkened kitchens, a thousand mill lofts gray," where their sisters toil with neither "bread" (money) nor "roses" (and the time to smell them).

The theme of bread and roses inspired others, including, according to anecdotal reports, the thousands of women who filled the streets of Lawrence, Massachusetts, a month after the poem was published, demanding higher pay and shorter hours in what came to be called the Bread and Roses Strike.[6]

THE SHORTER-HOURS MOVEMENT

Organized labor had not yet then accepted the definition of the good life as a goods life, in which the marker of progress was the consumption of stuff. Indeed, for more than half a century, the demand for shorter hours topped labor's agenda. In 1886, hundreds of thousands of workers filled American cities, demanding that an eight-hour workday be made America's legal standard. That didn't happen until 1938, when the Fair Labor Standards Act made the eight-hour day and forty-hour week the law of the land. And by then, labor leaders were fighting for a six-hour workday. It was needed, they argued, as much for spiritual as economic reasons.

"The human values of leisure are even greater than its economic significance," wrote William Green, president of the American Federation of Labor, in 1926. Green claimed that modern work was "meaningless, repetitive, boring," offering "no satisfaction of intellectual needs." Shorter working hours were necessary "for the higher development of spiritual and intellectual powers," Green claimed. His vice president, Matthew Woll, charged that modern production ignored "the finer qualities of life. Unfortunately, our industrial life is dominated by the materialistic spirit of production, giving little attention to the development of the human body, the human mind or the spirit of life."[7]

Juliet Stuart Poyntz, education director of the International Ladies Garment Workers Union, declared that what workers wanted most of all was "time to be human." "Workers," she observed, "have declared that their lives are not to be bartered at any price.... No wage, no matter how high" was more important than the time that workers needed.[8]

TIME TO KNOW GOD

Behind them, as Professor Benjamin Hunnicutt of the University of Iowa points out in his books *Work Without End* and *Free Time*, rallied prominent religious leaders, who worried that workers had no time for reflection and spiritual matters, no "time to know God." Jewish leaders challenged Saturday work as violating their Sabbath and led the fight for a five-day workweek. Catholic leaders backed Pope Leo XIII's call (in his encyclical *Rerum Novarum*, 1891) for a "living wage," or family wage, that would guarantee the breadwinner in working families sufficient income for a life of *"frugal* comfort." But beyond that, they believed that more time was more important to workers than more money.

During the 1920s, Monsignor John Ryan, editor of the *Catholic Charities Review*, pointed to Saint Augustine's claim that natural law demanded a "maximum" standard of living as well as a minimum one. "The true and rational doctrine," Ryan wrote, "is that when men have produced sufficient necessaries and reasonable comforts, they should spend what time is left in the cultivation of their intellects and wills, in the pursuit of the higher life." They should, he said, "ask, what is life for?"[9] The Jewish scholar Felix Cohen pointed out that, in the biblical tradition, work was a curse visited upon Adam for his sin in Eden and suggested that, with wasteful and unnecessary production abolished, it would soon be possible to reduce the workweek to ten hours![10]

THE GOSPEL OF CONSUMPTION

But industrial leaders in the 1920s had their own religion, the gospel of consumption. A reduction in working hours, they believed, might bring the whole capitalist system to its knees. Increased leisure, Harvard economist Thomas Nixon Carver warned, was bad for business:

> There is no reason for believing that more leisure would ever increase the desire for goods. It is quite possible that the leisure would be spent in the cultivation of

the arts and graces of life; in visiting museums, libraries and art galleries, or hikes, games and inexpensive amusements ... it would decrease the desire for material goods. If it should result in more gardening, more work around the home in making or repairing furniture, painting and repairing the house and other useful avocations, it would cut down the demand for the products of our wage paying industries.[11]

It would, you might say, reduce affluenza. He had a problem with that.

After the Model T began rolling from Henry Ford's assembly lines in 1913, a cornucopia of material products followed. Businesses sought ways to sell them—and the economic gospel of consumption—giving rise to an advertising industry that looked—and still looks—to psychology for help in pushing products.

"Sell them their dreams," a promoter told Philadelphia businessmen in 1923. "Sell them what they longed for and hoped for and almost despaired of having. Sell them hats by splashing sunlight across them. Sell them dreams—dreams of country clubs and proms and visions of what might happen if only. After all, people don't buy things to have things. They buy hope—hope of what your merchandise will do for them. Sell them this hope and you won't have to worry about selling them goods."[12]

The agrarian philosopher Ralph Borsodi warned Americans eloquently of where this was all heading in his 1929 jeremiad, *This Ugly Civilization*.

> Man has a habitable globe on which to spend his time—a veritable treasure trove and alchemist's library full of useful raw materials whatever his genius may lead him to design. Yet he burns the coal and the oil, cuts down and devastates the forest, pollutes and poisons the streams and lakes, and levels hills and mountains, not because this is the wisest use he can make of his time but merely that he may keep his factories busy and make the money with which to buy what they produce.... It is perhaps one of the gravest defects of the earn-and-buy economy, which the factory has brought into being that it has made money the measure of all things economic.... The true economy is not of money but of *time*, just as the true waste is not of money but of the irreplaceable materials of nature.[13]

But Borsodi's warnings fell on deaf ears at a time when the world's first mass-consumption society came in dancing the Charleston. Cash registers were ka-chinging, and the stock market soared—higher, higher, higher—like that of the '90s. People's wants, the captains of American industry declared, were insatiable, and business opportunities therefore boundless. During the '20s, their gospel of wealth had plenty of believers. There were those who thought it would never go down.

SHORTER HOURS DURING THE DEPRESSION

Then one day in October 1929, it all collapsed. "Wall Street Lays An Egg," declared the headline in *Variety*. Millionaires suddenly became paupers and leaped out of windows. Breadlines formed. With millions out of work, the idea of shortening work hours, "work sharing," was back in vogue. Even Herbert Hoover called shorter hours the quickest way to create more jobs.

Once again, labor leaders like William Green were demanding "the six-hour day and the five-day week in industry." Imagine their delight when word came from Washington on April 6, 1933, that the US Senate had just passed a bill that would make thirty hours the official American workweek. Anything over that would be overtime. Thirty hours. That was eighty years ago.[14]

The bill ultimately failed in the House by a few votes. President Franklin D. Roosevelt opposed it because he was convinced that federal job-creation programs—the New Deal—offered a better way to both reduce unemployment and keep industry strong.

But some businesses had already adopted thirty-hour workweeks, with excellent results. The cereal tycoon A.K. Kellogg took the lead, in December 1930. Kellogg was a paternalistic capitalist who ran his company with an iron hand. But he had a certain radical vision. In Kellogg's view, according to Hunnicutt, leisure time, not economic growth without end, represented the "flower, the crowning achievement, of capitalism." The vision came to Kellogg because he mourned his rigid childhood and his own addiction to long hours of labor. "I never learned to play," he once told his grandson, regretfully.

Kellogg offered his workers thirty-five hours' pay for a thirty-hour week, and he built parks, summer camps, nature centers, garden plots, sports fields, and other recreational facilities for them. The plan immediately created four hundred new jobs in Battle Creek, Michigan, where Kellogg's plants were located. Productivity rose so rapidly that within two years Kellogg could pay his thirty-hour workers what he had previously paid them for forty hours. Polling of Kellogg's workers during the '30s showed overwhelming support for the thirty-hour week; only a few single males wished for more hours and higher pay.

OLD EIGHT HOURS HAS GOT US ALL

But after Kellogg died, the company waged a long campaign to return to the forty-hour week. The reason: benefits. As benefits increasingly became a larger part of the wage package, it made more sense to hire fewer workers and keep them on longer. But the thirty-hour week at Kellogg's wasn't fully abandoned until 1985, when the company threatened to leave Battle Creek if the remaining thirty-hour workers (about 20 percent of the company, and nearly all women) didn't agree to work longer. The women held a funeral (complete with a casket) for the thirty-hour week at Stan's Place, a local bar, and one, Ina Sides, wrote a eulogy:

Farewell good friend, oh six hours
'Tis sad but true

Now you're gone and we're all so blue.
Get out your vitamins, give the doctor a call
'Cause old eight hours has got us all.[15]

While writing his book *Kellogg's Six-Hour Day*, Hunnicutt spent time with many former Kellogg workers. Most remembered the thirty-hour week with deep fondness. They remembered using their leisure well—to garden, learn crafts, practice hobbies, exercise, and share in a vibrant community life. "You weren't all wore out when you got out of work," said one man. "You had the energy to do something else."

Chuck and Joy Blanchard, a married couple who both worked at the plant, remembered that Chuck took care of the kids and was a "room parent" at their school "long before anyone heard about women's liberation." They also remembered that after the return to forty hours, volunteering in Battle Creek went down and crime went up. The Blanchards say they had little, but their lives, blessed with abundant leisure, were happier than those of young families today, who have so much more stuff but never seem to have time.

Never before or since in America had ordinary industrial workers traveled so far down that "other road"—the road of time instead of money. In that sense, the Kellogg's workers were, as Hunnicutt sees them, explorers in a new and wondrous land that all Americans might have come to if World War II had not intervened and—in demanding a vast national outpouring of labor—locked the gate. Today, we meet people who cannot quite believe that more than half a century ago, in a corner of the United States, full-time workers were spending only thirty hours a week on the job. But it happened. And it can happen again when we get a grip on affluenza.

CHAPTER 14

An emerging epidemic

> *How little, from the resources unrenewable by Man, cost the things of greatest value—wild beauty, peace, health and love, music and all the testaments of spirit! How simple our basic needs—a little food, sun, air, water, shelter, warmth, and sleep! How lightly might this earth bear Man forever!*
> —NANCY NEWHALL AND ANSEL ADAMS,
>   *This Is the American Earth*, 1960

During World War II, Americans accepted rationing and material deprivation. Wasteful consumption was out of the question. In every city, citizens gathered scrap metal to contribute to the war effort. Most grew some of their own food, in so-called victory gardens. Driving was limited to save fuel. Despite the sacrifices, what many older Americans remember most from that time was the sense of community, of sharing for the common good and uniting to defeat a common enemy.

But shortly after World War II ended, pent-up economic demand in the form of personal savings, coupled with low-interest government loans and mushrooming private credit, led to a consumer boom unparalleled in history. The GI Bill sparked massive construction of housing at the edge of America's cities, beginning with the famous Levittown development on Long Island. The average size of a Levittown bungalow was only 750 square feet, but its popularity encouraged other developers to build sprawling suburbs with larger homes.

New families filled the new homes as the baby boom began. Each family needed lots of appliances and—with transit service in the suburbs nonexistent—cars to get around. It's fascinating to watch the many corporate and government films produced during that period, both documenting and extolling the new mass consumption society.

THE GOODS LIFE

"The new automobiles stream from the factories," the narrator cheers, in one late-forties film. "Fresh buying power floods into all the stores of every community. Prosperity greater than history has ever known." In the same film, we see a montage of shots of people spending money and hear more peppy narration: "The pleasure of buying, the spreading of money! And the enjoyment of all the things that paychecks can buy are making happy all the thousands of families!" Utopia had arrived!

Another film proclaims that "we live in an age of growing abundance" and urges Americans to give thanks for "our liberty to buy whatever each of us may choose" (the words come with a heavenly chorus humming "America the Beautiful" and shots of the Statue of Liberty). A third reminds us that "the basic freedom of the American people is the freedom of individual choice" (of which products to purchase, of course).

One film appeals to women to take up where the soldiers of World War II left off and fight "the age-old battle for beauty." We've been told "you can't buy beauty in a jar," the narrator says, "but that old adage is bunk. We have the money to spend and we want all the lovely-smelling lotions, soaps, and glamour goo we can get with it." Joy in a jar. As women try on perfumes in an upscale department store, the narrator continues: "Our egos are best nourished by a well-placed investment in real luxury goods—what you might call discreetly conspicuous waste." "Waste not, want not," Benjamin Franklin once admonished, but the new slogan might have been "waste more, want more." Almost overnight, the good life became the *goods* life.

PLANNED OBSOLESCENCE

"The immediate postwar period does represent a huge change in the kinds of attitudes that Americans have had about consumption," says the historian Susan Strasser, author of *Satisfaction Guaranteed*.[1] "Discreetly conspicuous waste" got another boost from what marketers called "planned obsolescence." Products were either made to last only a short time so that they would have to be replaced frequently (adding to sales) or they were continually upgraded, more commonly in style than in quality. It was an idea that began long before World War II with Gillette's disposable razors and soon took on a larger life.

Henry Ford, who helped start the '20s consumer boom by paying his workers a then-fantastic five dollars a day, was a bit of a conservative about style, once promising that consumers could have one of his famous Model Ts in any color as long as it was black. But just before the Great Depression, General Motors introduced the idea of the annual model change. It was an idea that took off after World War II. Families were encouraged to buy a new car every year. "They were saying the car you had last year won't do anymore, and it won't do anymore because it doesn't look right," Strasser explains. "There's now a new car and that's what we want to be driving."

INSTANT MONEY

Of course, none but the richest of Americans could afford to plunk down a couple thousand dollars on a new car every year, or on any of the other new consumer durables that families wanted. Never mind, there were ways to finance your spending spree. "The American consumer!

Each year you consume fantastic amounts of food, clothing, housing, amusements, appliances, and services of all kinds. This mass consumption makes you the most powerful giant in the land," pipes the narrator in a cute mid-'50s animated film from the National Consumer Finance Association.

"I'm a giant," boasts Mr. American Consumer, as he piles up a massive mountain of stuff. And how does he afford it? Loans, says the film: "Consumer loans in the hands of millions of Americans add up to tremendous purchasing power. Purchasing power that creates consumer demand for all kinds of goods and services that mean a rising standard of living throughout the nation." You can probably already hear the drumroll in your mind.

A TV ad for Bank of America made about the same time shows a shaking animated man and asks, "Do you have money jitters? Ask the obliging Bank of America for a jar of soothing instant money. M-O-N-E-Y. In the form of a convenient personal loan." The animated man drinks from a coffee cup full of dollars, stops shaking, and jumps for joy.[2]

It was a buy now, pay later world, only to become more so with the coming of credit cards in the sixties.

AMERICA THE MALLED

During the 1950s and 1960s, the rush to suburbia continued (and hasn't stopped yet). In 1946 the GI Bill spurred it along. Ten years later, another government program did the same. President Dwight D. Eisenhower announced the beginning of a vast federal subsidy to create a nationwide freeway system. In part the system was sold as national defense—roads big enough to run our tanks on if the Russians invaded. The new freeways encouraged a mass movement to even wider rings of suburbs. All were built around the automobile and massive shopping centers, whose windows, according to one early '60s promotional film, reflected "a happy-go-spending world."

"Shopping malls," the film continues, "see young adults as in need of expansion [interesting choice of words, perhaps anticipating "supersize" meals]. People who buy in large quantities and truck it away in their cars. It's a big market!" Enthusiastically, the narrator continues, "These young adults, shopping with the same determination that brought them to suburbs in the first place, are the goingest part of a nation of wheels, living by the automobile." Going to the mall was, for these determined consumers, an adventure worthy of Mount Everest, at least according to this film, which later describes the consumers' hardest challenge as finding their cars again in the giant mall parking lots. Sound familiar?

By 1970, Americans were spending four times as much time shopping as were Europeans. The malls encouraged Sunday shopping, then as rare in the United States as it still is in Europe. To its everlasting credit, Sears, Roebuck & Company opposed opening its store on Sunday, on the grounds that it wanted "to give our employees their Sabbath." But by 1969 it caved to the competition, opening on Sundays "with great regret and some sense of guilt."[3]

THE BOX THAT ENLIGHTENED

The big economic boom wasn't the result of any one thing. A series of synchronous events made it possible: pent-up demand, government loans, expanded credit, suburbanization, longer shopping hours, and mallification. But perhaps no single cause was more responsible for the emerging postwar epidemic of affluenza than the ubiquitous box that found its way into most American homes by the 1950s.

Television showed everyone how the other half (the upper half) lived. Its programs were free, made possible only because of the sale of time to advertisers who hawked their wares during and between the features. Crude at first, the ads became increasingly sophisticated—both visually, because of improving technology, and psychologically, as batteries of experts probed the human mind to find out how to sell most effectively.

The early TV ads relied a great deal on humor—"Any girl can find a good husband, but finding the right man to do your hair, now that's a problem." Like many print and radio ads before them, they played on anxieties about personal embarrassment, warning of horrors like "BO" (body odor). But mostly, they just showed us all the neat stuff that was out there just waiting to be bought.

On TV, convenience was the new ideal, disposability the means. "Use it once and throw it away." TV dinners in disposable aluminum trays. "No deposit, no return" bottles. People in commercials danced with products. The airwaves buzzed with jingles. John still can't stop singing one that must have been on the tube every night when he was a kid: "You'll wonder where the yellow went, when you brush your teeth with Pepsodent."

AFFLUENZA'S DISCONTENTS

Of course, not everyone wanted Americans to catch affluenza. "Buy only what you really need and cannot do without," President Harry Truman once said on TV. By the early '50s, educational films were warning school kids about overspending. But those films were, in a word, boring. No match for TV's wit and whiz. In one, a nerdy-looking character called Mr. Money teaches students to save. One can imagine the collective classroom yawns it produced. In another, the voice of God says, "You're guilty of pouring your money down a rathole. You forget that it takes a hundred pennies to make a dollar." The visuals are equally uncompelling: a hand puts a dollar in a hole in the dirt labeled—you guessed it—"Rathole."

Meanwhile, far-sighted social critics from both Left and Right warned that America's new affluence was coming at a high price. The conservative economist Wilhelm Röpke feared that "we neglect to include in the calculation of these potential gains in the supply of material goods the possible losses of a non-material kind."[4] The centrist Vance Packard lambasted advertising *(The Hidden Persuaders*, 1957), keeping up with the Joneses *(The Status Seekers*, 1959), and planned obsolescence *(The Waste Makers, 1960)*. And the liberal John Kenneth Galbraith suggested that a growing economy fulfilled needs it created itself, leading to no improvement in happiness. Our emphasis on "private opulence," he said, led to "public squalor"—declining transit systems, schools, parks, libraries, and air and water quality. Moreover, it left "vast millions of hungry and discontented people in the world. Without the promise of relief from that hunger and privation, disorder is inevitable."[5]

The affluent society had met its members' real material needs, Galbraith argued at the end of his famous book. Now it had other, more important things to do. "To furnish a barren room is one thing," he wrote. "To continue to crowd in furniture until the foundation buckles is quite another. To have failed to solve the problem of producing goods would have been to continue man in his oldest and most grievous misfortune. But to fail to see that we have solved it, and to fail to proceed thence to the next tasks, would be fully as tragic."[6]

YOUNG AMERICA STRIKES BACK

During the following decade, many young Americans sensed that the critics of consumerism were right. A counterculture arose, rebuking materialism. Thousands of young Americans, inspired by books like Charles Reich's *The Greening of America*, left the cities for agricultural communes practicing simple living, the most successful of which still survive today.

Many of the young questioned American reliance on growth of the gross domestic product as a measure of the nation's health. In that they were supported by President Lyndon Johnson, whose "Great Society" speech warned that America's values and beauty were being "buried by unbridled growth."[7] His nemesis, the popular senator Robert F. Kennedy, agreed. During Kennedy's 1968 campaign for president (which ended when he was assassinated), Bobby Kennedy stressed that

> we will find neither national purpose nor personal satisfaction in a mere continuation of economic progress, in an endless amassing of worldly goods.... The gross national product includes the destruction of the redwoods and the death of Lake Superior.[8]

By the first Earth Day, April 22, 1970, young Americans were questioning the impact of the consumer lifestyle on the planet itself. Leading environmentalists, like David Brower, founder of Friends of the Earth, were warning that the American dream of endless growth was not sustainable.

Then, in 1974, a nationwide oil shortage caused many people to wonder if we might run out of resources. Energy companies responded as they still do today, by calling for more drilling. "Rather than foster conservation," writes the historian Gary Cross, "President Gerald Ford supported business demands for more nuclear power plants, offshore oil drilling, gas leases and drilling on federal lands," as well as "the relaxation of clean air standards."[9]

CARTER'S LAST STAND

But Ford's successor, Jimmy Carter, disagreed, promoting conservation and alternative energy sources. Carter went so far as to question the American dream in his famous "national malaise" speech of 1979. "Too many of us now tend to worship self-indulgence and consumption," Carter declared. It was the last courageous stand any American president ever made against the spread of affluenza.[10]

And it helped bring about Carter's defeat a year later. "Part of Jimmy Carter's failure," says the historian David Shi, "was his lack of recognition of how deeply seated the high, wide, and handsome notion of economic growth and capital development had become in the modern American psyche."

The Age of Affluenza had begun.

CHAPTER 15

The Age of Affluenza

> *Advertising separates our era from all earlier ones as little else does.*
> —CONSERVATIVE ECONOMIST WILHELM RÖPKE

> *Any space you take in visually, anything you hear, in the future will be branded.*
> —REGINA KELLY, Director of Strategic Planning, Satchi and Satchi Advertising

"It's morning in America," announced the 1984 TV commercials for Ronald Reagan, whose message that Americans could have their cake and eat it too had overwhelmed the cautious conservationist Jimmy Carter four years earlier. And indeed, it was morning, the dawning, you might say, of the Age of Affluenza. Despite economic ups and downs, the last twenty years of the twentieth century would witness a commercial expansion unparalleled in history. Those Reagan commercials, small towns and smiling people in golden light, seem quaint now, more like the sunset of an old era than the morning of a new one. For one thing, there are no ads to be seen anywhere in the America pictured in those political *commercials, no billboards, no product being sold except Reagan. That's not America anymore.*

Reagan's decade may have been that of supply-side economics, but it was also the decade of demand creation. Yuppies were made, not born. "Greed is good," chirruped Wall Street's Ivan Boesky. The message of Reagan's first inaugural ball and Nancy's $15,000 dress was clear: It's cool to consume and flaunt it. The tone of '80s advertising echoed the sentiment: "Treat Yourself. You *Deserve* a Break Today. You're Worth It." Look out for number one.

ADFLUENZA

That advertising's prime purpose is to promote affluenza is hardly a secret, as even its proponents have frequently stated in different words. As Pierre Martineau, the marketing director for the *Chicago Tribune*, put it back in 1957, "Advertising's most important social function is to integrate the individual into our present-day American high-speed consumption economy."[1] "The average individual doesn't make anything," wrote Martineau in his classic text *Motivation in Advertising*. "He buys everything, and our economy is geared to the faster and faster tempo of his buying, *based on wants which are created by advertising in large degree.*" This was no critic of advertising expressing himself, but one of its most prominent practitioners.

"Our American level of living is the highest of any people in the world," Martineau went on to say, "because our standard of living is the highest, meaning that our wants are the highest. In spite of those intellectuals who deplore the restlessness and the dissatisfaction in the wake of those new wants created by advertising and who actually therefore propose to restrict the process, it must be clear that the wellbeing of our entire system depends on how much motivation is supplied the consumer to make him continue wanting." Were Pierre Martineau still alive, he would doubtless be proud to see how much motivation is now supplied to keep consumers "wanting."

If, as the old saying goes, "a man's home is his castle," then Madison Avenue has battering rams galore. Two-thirds of the space in our newspapers is now devoted to advertising. Nearly half the mail we receive is selling something.

THE HIGH COST OF MOTIVATION

You could call it couch potato blight. The average American will spend nearly two years of his or her lifetime watching TV commercials.[2] A child may see a million of them before he or she reaches the age of twenty. There is more time devoted to them now—the average half-hour of commercial TV now has ten minutes of commercials, up from six two decades ago. And there are more of them—faster editing (to beat the remote control clicker), and the increasing cost of commercial time has shortened the length of the average ad.

They are phenomenally expensive: a typical 30-second national TV commercial now costs more than $300,000 to produce—that's $10,000 per second! By contrast, production costs for an entire hour of prime-time public television are about the same—$300,000, or $83 a second. Commercial network programming is somewhat more expensive but can't hold a candle to the cost of the ads. Is it any wonder that some people say they're the best thing on TV?

Moreover, it costs companies hundreds of thousands of dollars every time their ads are broadcast during national prime-time programming. In fact, thirty-second slots during the Super Bowl sold for as much as $4 million each.[3] Advertising, the prime carrier of the affluenza virus, is now a half-a-trillion-dollar-a-year industry worldwide, with the United States accounting for about a third of the total. Procter & Gamble alone spent nearly three billion, and Comcast, Verizon, Toyota, GM, Chrysler, ATT, News Corp, and Berkshire Hathaway all came in at over a billion each.[4]

It's paying off. In 1997, when NPR's Scott Simon asked teenagers at a Maryland Mall what they were buying, they ran off a list of brand names: Donna Karan, Calvin Klein, Tommy

Hilfiger, American Eagle. A recent study showed that while the average American can identify fewer than ten types of plants, he or she recognizes hundreds of corporate logos.[5]

WELCOME TO LOGOTOPIA

In the effort to create demand, marketers now seek to place commercial messages everywhere. By 2000, outdoor advertising was a $5-billion-a-year industry (and growing at a rate of 10 percent a year), with more than a billion spent on billboards alone. "Outdoor advertising is red-hot right now," says Brad Johnson in *Advertising Age*. "There's a shortage of space available."[6] Nearly fifty years after Lady Bird Johnson's Beautify America Campaign, our landscape is filled with more billboards than ever. The ad critic Laurie Mazur calls them "litter on a stick." "From a marketers perspective, billboards are perfect," says Mazur. "You can't turn them off. You can't click them with remote control."

Mazur points out that marketers themselves say the ad environment has become "cluttered," so smart sellers look for ever-new places to put ads. Schools, as discussed in the chapter "Family Fractures," are one target, reached in a myriad of ways, including corporate logos in math text books: "If Joe has thirty Oreo™ cookies and eats fifteen, how many does he have left?" Of course there's a big picture of Oreos on the page. The publisher might want to add another question: How many cavities does Joe have?

"Advertising is just permeating every corner of our society," says Michael Jacobson, coauthor with Mazur of *Marketing Madness*. "When you're watching a sports event, you see ads in the stadium. You see athletes wearing logos. You see ads in public restrooms. Some police cars now have ads. There are ads in holes on golf courses. And there are thousands of people who are trying to think of one more place to put an ad where nobody has yet put the ad."[7]

THE MARKETERS' MOON

The extreme idea for advertising placement, says Jacobson, "is the billboard that was proposed for outer space that would project logos about the size of the moon that would be visible to practically everyone on earth."

When the moon fills the sky like a big pizza pie, it's—Domino's! Imagine a romantic walk at night in the light of the full logo.

For now, the idea of logos in outer space is still a marketer's pipe dream, but, says Jacobson, "What is the limit? Maybe outer space, but down here on earth we're willing to accept just about everything."

*Get*SATISFIED

Night of the Living Consumer

Perhaps the biggest expansion of commercialism in the Age of Affluenza is occurring on the Internet. Ads are popping up like mushrooms on the information highway. In 2012, for the first time, total spending on Internet ads exceeded $100 billion, up from $72 billion in 2010. Nearly 40 percent is spent in North America. By 2016, more than a quarter of all advertising dollars will be digitally directed (it's one dollar in five currently).[8] And of course, this doesn't even consider the phenomenal increase in e-mail spam that all of us are tearing our hair out over these days. What was hailed as an educator's Eden has become a seller's paradise instead, as e-commerce attracts billions of investment and advertising dollars.

There is, admittedly, a bright spot in this grim scenario. We don't know about you, but since President George W. Bush signed the "Do Not Call" legislation in 2003, and we signed on, we've stopped getting those irritating dinner time calls from people who want to clean our carpets or sell us something we don't need. Apparently, even market-worshipping legislators were tired of having their dinners interrupted.

HYPERCOMMERCIALISM

Our hypercommercial era is one in which images are everywhere, and "image," as tennis star Andre Agassi says in the sunglasses commercial, "is everything." The daily bombardment of advertising images leaves us forever dissatisfied with our own appearance and that of our real-life partner. "Advertising encourages us to meet nonmaterial needs through material ends," says Mazur. "It tells us to buy their product because we'll be loved, we'll be accepted, and also it tells us that we are not lovable and acceptable without buying their product."[9] To be lovable and acceptable is to have the right image. Authenticity be damned.

Back in 1958, a prominent conservative economist and staunch defender of the free enterprise system warned that the twentieth century might well end up being known as "the

Age of Advertising." Wilhelm Röpke feared that if commercialism were "allowed to predominate and to sway society in all its spheres," the results would be disastrous in many ways. As the cult of selling grows in importance, Röpke wrote, "every gesture of courtesy, kindness and neighborliness is degraded into a move behind which we suspect ulterior motives."[10] A culture of mutual distrust arises.

"The curse of commercialization is that it results in the standards of the market spreading into regions which should remain beyond supply and demand," Röpke added. "This vitiates the true purposes, dignity and savor of life and thereby makes it unbearably ugly, undignified and dull."

Only by limiting the scope of its reach, claimed Röpke, could the free market system be expected to continue to serve the greater good. Extreme commercialization, the very sine qua non of our era, would, if not kept in check, "destroy the free economy by the blind exaggeration of its principle."

FINANCIAL COLLAPSE

In 2008, of course, it almost happened. Thirty years of deregulation, privatization, and tax cutting came to a head when the economy nearly collapsed following a major financial crash. "Capitalism at bay," sounded the alarm from *The Economist*. In the wink of an eye, trillions of dollars in financial wealth disappeared overnight. The precipitating incident was a sudden increase in mortgage failures, as many families were increasingly unable to make their house payments. In the years before, the authors of this book had warned that overextended borrowers were getting into big trouble.

To anyone watching the economy, this was not news. It was clear that real median wages for American workers had been stagnant for more than two decades, even while productivity doubled, since all the gains in income and wealth had accumulated at the top. Nonetheless, Americans had not stopped consuming more; indeed, through the nineties they spent as if there was no tomorrow. People were positively giddy about their ability to consume more in 1997, when the film *Affluenza* was first released. But greater consumption did not rest on higher incomes; rather, it was driven by more members of the family working, longer hours of work, and a massive expansion of consumer debt.

Much of this debt was fueled by rising housing prices. Those just entering the market were investing more than they could afford on the hunch that the price increases would continue indefinitely. Those already in the market, believing the value of their properties would continue to rise without limit, financed their consumption sprees by taking out second mortgages. These strategies were temporarily successful, but ultimately the growth of inequality and the flat growth in real median income caught up to them. People could simply not afford more expensive housing, and many could not keep up with their existing debt. The housing market fell as we, and many others, warned that it would.

After the crash, we were called by interviewers in the United States and from as far away as Norway and Brazil, credited with having predicted the financial crash. We had done no such thing; we only suggested that many individuals would lose their shirt. We were clueless about the possibility that these individual failures could take the entire economy down. But they did.

In the Age of Affluenza, the champions of deregulation and the "greed is good" ethic of Ivan Boesky had been quietly gambling away America's finances. For a clear, probing, and deliciously funny examination of all this, see the wonderful *Whoops!* by the British author John Lanchester.[11]

Arguing that limits on financial speculation (in place since the Glass-Steagal Act of 1933 had put a firewall between commercial and investment banks) would kill the goose that laid the golden egg of the booming housing market, the bankers lobbied Congress to repeal that law and to ban the effective regulation of new financial instruments called derivatives, which allowed the continual bundling and resale of home mortgages, opening up increasing capital to loan out new and even more risky mortgages to potential homeowners.

They did this by pushing homeownership on lower-income Americans, often for homes that were well beyond the buyers' means. In some cases, this included wholesale dishonesty (Banker: "Sir, what is your annual income?" Buyer: $30,000. Banker: "You need an annual income of $60,000 to be approved for this loan. Why don't we just write down that you make $60,000 a year instead?" Buyer: "You can do that?" Banker: "Sure, just sign here. You deserve a better house.") For all of this chicanery, the speculators took home fabulous bonuses, sometimes equal to what the average American earned in several decades.

The consumers' feverish expectations combined with the bankers' greed to create ever-more-risky mortgages that were then bundled with supposedly safer mortgages to create supposedly fail-safe derivatives, which earned AAA ratings from less-than-diligent oversight agencies. Meanwhile, a few smart investors realized what ticking time bombs these derivatives would be if enough mortgages failed. They were allowed to purchase what was essentially insurance on the derivatives (whether they owned them or not—imagine being able to buy fire insurance for every house in your neighborhood). Big insurance firms like AIG, initially unaware of the risks contained in the derivatives, were happy to sell trillions of dollars' worth of this insurance, known as "credit default swaps" in bank parlance.

We knew nothing about this, but its implications were huge. When individual mortgages began to fail, the supposedly safe derivatives also failed, taking down some of the banks that had sold them. Then, the holders of credit default insurance tried to collect on the failed derivatives, bankrupting firms like AIG, which did not have nearly enough funds on hand to meet their obligations. The whole house of cards, based on the values of affluenza—materialism and greed—fell apart. But the greediest, the purveyors of the crisis, didn't suffer. They were bailed out by the victims—everyday workers—to the tune of $700 billion. Remember another Golden Rule: *Those with the gold make the rules.*

Although they did take a short-term hit, the big banks are back in business. Wall Street has successfully protected itself against a new round of regulations that would have reinstituted Glass-Steagal and other economic protections. The housing market is starting to reheat, and we could see déjà vu all over again, to use the immortal expression of Yogi Berra. The financial crisis, like the World Trade Center attacks of 2001, did temporarily slow the march of affluenza, but only by imposing a round of fear-induced *involuntary* simplicity.

One senses that the American people have learned little from their brush with the deadly virus; indeed, the lesson for our politicians seems to be either that we are not deregulating *enough* or cutting rich Americans' taxes enough (Republicans), or that we simply need to spend our way back to the future (Democrats). But these two "solutions" are simply two sides to affluenza's counterfeit coin. Instead, the questions that need answering are

1. Austerity for whom? Conservatives seem to believe it is the *poor* who must be austere rather than the rich, whose greed promulgated the crisis.
2. Stimulus of what? Growth of what? In an age of ecological limits we cannot simply continue to grow. Progressives should be asked, "What should grow and what must shrink?"

But in the Age of Affluenza, these are precisely the questions we are least likely to hear.

CHAPTER 16

Spin doctors

> We have transformed information into a form of garbage.
> —NEIL POSTMAN, author of *Amusing Ourselves to Death*

> Government agencies are supposed to be watchdogs, but too often they are more like lap dogs.
> —JOHN STAUBER, founder of PRWatch

> In the public relations industry, the idea is to manage the outrage, not the hazard.
> —SHARON BEDER, author of *Global Spin*

What happens when we ignore the symptoms of a disease? It usually gets worse. That's why the epidemic of affluenza is spreading around the planet. Although symptoms like the stress of excess, the anxiety of resource exhaustion, and the depression of social scars are right in our faces, we tend to look the other way as we're told over and over again that the market will provide. But will it?

The author and "adbuster" Kalle Lasn tells a metaphorical tale about a large wedding party that takes place in a spacious suburban backyard.

The party oozes affluence and the good life: the live music is incredible, and everyone dances with abandon. The problem is that they're dancing on top of an old septic system, which causes the pipes to burst. "Raw sewage rises up through the grass," writes Lasn, "and begins to cover everyone's shoes. If anyone notices, they don't say anything. The champagne flows, the music continues, until finally a little boy says, 'It smells like shit!' And suddenly everyone realizes they're ankle deep in it."[1]

How many million Americans are now wheezing with affluenza, yet stubbornly in denial? "Those who are clued in apparently figure it's best to ignore the shit and just keep dancing," concludes Lasn. Meanwhile, the usual suspects (such as Phillip Morris, BP, the Fukushima nuclear power plant) may admit the pipes have cracked, but still, they try to convince us it'll never happen again.

According to trend watchers, at least fifty million Americans are ready for recovery programs to beat affluenza, but where can we turn for the advice we'll need? There seem to be as many quacks and spin doctors out there as real doctors. With a strict policy of concealing their funding sources, the quack scientists do their best to make the world "safe from democracy." The first step is to encourage us to do nothing, to keep ignoring the symptoms. They tell us in voices that sound self-assured, "Go back to sleep, the facts are still uncertain, everything's fine. Technology will provide. Just relax and enjoy yourself."

"TOXIC SLUDGE IS GOOD FOR YOU"

We all know how pervasive advertising is, because it stares us in the face. In fact, we pick up the tab for advertising in the products we buy—at least $900 a year per capita. But as John Stauber, past editor of the online resource *PRWatch,* comments, "Few people really understand the other dimension of marketing—an undercover public relations industry that creates and perpetuates our commercial culture." (In other words, it keeps us constantly exposed to the affluenza virus.) What is PR, exactly? "It's covert culture shaping and opinion spinning," says Stauber, whose informative book on PR is called *Toxic Sludge Is Good for You.* "Not only do PR professionals alter our perceptions, they also finesse the political and cultural influence that ushers those perceptions into the mainstream."[2]

Unreported by the blindfolded eyes of the media, PR-managed initiatives are often signed into law and adopted as standard operating procedures while the public's civic attention is diverted by the most current scandal, crime, or catastrophe.

Stauber first became involved in watchdogging the public relations industry when he was researching biotechnology. "We saw strong evidence of collusion between Monsanto and various government agencies and professional organizations," he says. "Government agencies like the FDA and USDA did their part by working with Monsanto to overcome farmer and consumer opposition to the emerging products." (The US Congress recently passed legislation referred to by stunned opponents as "the Monsanto Protection Act"—officially the "farmer assurance provision." This limits the ability of judges to stop Monsanto or farmers from using genetically modified seeds even if courts find evidence of potential health risks.[3]

"It is now common for lawyers to sit in the actual drafting sessions where legislation is written and to provide the precise language for new laws," writes Al Gore in his 2013 book, *The Future: Six Drivers of Global Change*. "Many US state legislatures now routinely rubber-stamp laws that have been written in their entirety by corporate lobbies." Gore notes that in the 1970s, only 3 percent of retiring members of Congress found work as lobbyists. "Now more than 50 percent of retiring senators and 40 percent of retiring House members become lobbyists." In 1975, recorded expenditures by lobbyists were $100 million. By 2010, they had $3.5 billion worth of influence on politicians.[4]

"The best PR is never noticed" is an unwritten slogan of an industry whose arsenal includes backroom politics, fake grassroots activism, organized censorship, and imitation news. The weapon of choice is a kind of stun gun that fires invisible bullets of misinformation. You can't remember how you formed a certain opinion or belief, but you find yourself willing to fight for it. For example, a popular corporate strategy staged by contracted PR firms is to form citizen advisory panels. This technique makes people feel included, rather than polluted. Citizens are carefully chosen to attend catered lunches around the corporate conference table, to discuss community issues. Similarly, on the advice of contracted PR experts, many corporations now fund and sponsor the very environmental groups that have dogged them for years. This "absorb the enemy" tactic accomplishes several things at once. It gives the company a buffed-up, green-washed image, and it distracts the environmental opponent-partner. Said one corporate partner, "We keep them so busy they don't have time to sue us."[5]

HOW MONEY TALKS

One of the most effective and powerful PR tactics is to fund "front groups" and give them friendly, responsible-sounding names, like the American Council on Science and Health, whose experts defend petrochemical companies, the nutritional value of fast foods, and pesticides. The mission of front groups is to supply the "right" information on a product or industry and to debunk the "wrong" information.

Front groups have a history of being staunch defenders of the rights of Americans, such as the right to have employee accidents (Workplace Health and Safety Council, an employer organization that lobbies for the weakening of safety standards); the right to pay more for less health care (the Coalition for Health Insurance Choices, founded in the 1990s to defeat the Clinton health care plan); the right to choose large, fuel-inefficient cars (the Coalition for Vehicle Choice); and the right to dismantle ecosystems for profit (the Wise Use Movement). Front groups portray themselves as champions of free enterprise—strongholds of fairness and common sense—an image that helps their PR products get circulated in influential circles. For example, Myron Ebell of the Competitive Enterprise Institute (who has publicly admitted he has no scientific training) poses in various media as an expert who's very skeptical of climate change. In a *Forbes* magazine article titled "Love Global Warming" he does what he's paid to do by funders like American Petroleum Institute and the extremist Koch Family Foundations: cast shadows of doubt on the urgent realities of climate change. "Rising sea levels, if they happen, would be bad for a lot of people," he writes. "But a warming trend would be good for other people. More people die from blizzards and cold spells than from heat waves."[6]

The problem is, crafted (and lucrative) statements like these have been working all too well; about two-thirds of Americans still believe that the consensus of *real* scientists is indecisive and controversial. Another industry and billionaire-funded front group is the Heartland Institute, called "the world's most prominent think tank promoting skepticism about man-made climate change" by *The Economist* magazine. Between 2008 and 2012 Heartland Institute sponsored seven International Conferences on Climate Change, convening a cadre of skeptics like Myron Ebell and Heartland's climate go-to guy, James Taylor, who's on record warning that taking action to reduce emissions would be a huge mistake that could cause a return to the "the Little Ice Age and the Black Death." Heartland Institute was on a roll until it launched an absurd billboard campaign associating acceptance of climate science with "murderers, tyrants, and madmen" including Ted Kaczynski, Charles Manson, and Fidel Castro. The first billboard featured the Unabomber's ungainly mug shot, with the caption, "I still believe in Global Warming. Do You?"[7]

INVASION OF THE MIND SNATCHERS

In effect, America's PR professionals create stage sets in which the rest of us play-act our lives. The PR industry cut its teeth in the 1920s on campaigns that promoted tobacco and leaded gasoline—products whose health effects badly needed to be swept under the carpet. Mark Dowie describes a classic perception coup executed by the PR pioneer Edward Bernays in 1929: "On the surface it seemed like an ordinary publicity stunt for 'female emancipation.' A contingent of New York debutantes marched down Fifth Avenue in the 1929 Easter Parade, each openly lighting and smoking cigarettes, their so-called 'torches of liberty.' It was the first time in the memory of most Americans that any woman who wasn't a prostitute had been seen smoking in public."

Bernays made sure publicity photos of the models appeared in worldwide press, and the tobacco industry quickly added sex appeal to its glorious if deadly parade through the twentieth century. In recent years, tobacco lobbyists persuaded the furniture industry to add flame retardant materials, so sleepy cigarette smokers were less likely to be blamed for burning down houses. A similar, hidden PR tactic was used in the 1920s to promote leaded gasoline (ethyl). The mission was to boost both automobile performance and the profits of General Motors, DuPont, and Standard Oil. These allies soothed and massaged the American public's justified fear of leaded gasoline by performing health effects research in-house, with precedent-setting approval from the federal government. Word from the corporate labs was "no problem," even as factory workers making ethyl were dying by the dozen. A 1927 ad in *National Geographic* urged, "Ride with Ethyl in a high-compression motor and get the thrill of a lifetime." The overt message was "Don't let others pass you by," but the hidden tag line was "...even if it kills you."

GOOD NEWS IS NO NEWS

Journalists simultaneously supply and divert the information stream. Depending on a journalist's sources and biases, we may come away from a news article knowing less than when we started. On perpetual deadline, and with a mandate for objectivity as well as controversy, journalists present both sides of an issue, often creating a sense that the truth is uncertain. Marching orders for the news media come from one of the half dozen or so remaining media conglomerates—including NBC, News Corp, CBS, Viacom, Disney, and Time Warner—whose CEOs and editors and producers dictate what's newsworthy and what's not. As recently as the 1980s, fifty corporations still had a slice of the media pie, but that elite clan has now shrunk to an incestuous handful that invest in each other's companies, are fattened by the same group of mega-advertisers, and get in-the-field reports from the same large wire services. These companies, whose primary goal is turning a profit, construct a reality that's either fearful or fun, merging entertainment and news. Everyone gets the same slice of reality, no matter what region they live in. Stories that interpret the underlying meaning of an event become an endangered species, making George Orwell's *1984* prophecies nearly complete: "The special function of certain Newspeak words ... was not so much to express meanings as to destroy them."[8]

According to the former managing editors of the *Washington Post*, the *New York Times*, and the *Wall Street Journal*, at least 40 percent of the news in those papers is generated by "spin doctor" PR journalists.[9] Because newspaper, magazine, and Internet writers must also compress their stories into a given number of inches, they have little room for context and complexity. The same is true of TV news, sandwiched between the commercials and crime reporting that now make up a third of network news content. In 1968, the average interview sound bite was forty-two seconds; in 2013, the standard is eight seconds.[10] Instead of political process, we get isolated events. Instead of context, we get vignettes about novelty and conflict. Information about change and reform takes too long to explain, so we are fed high-speed chases and newborn zoo animals instead. The goal is to keep us watching, not to keep us informed.

After journalists "dumb down" and abbreviate the remnants of the information stream, deep-pocketed advertisers divert more of the flow, often exerting enough pressure on editors to mop up a story altogether. Some advertisers issue policy statements to editors and news directors, requesting advance notice on stories that may put their products in an unfavorable light. Phone calls from CEOs of advertiser companies are like delete buttons on editors' computers: There goes a story from the front page of tomorrow's paper, or the six o'clock news.

By the time the truth about a subject like "fracking" reaches the American citizen, it's been siphoned and filtered down to a trickle of questionable pop science. Fracking—the hydraulic fracturing of drilled well sites to harvest natural gas—is coming soon to your town, it's not already there. In 2012, another 19,000 wells were drilled, bringing the grand total close to half a million. Yet how many Americans are aware of the hazards of this scraping-the-pot technology? The truth is, our impressions of fracking have been formed mostly by corporate PR. Many Americans believe fracking is completely safe because they've seen images in TV ads of cows grazing next to a fracking well. They've seen smiling faces of Americans who are prospering from the natural gas boom, and they've heard how these new energy supplies can reduce pollution and the threat of climate change.

But they haven't heard the other side of the story, because ads don't have to tell the other side. The media advocacy group FAIR (Fairness and Accuracy in Reporting) dug into television archives to compare the number of news stories on fracking that had aired from 2009 through 2011 on national TV news stations (ABC, CBS, NBC, CNN, and Fox News Channel). "All told," says FAIR magazine *(Extra!)* reporter Miranda Spencer, "we found only nine stories focused specifically on fracking." In contrast, during that three-year slice of news programming, there were 530 advertisements for "America's Oil and Gas Industry" or "America's Natural Gas." Says Spencer, "Consider this typical don't-worry-be-happy ad from the advocacy and lobbying group America's Natural Gas Alliance:

> All energy development comes with some risk. But proven technologies allow natural gas producers to supply affordable, cleaner energy while protecting our environment. Across America, these technologies protect the air, by monitoring air quality and reducing emissions; protect water through conservation and self-contained recycling systems; and protect the land by reducing our footprint and respecting wildlife. America's natural gas. Domestic, abundant, clean energy to power our lives. That's smarter power today.

"As the voiceover proceeds," Spencer explains, "images of workers at high-tech consoles and modest, tidy-looking drill rigs alternate with frolicking kids and tranquil nature scenes."[11] Contrast those rosy images with the realities of this nature-oblivious technology, summarized by Artists against Fracking:

> Hydraulic Fracturing (fracking) wells require large industrial sites, ranging from 5–15 acres.... Millions of gallons of water are mixed with sand and over 600 different chemicals, including known carcinogens and toxins like lead, uranium, and methanol. For each "frack," chemical fluid gets pumped deep under the earth's surface, where it can contaminate groundwater that cities and towns often use for drinking water. Finally, after the oil or natural gas is extracted, the waste fluid is left in open air pits to evaporate, releasing harmful VOC's (volatile organic compounds) into the atmosphere, contaminating ground level ozone and causing smog and acid rain.[12]

The waste from a Pennsylvania fracking well was recently rejected at a hazardous waste dump because it was ten times as radioactive as the town's allowable level. That wouldn't be much of a surprise to Jacki Schilke, a cattle farmer in northwest North Dakota whose teeth are falling out and who often has blood in her urine. When fracking began on thirty-two oil and gas wells within three miles of her 160acre ranch, the first sign of trouble was five dead cows. Then, other cows stopped producing milk for their calves. They lost from sixty to eighty pounds in a week, and their tails mysteriously dropped off. When a certified environmental consultant tested the ambient air, he detected elevated levels of benzene, methane, chloroform, butane, propane, toluene, and xylene—all compounds associated with drilling and fracking and also with cancers, birth defects, and organ damage.[13]

Schilke's story is just one of many that are finally coming to light, mostly in local and regional media. Fortunately, Josh Fox's *Gasland*, a documentary about natural gas drilling, was nominated for an Oscar in 2011 and has captured a wide national audience, helping concerned Americans understand what lies behind the PR. A chart measuring Google searches for the terms *fracking, shale gas,* and *Gasland* shows that before the release of the film, few people were searching for information about fracking. Only after a sharp spike in searches for the term *Gasland* is there a strong, steady rise in search activity for *fracking* and *shale gas*.

DELAYED, DISCOUNTED, AND DILUTED FEEDBACK

Scientists like Donella Meadows argue that we need to be sensitive to scientific signals—"feedback"—or we risk crashing our civilization into a brick wall. She compares our world to a speeding automobile on a slippery road. "The driver goes too fast for the brakes to work in time."[14]

At the scale of an entire society in overdrive, she observes that "decision makers in the system do not get, or believe, or act upon information that limits have been exceeded." Part of our dilemma is from insufficient feedback: We don't even realize that caution is necessary. Another part of the problem is the speed we're traveling: Our "pedal to the metal" economy is based on beliefs that resource supplies are limitless and that the earth can continually bounce back from abuse. These beliefs are in part scripted by public relations and advertising experts, just doing their job. What the heck, no harm done, right? Not exactly. Because of low-quality, incomplete information, we may be overlooking an obvious, and ominous, concept: The car will still achieve race car speeds as always, even if the tank is almost empty.

PART THREE
Cures

CHAPTER 17

Diagnostic test

The following situation, imagined by *Affluenza* coproducer Vivia Boe, has not occurred. Not yet.

You're watching TV, in the middle of a program, when the screen goes black for a moment. The scene cuts to a breaking news story. A large crowd is gathered outside an expensive home with some equally pricey cars parked out front. A well-dressed family of four stands on the stairs, looking grim. One of the children is holding a white flag. The reporter, in hushed tones speaks into his microphone: "We're here live at the home of the Joneses—Jerry and Janet Jones—the family we've all been trying to keep up with for years. Well, you can stop trying right now, because they have surrendered. Let's eavesdrop for a moment." The shot changes, revealing a tired-looking Janet Jones, her husband's hand resting on her shoulder. Her voice cracks as she speaks: "It's just not worth it. We never see each other anymore. We're working like dogs. We're always worried about our kids, and we have so much debt we won't be able to pay it off for years. We give up. So please, stop trying to keep up with us." From the crowd our reporter yells, "So what will you do now?" "We're just going to try to live better on less," Janet replies. "So there you have it. The Joneses surrender," says the reporter. "And now for a commercial break."

The Joneses haven't really surrendered. Not yet. But millions of Americans are looking for ways to simplify their lives. And in the rest of this book, you'll learn about some of the ways they've tried and how they are coming together to help create a more sustainable society, free from the clutches of affluenza. We suggest that you start by taking our affluenza self-test, an admittedly unscientific, but we think useful, means of determining whether you've got affluenza and, if so, how serious your case is.

OK, now the moment of truth. In the privacy of your own home, without anyone looking over your shoulder, take the following diagnostic quiz. If you discover you have affluenza, reader, you're not alone! There's help available in this part of the book, so read on. If you don't have it, read on to stay healthy.

AFFLUENZA SELF-DIAGNOSIS TEST

YES	NO	
_	_	1. Do you get bored unless you have something to consume (goods, food, media)?
_	_	2. Do you try to impress your friends with what you own, or where you vacation?
_	_	3. Do you ever use shopping as "therapy"?
_	_	4. Do you sometimes go to the mall just to look around, with nothing specific to buy?
_	_	5. Do you buy home improvement products in a large chain store rather than the neighborhood hardware store?

_	_	6. Have you ever gone on a vacation primarily to shop?
_	_	7. In general, do you think about things more than you think about people?
_	_	8. When you pay utility bills, do you ignore the amount of resources consumed?
_	_	9. Given the choice between a slight pay raise and a shorter workweek, would you choose the money?
_	_	10. Do you personally fill more than one large trash bag in a single week?
_	_	11. Have you ever lied to a family member about the amount you spent for a product?
_	_	12. Do you frequently argue with family members about money?
_	_	13. Do you volunteer your time less than five hours a week to help other people?
_	_	14. Do you routinely compare the appearance of your lawn and/or home with others in your neighborhood?
_	_	15. Does each person in your house or apartment occupy more than 500 square feet of personal space?
_	_	16. Do you routinely gamble or buy lottery tickets?
_	_	17. Do you check your investments at least once a day?
_	_	18. Are any of your credit cards "maxed out"?
_	_	19. Do worries about debt cause you physical symptoms like headaches or indigestion?
_	_	20. Do you spend more time shopping every week than you do with your family?

_	_	21. Do you frequently think about changing jobs?
_	_	22. Have you had cosmetic surgery to improve your appearance?
_	_	23. Do your conversations often gravitate toward things you want to buy?
_	_	24. Are you sometimes ashamed about how much money you spend on fast food?
_	_	25. Do you sometimes weave back and forth in traffic to get somewhere faster?
_	_	26. Have you ever experienced road rage?
_	_	27. Do you feel like you're always in a hurry?
_	_	28. Do you often throw away recyclable materials rather than take the time to recycle them?
_	_	29. Do you spend less than an hour a day outside?
_	_	30. Are you unable to identify more than three wildflowers that are native to your area?
_	_	31. Do you replace sports equipment before it's worn out in order to have the latest styles?
_	_	32. Does each member of your family have his or her own TV?
_	_	33. Is the price of a product more important to you than how well it was made?
_	_	34. Has one of your credit cards ever been rejected by a salesperson because you were over the limit?
_	_	35. Do you receive more than five mailorder catalogs a week?
_	_	36. Are you one of those consumers who almost never takes a reusable bag to the grocery store?

—	—	37. Do you ignore the miles per gallon of gasoline your car gets?
—	—	38. Did you choose the most recent car you bought partly because it enhanced your self-image?
—	—	39. Do you have more than five active credit cards?
—	—	40. When you get a raise at work, do you immediately think about how you can spend it?
—	—	41. Do you drink more soft drink, by volume, than tap water?
—	—	42. Did you work more this year than last year?
—	—	43. Do you have doubts that you'll be able to reach your financial goals?
—	—	44. Do you feel "used up" at the end of your workday?
—	—	45. Do you usually make just the minimum payment on credit card bills?
—	—	46. When you shop, do you often feel a rush of euphoria followed by anxiety?
—	—	47. Do you sometimes feel like your personal expenses are so demanding that you can't afford public expenses like schools, parks, and transit?
—	—	48. Do you have more stuff than you can store in your house?
—	—	49. Do you watch TV more than two hours a day?
—	—	50. Do you eat meat nearly every day?

SCORING YOUR RESULTS (GULP!)

Each "yes" answer carries a weight of 2 points. If you're uncertain as to your answer, or it's too close to call, give yourself one point. If you score:

0–25 You have no serious signs of affluenza, but keep reading to stay healthy.

25–50 You are already infected—keep reading to boost your immune system.

50–75 Your temperature is rising quickly. Take two aspirin and read the next chapters very carefully.

75–100 You've got affluenza big-time! See the doctor, reread the whole book, and take appropriate actions immediately. You may be contagious. There's no time to lose!

The Surrender of the Joneses

CHAPTER 18

Bed rest

> *Are you making a living or making a dying?*
> —JOE DOMINGUEZ

OK. You've taken the affluenza self-test and you're admitting to yourself you've got a few of the symptoms, maybe more than a few. You sit back in your chair, wipe the sweat from your brow, cough a couple of times, sneeze mightily, and rummage around for a thermometer. You're wondering, "What do I do now?"

Remember what the doctor once told you when you had a bad case of the flu? "Go home and go to bed, take some aspirin and call me in the morning." (Actually, they don't want you to call them anymore in this age of HMOs, but that's a different issue.) A case of affluenza calls for bed rest, too. We just define it a little differently. But the point is the same: Stop what you're doing. Stop now. Cut back. Take stock. Give yourself a break.

YOUR MONEY OR YOUR LIFE

Joe Dominguez was a former stockbroker, Vicki Robin a former actress. Believers in frugality and simple living, they taught others to get out of debt, save money, and work on saving the world. John got to know Joe Dominguez and had a chance to interview him less than a year before Dominguez died in 1997. By that time, Joe was a frail man, weak from fighting cancer for many years. But he had not lost any of the passion, moral courage, and biting sense of humor that had helped him influence the lives of thousands of people.

During one interview, Joe described the turnaround in his thinking that occurred while he was still a stock market analyst. "When I was on Wall Street," he said, "I saw that people who had more money were not necessarily happier and that they had just as many problems as the folks that lived in my ghetto neighborhood [in Harlem] where I grew up. So it began to dawn on me that money didn't buy happiness, a very simple finding." Simple indeed, but mighty rare in the Age of Affluenza.

Dominguez tried frugality. He found he enjoyed life more and he found a way to save so much that he was able to retire at the age of thirty-one and live (very simply—when he died, he was living on $8,000 a year) on his interest. "A lot of people would ask me, 'How did you do it?'" Joe recalled. "'How did you handle your finances so you're not an indentured slave like the rest of us?'"

So with his newfound time, he set out to teach other people how to cut their spending sharply. He soon met Vicki Robin, who became his partner for the rest of his life. Says Robin, "I found that I needed to learn how to fix things, and I became fascinated with living life directly and developing my skills and capacities and ingenuity, rather than just earning more money and throwing money at problems."

Together, Dominguez and Robin resettled in Seattle, and went from conducting workshops in people's homes to producing an audiotape course that thousands of people ordered. "Then the publishing industry came to us to write a book," Joe remembered, "and the rest is history." The book, *Your Money or Your Life*, was published in 1992 and soon became a best seller that has now sold nearly a million copies. If the letters from readers that Joe and Vicki have received are to be believed, *Your Money or Your Life* has transformed countless lives.

Dominguez contrasted *Your Money or Your Life* with the plethora of financial self-help books on the market. "It's not about making a killing in the stock market. It's not about how to buy real estate with no money down or anything of that sort. It's just the opposite. It's about how to handle your existing paycheck in a much more intelligent way that creates savings instead of leading you deeper and deeper into debt. It's the stuff our grandparents knew but we've forgotten or been taught to forget."

NINE STEPS TO FINANCIAL INTEGRITY

The book offers a nine-step "new frugality" program by which readers can get their financial feet back on the ground. When all steps are followed, many higher-income readers find that they can achieve "financial independence" in a decade or so, allowing them to devote time to work they find more meaningful than their current jobs. But even lower-income readers have found they can cut their expenses sharply. "In fact, the steps will be most useful to low-income people," Dominguez told John, "because they're the ones who really need to know how to stretch a buck." Even following a few of the initial steps makes a big difference for many readers, who, on average, cut their spending by about 25 percent.

The initial steps include these four practices:

1. *Making peace with your past.* Calculate how much money you've earned in your life, and then what you have to show for it, your current net worth. You may be shocked at the total you've squandered, what we might call the toll of affluenza.

2. *Tracking your life energy.* Calculate your real hourly income by adding hours spent in commuting and other work-related activities to your total workweek, and subtracting

money spent on things needed for work (such as commuting, business clothes). Then keep track of every cent that comes into or goes out of your life. Your working time is an expenditure of your essential life energy. What are you getting for it and using it for?

3. *Tabulating all of your income and spending for one month.*
4. *Asking yourself whether you've received real fulfillment for the life energy you spent.* Joe and Vicki recommend plotting a "fulfillment curve," which rises as you spend for essential needs, then begins to fall as you spend on luxuries that aren't that important to you. The top of the curve is the point called "enough"—the point when you should stop spending and start saving.[1]

Doing these things means stopping your regular routine of activity to take stock. When you've got the flu, go to bed. When you're walking off the edge of a cliff, step back. When you've got affluenza, stop and think it over.

Joe Dominguez and Vicki Robin gave away all the money they earned from their popular book. Though she still lives extremely frugally, no one who knows Vicki Robin would ever consider her poor. Money can most certainly be a blessing, not a curse, she would argue. But most of all when it is used to make the world a better place.

DOWNSHIFTING

Of course, the "Your Money or Your Life" model isn't the only bed to rest in. Thousands of Americans have found other helpful ways to slow down, cut back, and reassess. They've taken personal steps to live better on less income. Living in smaller homes is one step that many are finding provides a break for their wallets, and for the environment, while getting them away from "cocooning" and into a more satisfying public life with others. In Seattle and other cities, young single professionals are rejecting suburban megahomes for tiny "apodments," some of them less than 400 square feet.[2]

Like Europeans, they don't expect their homes to provide full entertainment systems or the space to host their five hundred closest friends. That's what cafés are for. They are stepping back from the rat race, giving themselves a break from affluenza, and generally feeling very good about it.

Bill Powers, a friend of John's who spent many years working in Bolivia, went even further. He writes about his time living off the grid in a 12-by-12 house.

> Surprisingly, I enjoyed life without electricity. No humming refrigerator, no ringing phones, and none of the ubiquitous

"stand-by" lights on appliances—those false promises of life inside the machines. Instead: the whippoorwill's nocturnal call, branches scraping quiet rhythms in the breeze.... Most luxurious of all, each night was blessed with the glow of candles. Sometimes I'd step outside and look in through the windows, a dozen or so candles inside, as cheery as a birthday cake—the 12x12 point lit with primordial fire amid dark woods.

But you don't have to live in a 12x12 house to discover more inner joy and contribute to global healing. Each of us, no matter where we live, can ask ourselves, "What's my 12x12?" Even in large cities—I now live in New York—it is possible to scale back from overdevelopment to enough. By planting a windowsill or community garden; doing yoga or meditation; walking and biking; and carrying out at least one positive action for others every day. We decide what gets globalized—consumption or compassion; selfishness or solidarity—by how we cultivate the most valuable space of all: our inner acre.[3]

More recently, with a new child in the family, Bill and his wife, Melissa, moved to Santa Fe to be a bit closer to nature, but they are still living simply. Colin Beavan, who still lives in New York, scaled back even further, as part of an effort to reduce his "ecological footprint" to as close to zero as possible. For one year, he "swore off plastic and toxins, turned off his electricity, went organic, became a bicycle nut, and tried to save the planet from environmental catastrophe while dragging his young daughter and his Prada-wearing wife along for the ride."[4]

His adventures are detailed in the book and the film *No Impact Man*. Beavan and his family engaged in this effort out of what he admits was a liberal's guilt about the environment and his impact on the planet, but they say they found that "noimpact living is worthwhile—and richer, fuller, and more satisfying in the bargain." Beavan then created the No Impact Project (www.noimpactproject.org), which encourages students and communities to organize "No Impact Weeks," and see how it feels. For some, Beavan's cold-turkey approach goes too far, but most find that even if they can't keep up a truly no-impact lifestyle, they can cut back appreciably on their consumption and enjoy life more. Beavan himself has concluded that personal efforts like his, while important, aren't enough to drive the urgent change to a more sustainable lifestyle that we need. In 2012, he ran as a Green Party candidate for office in Brooklyn.

Oh we don't need anything—we're already satisfied.

The *US News & World Report* correspondent Amy Saltzman originally called people like Vicki Robin, Bill Powers, and Colin Beavan "downshifters." A 1995 poll found that 86 percent of Americans who voluntarily reduced their consumption said they were happier as a result. Only 9 percent reported feeling worse.[5] People choosing to downshift can find tips for living more simply and less stressfully from dozens of journals and books, many of which are included in our bibliography. You can find others at your library or local bookstore. Websites offer many more resources.

One of the best is the Center for a New American Dream (www.newdream.org), an organization with tens of thousands of members, which in its words is "providing tools and support to families, citizens, and activists to counter our consumerist culture and to create new social norms about how to have a high quality of life and a reduced ecological footprint.... New Dream's Beyond Consumerism program strives to create a vision of life beyond over-consumption, disposable lifestyles, and perpetual marketing, and to provide the tools to help families, citizens, educators, and activists rein in consumerism in their own lives and in broader society."

The New Dream website offers tips for Rethinking "Stuff," Reclaiming Our Time, Avoiding Advertising, Promoting Self-Reliance, and dealing with Kids and Commercialism. Visually inviting and simple to navigate, it features helpful blogs, videos, and excellent articles, plus a very helpful monthly newsletter.

One important "bed rest" technique is "mindfulness," an approach similar to meditation. Rick Heller writes that mindfulness "involves slowing down, paying more attention, and taking more pleasure out of the ordinary world around us.... Unless we can learn to be mindful, we'll be at the mercy of advertisers who crank up the consumer treadmill to run faster and faster. It is the cultivation of attention."[6] It works. Kirk Warren Brown, a Virginia Commonwealth University professor, has found that mindfulness training reduces financial desire.[7]

268

When you're sick, the first thing to do is take time out.

CHAPTER 19

Affluholics anonymous

Think, for a moment, back to your childhood. You were sick in bed with the flu and Mom came in with a little TLC. Words of comfort and maybe some medicine—aspirin for your fever, lozenges for your cough. And a bowl of hot chicken soup just to make you feel better. But the most important thing was having Mom there with her sympathy, so you wouldn't have to suffer alone.

The same goes for affluenza. To conquer it, most of us need to know we're not all by ourselves in the battle. Like alcoholics trying to stay on the wagon, we need support from others who are fighting the disease. Every addiction nowadays seems to have support groups like Alcoholics Anonymous for its victims, and conquering affluenza, the addictive virus, may require them even more, because there isn't any social pressure to stop consuming—just the opposite. But there is, you might say, an AA for affluenza.

Get SATISFIED

I may be losing the rat race, but at least I'm still a rat.

STUDY CIRCLES CAN SAVE THE WORLD

Cecile Andrews, a former teacher who now lives in Santa Cruz, California, has a childlike sense of awe and wonder—and an ability to make people laugh that any stand-up comedian would envy. She was promoting adult education classes as a community college administrator in Seattle in 1989, when she read a book called *Voluntary Simplicity*, by Duane Elgin. "I was really excited about it," she says, "but no one else was talking about it." She decided to offer a course on the subject. "But only four people signed up, so we had to cancel," she says with a laugh.

"Then we tried it again three years later for a variety of reasons, and that time we got 175."

Afterward, participants told Cecile that her voluntary simplicity workshop had changed their lives. It wasn't the kind of thing a community college administrator hears every day, she says. "So I ended up resigning my full-time position and devoting myself to giving these workshops."

She also remembered an idea she'd learned in Sweden. There, neighbors and friends organize discussion groups, called study circles, which meet in people's homes. Cecile began to organize her would-be voluntary simplicity students into such groups. Participants started with a short reading list, but most of the discussion focused on their personal experiences. People began to tell their own stories, "why they were there, that they have no time, they are working too much, they have no fun, they're not laughing anymore."

Some of the groups that Cecile began in 1992 still continue today. Participants give each other advice and build networks for tool sharing and other activities that increase their sense of community. They find ways to help each other out that reduce their need for a high income. They meet frequently in each other's homes and share tips, stories, and ideas for action. Everyone is expected to talk, and an egg timer, passed around the room, limits the time each can speak, preventing anyone from monopolizing the conversation.

The discussion often moves from the personal to the political. "People begin to talk about what institutional changes need to happen so they can find community and stop wasting money and resources," says Andrews. They talk about open space, parks for their kids, improved public transit, longer library hours, more effective local government. "Voluntary simplicity is not just a personal change thing. Study circles can save the world," Andrews adds with a wink.

SIMPLICITY AS SUBVERSION

Since 1992, Cecile Andrews has helped start hundreds of voluntary simplicity study circles. Her book, *The Circle of Simplicity*, explains how anyone can start them. Most important, says Andrews, is that participants not see voluntary simplicity as a sacrifice.

"One person I know calls what we're doing the 'self-deprivation movement,' but it's not," she argues. "The way to fill up emptiness is not by denying ourselves something. It's by putting positive things in place of the negative things, by finding out what we really need, and that's community, creativity, passion in our lives, connection with nature. People help each other figure that out. They learn to meet their real needs instead of the false needs that advertisers create. They learn to live in ways that are high fulfillment, but low environmental impact."

In the best sense of the word, Andrews sees herself as a subversive (imagine Emma Goldman as Grandma Moses). "The thing about the voluntary simplicity movement is that it looks so benign," she suggests. "Like, 'Isn't that sweet? They're trying to cut back, to live more simply.' So people don't understand how radical it is. It's the Trojan horse of social change. It's really getting people to live in a totally different way."

Andrews is now promoting a similar idea she calls the "living room" revolution. " What needs to happen? It all starts with local," she says. "And *local* starts with small groups, meeting in places like people's living rooms, cafés, meeting rooms, and auditoriums." Andrews is clear that once people know they want change and take a step back from affluenza—the "bed rest" of the previous chapter—they need to work with others to make progress. And for most, the process needs a small-group component with real connection to others, not simply involvement in big social-change outfits. The anthropologist Margaret Mead once said that we should not underestimate the ability of a small group of committed people to change the world: "Indeed, it's the only thing that has." But such groups can take many forms in addition to the free-flowing style promoted by Andrews.

THE ROYS OF DOWNSHIFTING

In Portland, Oregon, Dick and Jeanne Roy used study groups to take the battle against affluenza into unexpected places. Until he reached the age of fifty-three, Dick Roy was a leader in the most traditional fashion: president of his class at Oregon State University; officer in the Navy; and finally, a high-priced corporate attorney in one of America's most prestigious law firms, with an office on the thirty-second floor overlooking all of Portland. But he was also married to Jeanne, a strong environmentalist and a believer in frugality.

So despite their six-figure income, the Roys lived simply and often had to weather teasing from their friends about their old clothes and used bicycles. They went backpacking on their vacations. Once they took their children to Disneyland—by bus, walking with backpacks on through the streets of Anaheim, California, from the bus station to their motel.

Jeanne, in particular, found many ways to reduce consumption: using a clothesline instead of a dryer; sending junk mail back until it stopped coming; carefully saving paper; buying food in bulk and using her own packaging. Eventually, to the amazement of all her neighbors, she reduced the amount of landfill-bound trash the Roys produced to only one regular-sized garbage can a year! She says it wasn't a sacrifice. "If you ask people what kinds of activities bring them pleasure, it's usually contact with nature, things that are creative, and relationships with people, and the things we do to live simply bring us all of those satisfactions."

Eventually, Jeanne took a leadership role in Portland's recycling program, conducting group workshops in people's homes to teach them how to save energy and water and use resources to maximum effectiveness. Meanwhile, Dick raised a few eyebrows at work by putting in the fewest billable hours of anyone in the firm so that he could spend more time with his family. Such behavior almost brands you as a heretic in the legal profession, but Dick was a darned good lawyer and he got along well with his colleagues, so they overlooked his transgressions. Yet eventually he grew tired of corporate law. His children were grown and he wanted to do something that more directly expressed his values, especially his concern for the environment. In 1993, Dick Roy left his job to live on his savings and devote his time to saving the earth.

WIDENING THE CIRCLES

The Roys founded the Northwest Earth Institute in Portland (www.nwei.org), an organization that promotes simple living and environmental awareness by running discussion groups in existing institutions. Dick Roy's corporate connections helped him bring workshops—Voluntary Simplicity, Choices for Sustainable Living, and Discovering a Sense of Place—into many of Portland's largest corporations. Interested employees were encouraged to meet during lunch hours, in groups of a dozen or so, and conduct structured conversations that, Dick hoped, would lead to personal, social, and political action.

While the Roys have moved on to other projects, two decades later, the Northwest Earth Institute can look back at a surprising track record of success:

- Hundreds of discussion courses conducted in private businesses (including such giants as Nike and Hewlett-Packard), government agencies, schools, and nonprofits throughout the Pacific Northwest
- Dozens of church discussion groups in the Northwest
- Establishment of outreach courses and sister Earth Institutes in all fifty states
- Involvement of more than 25,000 people in its courses

One difference between Cecile Andrews's study circles and the Earth Institute groups is that Andrews starts hers with a conversation of what a happy but less consumptive life would look like for people, while the initial impetus at Earth Institutes is on the environment. Another is that the Earth Institute groups use a more traditional approach, incorporating intensive study guides, including a multiplicity of reading materials and other resources, to get the conversation going. They also focus on changing behavior, not merely thinking. Northwest Earth Institute points out that while 88 percent of Americans say recycling is important, only 51 percent actually do it; 81 percent advocate taking your own reusable bag to the grocery story, but only 33 percent do; 76 percent like the idea of buying locally grown food, but only 26 percent actually do so; and 76 percent think it's better to walk or bike than drive, but only 15 percent practice what they preach.

We leave the choice of what kind of small-group Affluholics Anonymous study model is best for you. The point is not to go it alone. Find others to help you combat your own affluenza and change our social and economics priorities at the same time.

FINDING EACH OTHER

One place to begin to find folks to team up with is the Internet. Twenty years ago, when Cecile Andrews and the Roys began their voluntary simplicity work, only 0.02 percent of the world's people had access to the Net (which then contained very little information). Today, 35 percent have Internet access, and in countries like the United States coverage is near total. Search engines like Google and social networking sites like Facebook and Meetup allow the opportunity to find potential collaborators in your community to a degree unimaginable in the past. An Internet search on *voluntary simplicity*, for example, immediately turns up a million references to the term. Add the word *Facebook* and you find a hundred thousand connections, while adding *Meetup* brings in 17,000 more. Adding *support groups* churns up another 180,000 references, many of them being groups of people who are actually getting together! Surely one is near you. Get creative. Try a combination of key words. Or start your own group.

PROGRESSIVE SIMPLIFICATION

In the late seventies, Duane Elgin conducted a study for the Stanford Research Institute of people who were choosing simpler, less consumptive lives. He found they were "eating lower on the food chain"; tending to vegetarian diets; wearing simple, utilitarian clothing; buying smaller, fuel-efficient cars; and cultivating their "inner" lives—living "consciously, deliberately, intentionally," mindful of the impacts of their activities. Naturally, we interviewed him for the *Affluenza* documentary and have remained in contact since then.

Elgin published his findings in the book *Voluntary Simplicity*. His timing was off by a bit. The book came out in 1981, just as Ronald Reagan was encouraging a return to excess and trend watchers were discovering the yuppies. By

2000, Elgin, a gentle man with a gray beard and twinkling eyes, was an acknowledged leader in the new voluntary simplicity movement. Elgin believes that "the power of commercial mass media to distract us from real ecological crises and focus our attention on shampoo" are "creating a mindset for catastrophe."

But he now sees hopeful signs that weren't there during the seventies' emphasis on simplicity. Elgin points to the countless ways that seekers of a cure for affluenza can now connect with one another: a plethora of magazines, some real, some merely opportunistic; valuable Internet resources; websites for dozens of simple-living organizations; chat groups; radio programs; books filled with practical tips and inspiration. Ten percent of the population, Elgin says, is making changes. "For a long time, they felt alone, but now they're beginning to find each other."

The change will take a generation, he feels, and he fears that's about all the time we have before we run into an ecological wall. "The leading edge of those people choosing a simple life," Elgin says, "have been relatively affluent. They've had a taste of the good life and have found it wanting, and now they're looking for a different kind of life." In that sense, the movement might be seen by some people as elitist. Yet, says Elgin, "it's only when such people begin moderating their consumption that there is going to be more available for people that now don't have enough."

Elgin likes to talk about Arnold Toynbee's law of progressive simplification. He points out that the great British historian studied the rise and fall of twenty-two civilizations and "summarized everything he knew about the growth of human civilizations in one law: *The measure of a civilization's growth is its ability to shift energy and attention from the material side to the spiritual and aesthetic and cultural and artistic side.*"

Thousands of Americans are coming together in small groups all across the country, trying to bring about that shift. Like Uncle Sam pointing from a World War II "Wanted" poster, they need you.

CHAPTER 20

Fresh air

> Given a chance, a child will bring the confusion of the world to the woods, wash it in the creek, and turn it over to see what lives on the unseen side of that confusion.
> —RICHARD LOUV,
> Last Child in the Woods

> Instead of doing something, something is done to us.... We stumble across a roaring, resplendent waterfall in the middle of a quiet forest, and we become profoundly entranced.
> —THOMAS MOORE,
> The Re-enchantment of Everyday Life

On an early summer day in 2013—on the first day of National Pollinator Week—more than twenty-five thousand bumblebees fell dead on a Target parking lot in Wilsonville, Oregon. Landscapers had erroneously sprayed the lot's sixty-five European linden trees with the potent insecticide Safari, marketed by Valent U.S.A as "a super-systemic insecticide with quick uptake and knockdown." (Ironically, Valent is a cosponsor of National Pollinator Week, which celebrates the value of bees.)[1] This unfortunate event, happening in *similar ways all over the country, is a metaphor for our distracted culture. Busy with our digital devices, inhabiting the great air-conditioned indoors, we are almost as clueless as the pesticide applicators who sprayed according to schedule rather than observing that the trees were in full bloom and buzzing with life.*

In the last few decades, the aphorism "Stop and smell the roses" sank to a more cynical "Wake up and smell the coffee." We didn't have time for nature anymore. We learned to just ignore the damn roses and let the landscaper take care of them. This chapter challenges a widespread belief that if you make enough money, you don't need to know anything about nature or have contact with it. Conversely, we suggest that the stronger our bonds with nature—both individually and collectively—the less money we'll need, or *want*. If kicking affluenza is the overall goal, proven natural remedies may be the way to go.

FOR THE CHILDREN

Nature isn't just something pretty to look at, not just a backdrop for our busy lives; it's where we live and what we *are*. It's what flows in our arteries and endocrine systems, and it's the whole-grain cereal that gives us energy to start the day. But the more sidetracked we get chasing possessions and the money to buy them, the more distant nature becomes from our everyday lives. And the distance between nature and popular culture has become a canyon: for example, recent data suggests children are tethered to electronic media (computers, phones, television, games) more than fifty hours a week, while spending less than forty minutes outside.[2] This disconnect between children and their Mother Earth—like the gradual loss of one's hearing or sight—is poignant but stupidly careless at the same time. Certainly, it's a poorly conceived strategy for human growth and development.

After a seventeen-year absence from the classroom, the biology teacher Fred First saw a lot of changes in student behavior: "Out of 120 on field trips near campus along Virginia's New River that semester, only one student could call one of some 50 observed living things by name: poison ivy. Everything else—birds and bushes, wildflowers and vines, insects and fungi—were anonymous strangers."[3]

On a similar natural exploration, the naturalist Annette Hurdle heard a frightened child call out, "A plant touched me! What should I do?" Another child poked a stick at a dead beetle, commenting to her friend that the insect's batteries must have run out. Is nature becoming just so much nostalgia in our virtualized world? Richard Louv, author of the pivotal book *Last Child in the Woods* and cofounder of the Children & Nature Network, recalls that when he started interviewing children and their families in the

1980s, "They'd watch reruns of *Lassie* on TV, and see Jeff and Porky build a tree house in the woods, get lost, and have adventures. One boy said that, to him, that kind of life seemed like living on Mars. The disconnection has accelerated over the past three decades." But is it children's fault that the woods is now Fox Run Development, that some school playgrounds have signs that say, No Running, or that homeowners' associations often forbid residents to have basketball hoops and trampolines? Don't we need to change our priorities and design our cities and towns for natural diversity and resilience? William McDonough designs buildings brimming with biologic. On a recent visit to the architect's office, Richard Louv saw plans for a hospital building in Spain that will heal more than sick humans:

Get SATISFIED

The Original Stimulus Plan

    The bottom floor of the hospital will be all glassed in and anybody who walks into that hospital may have a butterfly—the butterfly that is threatened with extinction in that region—alight on them. The hospital's bottom floor will become a "butterfly factory."

    The butterflies emerge from their chrysalises in a synchronized fashion. Their emergence will become a community ritual. When they emerge, the hospital will open the doors and let them loose into the surrounding community. And the idea doesn't stop there. The hospital staff will reach out to every school, place of worship, business, and home and say, "You can do this, too. We can bring this butterfly back."[4]

Louv somehow remains optimistic that we can reconnect humans with nature. We can beat "nature-deficit syndrome," he believes, "if we begin to spend less time in front of screens and more time in front of streams."

NATURAL REMEDIES, SMALL AND LARGE

For individuals and families:
- Protect "nearby nature," such as a creek behind your house or a little woods at the end of your cul-de-sac. Maintain a birdbath. Replace part of your lawn with native plants. Build a bat house. Collect lightning bugs at dusk, release them at dawn.
- Make your yard a National Wildlife Federation Certified Wildlife Habitat.
- Encourage your kids to go camping in the backyard. Buy them a tent or help them make a canvas tepee, and leave it up all summer.
- Play "find ten critters"—mammals, birds, insects, reptiles, snails, other creatures. Finding a critter can also mean discovering footprints, mole holes, and other signs that an animal has passed by or lives there.

- Become a more effective recycler to conserve natural resources; consider green alternatives to standard products like cleaners, personal care products, clothes, and building materials.
- Become a habitual walker who observes the cycles of nature at the park or in neighbors' yards.
- Let your thumb turn green, maybe starting with a single plant, such as your favorite variety of tomato.
- Shop for products that have green labels such as USDA Organic (food), Energy Star (appliances), the recycle logo (products, packaging), Fair Trade (coffee, chocolate), LEED (buildings), Forest Stewardship Council (lumber), Friend of the Sea (seafood), and Marine Stewardship Council (seafood). These designations help ensure practices that are nature friendly.

For educators:

- Move nature conceptually from the "recreation column" to the "health" column.
- Teach children about nature interactively; for example, teach about birds by letting them craft wings out of cardboard boxes and build nests out of plant leaves and sticks.
- Let them love the earth before being asked to save it.

For governments:

- Launch programs that support reconnection with nature, such the "No Child Left Inside" programs adopted by Connecticut, Colorado, Illinois, Massachusetts, and Wisconsin.

  For medical personnel:
- Conduct research on the benefits of exposing children to nature instead of pharmaceuticals; incorporate the health benefits of nature into medical and nursing school curricula; encourage pediatricians to prescribe nature time for stress reduction and as an antidote to child obesity.[5]

IF IT AIN'T FIXABLE, DON'T BREAK IT

In our current way of thinking, nature is at worst an evil enemy we've been battling for eons, and at best a warehouse of resources we can convert to cash. "Pay no attention to the pests, toxic chemicals, weeds, slash piles, and tailings ponds that are side effects of industry," we coach each other, "because that's the shape of money." But the truth is, nature is far from being a problem; rather, it's a living tapestry of tried and true solutions. Why should we care if this might be the last century for biological celebrations such as abundant schools of wild seafood; silent, old-growth forest; determined songbird migrations; and the annual spring "turnover" of pristine mountain lakes? Well, no need to care about such things—unless we have a fondness for life as we know it. Unless we have some use for clean air and water, healthy food, flood control, soil fertility, waste recycling, pest control, pollination, raw materials for goods, climate control, seed dispersal, erosion control, recreation, and medicine. A survey of the top 150 prescription drugs used in the United States found that 118 are based on natural sources: plants (74 percent), fungi, bacteria, and snakes.[6]

In research studies, when people view slides of nature, their blood pressure falls; and when those with ADHD spend time in nature, the results are often as effective as if they'd taken the widely used drug Ritalin. Nature is where we feel most comfortable. A classic ten-year study reported in the *American Journal of Preventive Medicine* documented that hospital patients with a view of trees went home much sooner than those who viewed a brick wall. In a similar study, Michigan prisoners whose cells overlooked a prison courtyard had 25 percent more visits to health care facilities than those whose cells looked into farmland.[7]

A CIVILIZATION ON LIFE SUPPORT?

One after another, services that used to be provided free by nature have been packaged and put on the market. Take bottled water, home-delivered in five-gallon bottles, or tanning salons, where creatures of the great indoors bask in simulated sunlight. Why build with durable stone and brick when petrobricks and faux rocks are cheaper? Many educators and thinkers refer to an "extinction of experience" that accompanies our pullback from nature. Like a washed-out sprig of parsley on a dinner plate, the community park is often biologically bland—and sometimes not secure from crime. The only way some know nature is by mentally crunching images of it on TV, like popcorn.

But television can't communicate a multidimensional, sensuous, interactive reality. It shows only the visual realm—and that through the tunnel of a lens. We're not actually *there* to smell nature, and touch it, and feel the breeze. Besides, televised nature is often scripted nature—as fake as a paper ficus. Spliced together from hundreds of nonsequential hours of tape, a typical nature program filmed in Africa zooms in on a majestic lion, relentlessly on the prowl for wildebeests, jackals, and gazelles. The reality is, lions are as lazy as your housecat, sometimes sleeping twenty hours a day. Even so, footage of two lions mating is predictably followed by "cubs, tumbling out after a two- or three-minute gestation, full of play. The timeless predatory cycle repeats...."

In *The Age of Missing Information,* Bill McKibben compares and contrasts the information contained in a daylong hike in upstate New York with the information content of a hundred cable TV stations, on the same day. Writes McKibben, "We believe that we live in the 'age of information,' that there has been an information 'revolution.' ... Yet vital knowledge that humans have always possessed about who we are and where we live seems beyond our reach." In one hundred hours of programming, he found very little to enrich his life.

Yet his real-world experiences made him feel actively, rather than passively, alive. In the closing sentences of *The Age of Missing Information*, McKibben reminds us of the virtual canyon we've put between ourselves and the natural world:

> On *Now You're Cooking*, a lady is making pigs-in-a-blanket with a Super Snacker. "We have a pact in our house—the first one up plugs in the Super Snacker."
>
> And on the pond, the duck is just swimming back and forth, his chest pushing out a wedge of ripples that catch the early rays of the sun.[8]

KICKING ECOPHOBIA

The educator David Sobel terms our separation from nature "ecophobia"—a symptom characterized by an inability to smell, plant, or even acknowledge the roses. "Ecophobia is a fear of oil spills, rain forest destruction, whale hunting, and Lyme disease. In fact it's a fear of just being outside," Sobel explains. A fear of microbes, lightning, spiders, and dirt. Sobel's first aid for ecophobia emphasizes hands-on contact with nature. "Wet sneakers and muddy clothes are prerequisites for understanding the water cycle," he says. In the book *Beyond Ecophobia,* he describes the magic of overcoming "timesickness" and regaining a more natural pace:

> I went canoeing with my six-year-old son Eli and his friend Julian. The plan was to canoe a two-mile stretch of the Ashuelot River, an hour's paddle in adult time. Instead, we dawdled along for four or five hours. We netted golf balls off the bottom of the river from the upstream golf course. We watched fish and bugs in both the shallows and depths of the river. We stopped at the mouth of a tributary stream for a picnic and went for a long adventure through a maze of marshy streams. Following beaver trails led to balance-walking on fallen trees to get across marshy spots without getting our feet wet. We looked at spring flowers, tried to catch a snake, got lost and found. How fine it was to move at a meandery, child's pace![9]

NATURE'S MADNESS

The wilderness leader and ecopsychologist Robert Greenway has spent many years on the trail and has allowed the child in himself to remain active. He tries to bring out that trait in others, too, with tangible results. Comments from more than a thousand wilderness-trip participants (both adult and child) indicate that nature is indeed working its magic:

- 90 percent described an increased sense of aliveness, well-being, and energy
- 77 percent described a major life change upon return (in personal relationships, employment, housing, or lifestyle)
- 60 percent of the men and 20 percent of the women stated that a major goal of the trip was to conquer fear, challenge themselves, and expand limits
- 90 percent broke an addiction such as nicotine, chocolate, and soda pop
- 57 percent of the women and 27 percent of the men stated that a major goal of the trip was to "come home" to nature
- 76 percent of all respondents reported dramatic changes in quantity, vividness, and context of dreams after seventy-two hours in the wilderness[10]

COMING BACK TO OUR SENSES

A few years ago, Lana Porter began to come to her senses. The garden she cultivates in Golden, Colorado, is far more than a lush, reclaimed vacant lot—it's a biological extension of herself and a way of life. "I eat very well out of this garden, just about all year round," she says, "and the organic produce gives me energy to grow more produce and get *more* energy. It's a cycle of health that has cut my expenses in half. My grocery bills are lower, my health bills are lower, I don't need to pay for exercise, and my transportation costs are lower because I don't have to travel so much to amuse myself."

Asked what she likes best about her personal Garden of Eden, Porter replies, "I like what it does for my head. Sometimes, when I'm watering a healthy crop, or planting seeds, or cultivating between rows, I'm not thinking anything at all—a radical switch from my previous life as an overworked computer programmer. People tell me I should take care of my crops more efficiently—with irrigation systems on timers, designer fertilizers, and pesticides—so I could spend less time out here. But that way of growing disconnects the grower from the garden. The whole point is to spend *more* time with the plants, taking care of things, and less time trying to reshape myself to fit the changing whims of the world."[11]

When we experience nature with our own noses, skin, lungs, and reptilian brains, we feel silly about the stress of obsessive projects and timelines. Self-importance begins to dissolve into something larger. We see that we're integral members of a club called Life on Earth, and it feels great! Rather than perceiving ourselves as simply human-paycheck-house-car, we finally understand who and where we are. We see that in reality, we're human-soil-grains-fruits-microbes-trees-oxygen-herbivoresfish-salt marshes, and on and on and on! We begin to question the logic and the ethic of parting nature out like a used-up car. Then, if we have the guts, we begin to speak out about protecting nature and supporting policies and even companies that help it regenerate. We begin to see nature as a sacred garden that can't tolerate any more abuse and as a haven that can restore our psyche and our health.

CHAPTER 21

Back to work

Markets flatter our solitary egos but leave our yearnings for community unsatisfied. They advance individualistic, not social, goals, and they encourage us to speak the language of "I want" not the language of "we need."
—BENJAMIN BARBER, *A Place for Us*

It is illogical to criticize companies for playing by the current rules of the game. If we want them to play differently, we have to change the rules.
—ROBERT REICH, *Supercapitalism*

If you think your actions are too small to make a difference, you've never been in bed with a mosquito.
—ANONYMOUS

The work of building and rebuilding a culture is never finished, because the context—the environment and human activities—is constantly changing. At this moment in history, it's clear that overconsumption as a way of life can't continue, but what will take its place? That's the weighty issue facing us on our desks, on our blog sites, in our state legislatures.

Our mission is to invent equitable and efficient ways of meeting our needs in a world of diminishing resources, a changing climate, and a still-rising global population. This is a big moment, and these changes will not be automatic.

Think of the work that was accomplished more than two hundred years ago! In 1776, two civilization-shifting works were published. The pamphlet *Common Sense,* by Thomas Paine, was read by more than a third of Paine's fellow colonists and inspired American revolutionaries to put their lives on the line for freedom and equality. Comments Marianne Williamson about its underlying theme, democracy: "The phrase, 'Life, liberty, and the pursuit of happiness' is not just an early American public relations slogan. It is a bright light shot like a laser through thousands of years of history."[1] Simply put, democracy is a keeper, and we need to safeguard it. As we tell our children when they receive their first grown-up gift, "You can have it, but you have to take care of it."

The second transformative book, *The Wealth of Nations,* by the Scottish economist Adam Smith, helped launch one of the most vigorous and challenging periods in the history of humanity: the age of capitalism, in which individuals and companies in free market countries are given society's blessing to accumulate as much material wealth as possible and as a bonus, receive kudos for contributing to the general good. (But isn't this a little like telling our children, "Feel free to eat all the candy you want, because profits from candy sales are good for everyone?")

In our time, Smith's well-meaning formula is becoming obsolete, and toxic. As a flagship of civilization, it's badly in need of course correction. Here's why: In Smith's time, most people lived in close-knit towns supplied by village-scale enterprises. Residents knew each other by name, and these connections provided accountability and conscience-by-community. If the butcher sold spoiled meat, not only would he get a bad "customer review" in the town, but the townspeople also probably wouldn't let a daughter marry his son.

What would Adam Smith say now? Global population has expanded eightfold, and the world's "local" butcher shop has morphed into monster companies like Tyson and Cargill that slaughter and pack sixty thousand cattle each day. Corporations like these pay celebrity CEOs outrageous salaries; move jobs overseas where wages are lower; substitute robots for people; bust unions; elbow small businesses out of the marketplace; abandon communities for sweetheart deals elsewhere; and exploit resources as if they were limitless, all in quest of short-term profits. In our day, the thousand largest publicly traded corporations control 80 percent of the world's industrial output, and fifty-three of the largest hundred economies in the world are companies, not countries.[2] How do we hold titans like these accountable? Maybe the underlying purpose of trends toward localism, cooperative ventures, and the decentralization of technologies is an instinctive attempt to bring Thomas Paine's thinking back into our lives.

THE SOFTWARE OF SUSTAINABILITY

In the brilliantly researched book *Owning the Future,* Marjorie Kelly opens the door just a crack to a new kind of economy—a democratic one, in which profits share the stage with other values such as the well-being of employees, the health of communities, the pride of producing high-quality products and services, and the regeneration of nature. After years as the cofounder and editor of *Business Ethics* magazine, she had an epiphany: "You don't *start* with the corporation and ask how to redesign it. You start with life, with human life and the life of the planet, and ask, how do we generate the conditions for life's flourishing?"[3]

One of many examples of stakeholder ownership she cites is a hometown bank reminiscent of Bailey Building and Loan in the movie *It's a Wonderful Life.* Beverly Cooperative Bank, one of about eight hundred "mutual" banks in the country, doesn't have outside investors who demand higher short-term earnings. This gives its owners more leeway to follow the bank's mission: to create and maintain a great community filled with satisfied residents. The bank considers it a successful year when, for example, there are zero foreclosures on mortgage loans. Kelly writes, "Just as cows eat grass because their stomachs are structured to eat grass, Beverly Cooperative Bank makes good loans because it's structured to serve its community."[4]

Kelly sees ownership as the underlying architecture of an economy, but when that architecture is poorly designed, "it locks us into behaviors that lead to financial excess and ecological overshoot." In contrast, the member-ownership architecture of the nation's eight thousand credit unions keeps money (more than $10 billion each year) in the hands of ninety million Americans who pay lower interest rates on credit cards, car loans, and mortgages. When megabanks were receiving bailouts in the recession, the vast majority of credit unions didn't need help, because they had steered clear of toxic mortgage securities that tempted the officers of other banks. In credit unions, profits are just one slice of a pie that also includes the financial health of members—who won't go along with their money being gambled away in high-risk "casinos."

Kelly emphasizes that systems do what they're designed to do. For example, most publicly traded banks are *designed* to maximize profit and minimize risks and expenses, including expenses like livable wages and contributions to the community. "Too big to fail" banks like Lehman Brothers and Goldman Sachs were once partnerships that changed their ownership design to publicly traded firms, and that's where the trouble began. Onetime trader Michael Kelly observes, "We took some risks, but because firms were partnerships, we were using our own money. If all of a sudden you're using shareholders' money, they end up taking all the risk while you make all the money."[5]

"We know the next economy will require things like wind turbines, limits on carbon emissions, and sustainably managed forests," writes Marjorie Kelly. "The question is, who will *own* these, who will control them?" Many farmers in the United States are now leasing wind rights to absentee developers who take home most of the profits. In tiny Luverne, Minnesota, farmers asked, "Why shouldn't we pool our resources and own the wind developments ourselves?" They quickly raised $4 million by selling shares for $5,000 apiece—enough to construct four huge turbines. The architecture of Minwind's contract requires all shareholders to be Minnesota residents, and 85 percent must be from rural communities. With this kind of agreement in place, the wealth stays local, by design, and in the hands of people who care about their land and communities.

Similarly, the community forests of Mexico (and many other countries) provide income and stewardship of the environment at the same time.

Sixty to 80 percent of Mexican forests are managed by local stakeholders. For example, in Ixtlan, Mexico, the forests provide income for three hundred employees who harvest timber, make furniture, and sustainably manage the forest. Marjorie Kelly emphasizes, *"When ownership rights are in the hands of those whose self-interest depends on the health of the forests, the fish, and the land, they have a natural tendency toward stewardship. Self-interest and the interests of the whole become one and the same."*

Kelly's groundbreaking book explores the sustainable software of community land trusts; community development financial institutions; community-owned utilities; conservation easements; catch shares (biologically calibrated fishing rights); employee-owned businesses (more than eleven thousand in the United States); consumer-owned food cooperatives; producer-owned farming and fishing cooperatives like Organic Valley and North End Lobster Co-op; and many other highly democratic forms of ownership. There's a common thread in these ventures: instead of capital hiring labor—and often suppressing it—labor in effect hires capital, setting precise rules to achieve specific outcomes such as employee stock options or protection of an ecosystem. It's not that megacorporations are (all) run by crooks; they are just designed selfishly; their mission is to siphon money from living systems (including us) to Wall Street. The famed economist John Maynard Keynes saw this coming in 1933 when he wrote, "Remoteness between ownership and operation is an evil."[6]

The lack of connection is convenient for corporate managers who don't have to see the life cycle of their profits—remote sweatshops, strip mines, and toxic waste landfills. Their emotions and instincts can't gum up the works of "rational" free market profiteering. They can focus on spreadsheets rather than livable wages or natural diversity. But there are many signs that economic rules are changing, and Adam Smith would probably approve.

"GOOD MORNING, BEAUTIFUL BUSINESS"

Judy Wicks, a tireless activist for "local living economies," would much rather make financial agreements with people she knows. Thirteen years ago, she sold her stocks and put her life savings into the Reinvestment Fund, a Philadelphia community investment group that lends money to support things like affordable housing, local businesses, and community centers. "I soon discovered that the wind turbines producing renewable energy for our region, including my own home and business, were financed by the Reinvestment Fund," she recalls. "So, from my local investment, I receive not only a modest financial return (which has recently outperformed the stock market), but also a 'living return'—the benefit of living in a more sustainable community."[7]

For twenty-six years, Wicks poured her energy into managing the White Dog Café in Philadelphia. The restaurant started and remained relatively small, because she's never bought into the dominant paradigm that growth is defined solely by increased profits, though she does believe that economic exchange can be satisfying and meaningful. As Wicks sees it, growth is also about increasing knowledge, expanding consciousness, developing creativity, deepening relationships, increasing happiness and well-being—and having fun. She made a conscious decision to stay small, to be one special restaurant rather than a chain. She hung a sign in her closet that she'd see each morning: *Good morning beautiful business*. The sign reminded her of the farmers who were already out in the fields picking fresh organic fruits and vegetables; and the pigs, cows, chickens that were out in the pastures, enjoying the morning sun and fresh air. She would think of the restaurant's bakers coming early in the morning to put cakes and pies in the oven, and the coffee growers who produced the organic fair trade coffee beans that made her restaurant so fragrant each morning.

The White Dog became an education and support center for Philadelphia residents. When the farmer who supplied the restaurant with organic pork needed a refrigerator truck to expand his business and supply other restaurants,

Wicks lent him $30,000, which he has since paid back. Every year, Wicks staged a Green Dog Day to talk about green business practices and launch green initiatives, which included a project that supplied compost to inner-city school gardens; a solar hot water system to heat dishwasher water; and a ban on bottled water in the restaurant.

Choosing a place and taking responsibility for it is the first step in building a local living economy, she asserts. Other key principles of the movement include democracy and decentralized ownership, not concentrated wealth; a living return, not the highest return; a fair price, not the lowest price; a life-serving approach, not a self-serving one; cooperation, not competition; and cultural diversity, not a monoculture.

THE SHARING ECONOMY

Bending Marjorie Kelly's ownership perspectives in a different, yet still innovative, direction, millions of Americans are practicing leasing rather than owning. (All they want to own is *access* to goods and services.) The digital revolution has provided online communities where virtually anything can be bought and sold; capital can be lent, borrowed, and invested; and cars, houses, even appliances, can be leased rather than purchased. Writes the green economy expert Van Jones, "Warren Buffett's MidAmerican

Energy made news recently with its investment of more than $2 billion in two solar power plants in California. But you know who has more money than even Buffett? All of us combined. Together, consumers can start rebuilding the economy from the community up."[8] The New Age term for cooperative investing is *crowdsourcing,* or *crowdfunding,* which can quickly parlay many small contributions or investments into large pools of money. Referring to the online energy investment company, Mosaic, Jones explains, "Mosaic connects investors to solar projects in need of financing. The projects generate revenue by selling the electricity they generate, which allows the investors to get paid back with interest."

The Human Race

Maybe a solar project at a convention center in Wildwood, New Jersey, appeals to you, or an affordable housing complex in San Bruno, California. You can invest as little as $25 and get returns starting at 4.5 percent annually. Or what if you want to invest in a mini-power plant on your own roof, but you don't have the cash? Hire a company like SolarCity and lease a solar electric system from them. "We'll handle everything for your project including engineering, permits, installation and ongoing monitoring of system performance," explains the company's website. Essentially, you'll be sharing the value of your roof space with SolarCity, while powering your home with clean energy and reducing your utility bills. Arrangements like this leave utility managers stuttering, because the very need for centralized power plants is being questioned. In 2012, there were more than ninety thousand PV installations in the United States, including eighty-three thousand in the residential market alone. According to the Solar Energy Industries Association, the United States now has over 8,500 megawatts of cumulative installed solar electric capacity, enough to power more than 1.3 million average American homes.[9] (Add the more than 60,000 megawatts of installed wind generators already installed in 2013, and renewable energy in the United States begins to look formidable.)

The success of the online company AirBnB demonstrates that Americans are interested in innovative approaches, cost savings, and less conventional lodging when they travel, made possible by the smartphones, tablets, and laptops that allow access to lodging options from virtually anywhere. AirBnB's platform for short-term rentals includes a quarter million or more listings of private rooms, apartments, castles, boats, manors, tree houses, tepees, igloos, and private islands in 192 countries. What was once considered one step beyond freeloading is going mainstream, or nearly so. What makes a service like this one work is reciprocal customer reviews and renter evaluations that establish trustworthiness.

Similarly, five years ago, consumers of car-sharing services were often assumed to be on the fringe, probably just too poor to afford cars. But recently Avis Budget Group bought the Zipcar franchise ("Wheels when you want them") for a whopping $500 million, to compete with Hertz's and Enterprise's new car-sharing ventures. Here's why car sharing makes sense: cars spend 95 percent of their lives parked, *not* doing what they were built to do—taking people where they want to go. Why not get full service out of our collective fleet of vehicles? If renting a car by the hour is the free market's way of distributing value, even Adam Smith would probably drive a Zipcar, or even become a member of peer-to-peer car sharing ventures like RelayRides and Getaround (with a combined fleet of fifty thousand or more), in which privately owned cars are rented out by people like you and me.

"You can get anything you want at Alice's restaurant," sang Arlo Guthrie, and it's clear that our economy (and especially the Internet) has become that kind of place. Need a bike in a foreign city? No worries. More than five hundred cities in forty-nine countries now host advanced bike-sharing programs, with a combined fleet of over half a million bicycles.[10] Says New York City's Mayor Bloomberg, "We now have an entirely new transportation network without spending any taxpayer money." (The pay-by-the-hour program called Citi Bike launched in 2013 with six thousand bikes at more than three hundred stations.) With a Spotify subscription, you'll have access to your favorite music without having to own CDs. Same deal with Netflix movies, as thirty million Americans have already discovered. A Community Supported Agriculture subscription brings fresh produce to your table and at the same time reduces the grower's financial risk.

Need designer jeans but can't believe how much they cost? Go to Mud Jeans, online, and rent them by the month. Philips Lighting will lease high-efficiency lights to you, and Interface will rent, install, and maintain modular carpet tiles. Textbooks, office space for "coworking," handbags, jewelry, computers, guitars—all are for rent. This new way of having access without the burden of ownership is just one symptom of an invisible hand that's reaching for efficiency and sustainability.

DESIGNING FOR A HEALTHY PLANET

When a toaster is designed well, it makes the day go better, because the toast comes out golden brown, and the appliance itself is so stylish! If the toaster is designed to be repairable, that's also a good thing, and if it can easily recycled, we have a smart product that creates a minimum of impact, by design. Most countries in western Europe now mandate "extended producer responsibility," which requires companies to take back products at the end of their lives. In the future, your toaster might "swim upstream" to be recycled at the very factory where it was manufactured. This mandate is conceptually brilliant, stimulating manufacturers to design a product that's recyclable, durable, and nontoxic. But it's not just products that need brilliant design; entire systems need to be rethought. Partly because our era is infected with the assumption of consumption, systems like energy, food supply, manufacturing, and city planning are in turn infected with coal-fired power plants, suburbs without stores, poorly designed packaging, processed food, out-of-season fruit from distant continents, communities with no recycling services, thirty million acres of thirsty, hungry lawn in America. If we integrate values such as efficiency, moderation, and fairness into our designs, along with tools such as precision, prevention, and participation, we stand a chance of creating a realistic, holistically abundant civilization. However, if we integrate the spoiled assumptions of our current era into our products, buildings, and landscapes, we'll lock ourselves into a future that is literally designed to fail. Fortunately, brilliant minds are coming up with innovative designs to help restructure these systems and cool the fever of enormous challenges such as climate change. To give just two examples:

- The cement industry accounts for 6 percent of global CO_2 emissions (twice as much as the aviation industry). That percentage will get higher as Asia and eastern Europe continue to build infrastructure. Calera Corporation in California is challenging a cement-making paradigm that has remained constant for more than 2,300 years with a process that's similar to the way coral reefs self-assemble. Calera injects carbon dioxide emissions from power plants into seawater, which creates a chalky carbonate that is added to gravel and water to make concrete. This process avoids the need for the high temperatures typically supplied by coal-fired

kilns, creating a cement that is 40 percent solidified carbonate by weight.
- Touted by designers as the world's greenest office building, the Bullitt Center in Seattle produces as much electricity with solar energy as the building needs, making it "net zero." Rainwater is collected in cisterns, and gray water from sinks and showers irrigates the building's green roof. The project complies with the Living Building Challenge, even more rigorous than the more familiar LEED certification for sustainable buildings. Building materials come from sustainable sources. Exposed wood, certified as sustainably harvested by the Forest Stewardship Council reflects the local Pacific Northwest natural environment.

WHERE WE LIVE TO CONSUME, OR WHERE WE COME TO LIFE?

We tend to use the question, "Where do you live?" automatically, without really thinking about what it means, or could mean. All too often it means, "How far do I have to drive to get there?" or "Do you live in an exclusive neighborhood?" In a distracted, unhealthy culture, where you live is just a place where you park your car, watch four hours of TV a day, and generate four pounds of trash. Ideally, of course, where you live is so much more: Where you come to life. Where you have your best relationships, your most creative ideas ... Where do you feel the most content, and energized.

About eighteen years ago, Dave joined a group of people interested in designing a neighborhood from scratch, where basic needs could be met directly. The group took the formula for cohousing, a design concept imported from Denmark, and applied it to a chunk of land in Colorado. They found a scenic ten-acre property west of Denver, and with help from an architect and a developer, they designed and contracted twenty-seven private homes, a workshop, a garden-orchard and a common house. (The common house is used for community meals once every week and a half or so, and for meetings, parties, rehearsals, house concerts, late-night soul sessions, and whatever else.) The common house is owned collectively yet adds individual value because members don't need a big living room to entertain in, or a guest room, since there are several available.

Before construction began, many visioning sessions made even a slow-moving process exciting. The group imagined the pedestrian walkways, the community garden, the kids' playgrounds, and various rooms in the common house. Since the architecture is southwestern, they pictured a mission bell in a bell tower. Years later, that imaginary bell has a very real clang, and kids love to be asked to pull the rope that rings it. Salvaged from an old farm where one of the members grew up, the massive bell calls everyone in the community (called Harmony Village) for meals, meetings, and celebrations.

By clustering homes in blocks of two and four, Harmony residents preserved both land and energy, since heat is "borrowed" from the walls of neighboring homes. And by mandating that cars be parked in garages and parking spaces at the edge of the neighborhood, the group preserved the sanity of its members. There's a sense of calmness in the center of the neighborhood, kind of like a courtyard in a college campus. The design also helps the neighborhood's security, because there's usually activity in the common area, and there's also a good chance of having "eyes on the green" as people make dinner or do the dishes.

Though the residents don't call their neighborhood Utopia, they're learning trialby-fire citizenship—an exciting and challenging, if sometimes frustrating, proposition. Cohousing is only one of many ways to create vital, people-friendly neighborhoods, and it doesn't have to take place in newly constructed buildings. (The Nomad community in Boulder, Colorado, for example, shares public space with an existing theater, while the On-Going Community in Portland, Oregon, rehabilitated old neighborhood houses that members were able to purchase cheap.) Whenever developers, city leaders, and active citizens create a place that optimizes social opportunities and minimizes wasted effort (including resources, time, and money), they are taking a swipe at affluenza.

CHAPTER 22

Building immunity

An ounce of prevention is worth a pound of cure, or so the old saying goes. Many of us take that suggestion seriously each fall when we line up dutifully for flu shots. When we feel a virus coming on, we pop some vitamin C tablets into our mouths, hoping Linus Pauling knew what he was talking about (turns out, he didn't). Of course, there are no real shots or pills that can prevent or soften the impact of affluenza. (There's one exception: for the small percentage of Americans who are truly addicted—that is, compulsive shoppers—psychiatrists sometimes prescribe anticompulsion drugs and antidepressants, with promising results.) But in a metaphorical sense, some powerful antiviruses are floating around that can help vaccinate us against affluenza, and so are some equally effective vitamins that can help keep us from harm's way.

Vancouver, British Columbia, might be called the headquarters of anti-affluenza vaccine research. It's the home of Kalle Lasn, the author of *Culture Jam* and publisher of a magazine called *Adbusters*. The magazine became popular with its clever "uncommercials," anti-ads that often mock real ads. For example, a parody of Calvin Klein's Obsession perfume ads shows men staring into their underwear, while another mocking Absolut

Vodka shows a partially melted plastic vodka bottle, with the caption "Absolute Impotence" and a warning in small print that "drink increases the desire but lessens the performance."

John's favorite ad mocks no real product but shows a handsome young businessman who says he's one of many who are turning to mammon, because "I want a religion that doesn't complicate my life with unreasonable ethical demands." It's an obvious play on Christ's declaration that "you cannot serve both God and mammon." "We're not the biggest player in the spiritual arena, but we're the fastest-growing," the mammon anti-ad declares. It's a subtle but powerful reminder of the decline of true spirituality in the Age of Affluenza.

Perhaps the most successful of *Adbusters'* parodies were its antismoking ads. In one, two Marlboro Man–type cowboys ride side by side in the sunset. "I miss my lung, Bob," reads the caption. A series of anti-ads mocks Joe Camel, a cartoon character devised to sell cigarettes to kids, according to antismoking critics. Joe Camel becomes Joe Chemo, a camel dying of cancer, lying in a hospital bed hooked to an array of life-support equipment, or already dead from cancer and lying in his coffin. In Seattle, the city's public health department paid to put Joe Chemo on outdoor billboards.

TURNING ADVERTISING AGAINST ITSELF

The anti-ads work like vaccines because they use the virus itself to build up resistance. "We discovered early on in the publication of *Adbusters* that if we come up with an ad that looks like a Chevron ad or a Calvin Klein ad and fool people for a couple of seconds before they realize it's saying exactly the opposite, then we have created a kind of moment of truth that forces them to think about what they've seen," says Lasn.

Born during World War II in Estonia, Lasn spent the early years of his life in a refugee camp. He remembers those early years as tough in a material sense, "but it was a time when our family was very together, when the community in which we lived was very together, and I recall it with fondness." Lasn moved around a lot, from Germany to Australia to Japan, where he worked for ten years in marketing until he had a sudden change of heart. He emigrated to Vancouver and became a documentary filmmaker. In 1989 Lasn produced his first television "uncommercial," a parody of British Columbia Tourist Commission ads that showcased the province's stunning natural beauty. Lasn's spoof showed what was happening to that beauty as logging companies clear-cut BC's ancient forests. Not surprisingly, television stations refused to air the uncommercial even though Lasn was willing to pay for the airtime.

Many of the uncommercials are produced by people who work in the advertising industry. "They have qualms about the ethics of their business," says Lasn, "so clandestinely they come and help us to come up with our messages, which are trying to use television to change the world for the better."

BUY NOTHING DAY

Lasn's group has been promoting an idea called "Buy Nothing Day," since 1992. Buy Nothing Day is now celebrated in more than sixty-five other countries. In the United States, it is held on the day after Thanksgiving, Black Friday, traditionally one of the biggest shopping days of the year. According to *Wikipedia*, Buy Nothing Day now includes a wide range of possible activities aimed at targeting consumerism and affluenza:[1]

- Credit card cut-up: Participants stand in a shopping mall, shopping center, or store with a pair of scissors and a poster that advertises help for people who want to put an end to mounting debt and extortionate interest rates with one simple cut.
- Free, noncommercial street parties.
- Zombie walk: Participant "zombies" wander around shopping malls or other consumer

havens with a blank stare. When asked what they are doing participants describe Buy Nothing Day.

- Whirl-mart: Participants silently steer their shopping carts around a shopping mall or store in a long, baffling conga line without putting anything in the carts or actually making any purchases.
- Buy Nothing Day hike: Rather than celebrate consumerism by shopping, participants celebrate the earth and nature.
- Buy Nothing Day paddle along the San Francisco waterfront: In this event, promoted by the Bay Area Sea Kayakers, you can kayak along the notoriously consumptive San Francisco waterfront.
- Winter coat exchange (an idea that started in Rhode Island and has spread to Rhode Island, Kentucky, Utah, and Oregon): Coats are collected from anyone who wants to donate, and anyone who needs a winter coat is welcome to take one.

"Buy Nothing Day has exploded," says Lasn. "It's becoming a truly international celebration of frugality and living lightly on the planet, and of voluntary simplicity." Lasn believes the spirit of Buy Nothing Day must catch on as an effective vaccine against affluenza, because the North American lifestyle is simply unsustainable. "Overconsumption is the mother of all of our environmental problems," he says. Lasn and his associates were also the creative spark for the Occupy Movement, which has challenged the right of Wall Street, and the 1 percent to appropriate the wealth of our society. One project of Occupy was Occupy Christmas, which calls for supporting the local economy in gift giving, while also encouraging gifts of time and personal energy instead of stuff.

If only they'd at least buy something

THE (EN)RICH LIST

In the spirit of the *Adbusters* anti-ads, the Post-Growth Institute, based in Sydney, Australia, has found another to poke fun at an institutional bulwark of affluenza, *Forbes* magazine's vaunted Rich List of the hundred wealthiest Americans.

The institute, which promotes a less consumptive, "steady state" economy, publishes its own (En)Rich List (enrichlist.org/the-complete-list), honoring people around the world, living and dead who, in the institute's opinion, have been the leading lights of sustainability. The hundred people featured on the list include such luminaries as E.F. Schumacher, Donella Meadows, David Suzuki, Bill McKibben, and our foreword writer, Annie Leonard, as well as such obscure personages as this book's cowriter, John, for whom the honor came as a magnitude 10 shock. To add to the parody, the (En)Rich List includes the "net worth" of its members, measured in Internet references rather than dollars, as with Forbes. The idea is that the Internet references are a proxy for how effectively members have been spreading the word for sustainability: Annie is worth 1.97 million, and John 1.07 million.

VACCINATING KIDS

To be truly effective, vaccination programs for affluenza will have to start with children, especially now, when marketers have them squarely in their crosshairs. Websites providing valuable advice in this area include Consumer Jungle (www.consumerjungle.org), a Wenatchee, Washington–based site that offers activities for teachers, parents, and high school kids, helping them become savvy consumers; and Share Save Spend (www.sharesavespend.com), created by

Nathan Dungan, the Minneapolis author of the excellent book *Prodigal Sons and Material Girls: How Not to Be Your Child's ATM*. Dungan's site promotes what we think is a very healthy philosophy. It starts with teaching children the value of giving, then shows them how to save money, and finally, how to spend it wisely when they need to.

In many schools around the country, teachers help their students protect themselves from affluenza-carrying commercials by teaching them to analyze how media messages manipulate them. The concept is called "media literacy" and in the Age of Affluenza it may be as important as learning to read. Students dissect television ads to discover the psychological techniques the ads use to persuade them to buy. They analyze what needs each advertisement suggests the product might fill, then ask if there are better, less costly ways to meet the same needs. Increasingly, enlightened school districts require media literacy courses. Around the United States, students who have been exposed to media literacy are also learning about the deplorable wages and working conditions in factories that make some of the products and brands teenagers have been taught to desire. They demonstrate against child labor and sweatshops in other countries where their products are made and refuse to be walking billboards for global corporations.

THE STORY OF STUFF

In our view, one of the most effective vaccinations for building immunity against affluenza has been a funny and provocative twenty-minute video called *The Story of Stuff* (www.storyofstuff.org), which the *New York Times* reports "has become a sleeper hit in classrooms across the nation." The video is a compelling, simply animated monologue by Annie Leonard, a former Greenpeace activist who spent more than a dozen years studying the disposal of waste around the world and the impact of overconsumption on planetary ecosystems. Hundreds of teachers have shown the video, inoculating thousands of students by showing them the real impact of an affluenza-driven, stuff-centered economy. Millions of viewers have seen the video online, and it has so far been translated into more than two dozen languages. In commercial parlance, it's been a megahit, even though you can watch it for free—do it, by the way!

The success of *The Story of Stuff* has spawned an entire project directed by Leonard, and since she made the video in 2007, she's produced many others that can also be found on the project's website, including penetrating looks at the real costs of bottled water, cosmetics, and electronic gadgets. One of the videos on the site, *The Story of Broke*, examines the causes and consequences of our debt crisis.

Of course, not everyone has agreed with Leonard's anticonsumerist message and its proven ability to reach kids. Glenn Beck labeled the video an "anticapitalist tale that unfortunately has virtually no facts correct." Leonard's facts are actually well documented. Still, in a 4–3 vote, one Montana school board banned the screening of the film in a biology classroom. Parents in the district rose up against this decision, got the policy changed, and gave an award to the teacher who screened the film. Sometimes justice prevails.[2]

Those who help vaccinate our kids to build affluenza immunity are going to be targeted by purveyors of the disease, and for them, Annie Leonard is a courageous role model. With humility and grace, she fights back, a superstar for simplicity. In her quiet way, Carol Holst is taking the same message to adults.

Though far too humble to agree with our characterization of her, Holst might be simplicity's saint, a woman who has sacrificed much to challenge the consumer culture. In the late nineties she started an organization called Seeds of Simplicity to promote voluntary simplicity study circles in the Los Angeles area, where she lives. The organization quickly achieved national stature, attracting support from popular television stars Ed Begley Jr., best known for his starring role in the drama *St. Elsewhere*, and former Baywatch star Alexandra Paul as well as the prominent neuroscientist Peter Whybrow, author of *American Mania*.

Holst has since begun another organization, Postconsumers (www.postconsumers.com), to promote "the satisfaction of enough," a message that simpler living can be happier living. To keep the organization going, Holst works two regular jobs, scrimps on her own provisions, and hires a team of consultants to update the Postconsumers website. In this work, she is supported by donations of clever cartoons by Mike Swofford, who has been a Hollywood film animator and whose work, with that of David Horsey, adorns this book—courtesy of Swofford and Holst. Their site includes interactive games and dozens of helpful tips and articles that help build affluenza immunity. The big message is that people have been looking in the wrong places for happiness.

EXPERIENCES INSTEAD OF STUFF

Research psychologists like Leaf Van Boven of the University of Colorado and Ryan Howell of San Francisco State University have come to similar conclusions. In their view, stuff simply doesn't offer as much bang for the buck as experiences do in promoting lasting well-being. Their research suggests that taking a vacation—and it need not be expensive—leads to more lasting pleasure than buying a product. Other resource-minimal experiences—theater or live music, for example, can also be far more satisfying than resource-intensive consumer purchases. Howell has developed a website called Beyond the Purchase (www.beyondthepurchase.org), which was recently featured in *Time* magazine,[3] to "explore happiness and the quality of life, and the outcomes of different purchasing and money-management choices, as well as the motivations behind them."

"With these insights, we can better understand the ways in which our financial decisions affect well-being," says Howell, a new father who has concerns about the sustainability and quality of the world his daughter will inherit. "Also, our goal was to create a site that would be useful and interesting to users, particularly consumers who are interested in how their purchasing styles impact their well-being." One great thing about the Beyond the Purchase site is the number of fascinating questionnaires that can be found there, helping people explore their own purchasing behavior and think more clearly about making effective and sustainable choices.

One doesn't build immunity by beating oneself over the head, and the likelihood is that few of us will ever get our affluenza down to the low-impact levels of a Colin Beavan. On the other hand, we can move in that direction and at the same time do positive things that can neutralize the negative impact of some of our lifestyle. By helping make larger changes happen, you can even have a "net positive" impact on the planet. The idea is to create an ecological "handprint" (putting the stamp of your hand on positive change) that exceeds your ecological footprint. Handprinting (www.handprinter.org) is the brainchild of Greg Norris, a soft-spoken life-cycleassessment researcher at the Harvard School of Public Health. "The big question we all have to ask," says Norris, "is, Would the planet be better off without me? Handprinting is about trying to be sure the earth would be better off with us than without us."[4]

According to the website:

> Handprinter lets you calculate your environmental footprint based on your country, income, and air travel habits. Second, it offers suggestions for simple actions you can take to lower your impact on the planet, and gives you the ability to suggest new actions for our collection. Finally, Handprinter lets you spread your ideas and actions around the world, and measure their progress. When you refer your friends to Handprinter, and when their friends sign on, their handprints will become part of yours. Inspire enough people, and your handprint eventually outweighs your footprint.

You can calculate your changing handprint using a test on Norris's website. When you see progress as your handprint grows relative to your footprint, you are encouraged to keep doing more of the right thing, just as getting more in shape encouraged you to exercise even more and eat even better.

The kind of immunity building this chapter promotes comes from learning to make better personal choices. That's necessary to overcome affluenza, but not, by itself, sufficient. We also need to change the rules. You can help prevent malaria by using bed nets and taking pills, but sometimes you also need to drain the swamp.

CHAPTER 23

Policy prescriptions

Despite thirty-five years of collective bad-mouthing that has left the American public deeply cynical about whether government can ever do anything right, we believe it can play an important role in helping create a society that is affluenza unfriendly, or, to put it in more positive terms, simplicity friendly. We line up squarely on the side of those who say our social ills won't be cured by personal action alone. Just as the symptoms of affluenza are many and interconnected, so must be public efforts to quarantine it. There is no silver bullet that by itself will do the trick. It will take a comprehensive strategy, at all levels of government from local to federal, around several key areas of action:

- A reduction in annual working hours
- A restructuring of the tax and earnings systems
- Corporate reform that includes responsibility for entire product cycles
- Investment in a sustainable infrastructure
- Redirection of government subsidies
- A new concept of child protection
- Campaign finance reform
- And, finally, new ideas about economic growth

BACK TO THE ROAD NOT TAKEN

First of all, if we want to put a lid on the further spread of affluenza, we should restore a social project that topped organized labor's agenda for half a century, then suddenly fell from grace.

In chapter 13 we argued that since World War II, Americans have been offered what economist Juliet Schor calls "a remarkable choice." As our productivity more than doubled, we *could* have chosen to work half as much—or even less—and still produce the same material lifestyle we found "affluent" in the '50s. We could have split the difference, letting our material aspirations rise somewhat but also taking an important portion of our productivity gains in the form of more free time. Instead, we put all our apples into making and consuming more.

Established as law in 1938, the forty-hour workweek is still our standard (though most full-time American workers average closer to 45 hours a week). By law, we could set a different standard, and we should. It need not be a one-size-fits-all standard, like a thirty-hour week of six-hour days as proposed in the 1930s (and more recently in a 1993 congressional bill written by Democratic representative Lucien Blackwell of Pennsylvania) or a thirty-two-hour week composed of four eight-hour days, though for many working Americans either of those choices would be ideal.

More important, perhaps, is to get annual working hours—now averaging about 1,800 per year and exceeding those even of the workaholic Japanese—under control. Were the average workday to be six hours, we'd be putting in less than 1,500 hours a year, the norm in several western Europe nations. That's an additional 300 hours—seven and half weeks!—of free time. So here's a suggestion: Set a standard working year of 1,500 hours for full time, keeping the forty-hour a week maximum. Then allow workers to find flexible ways to fill the 1,500 hours.

FLEXIBLE WORK REDUCTION

Polls have shown that half of all American workers would accept a commensurate cut in pay in return for shorter working hours.[1] But the cut needn't be based on a one-to-one ratio. Workers are more productive per hour when they work fewer hours. Absenteeism is reduced and health improves. Therefore, as W.K. Kellogg recognized in the 1930s, their thirty-hour weeks should be worth at least thirty-five hours' pay and perhaps more. In fact, in the 1990s, Ron Healey, a business consultant in Indianapolis, persuaded several local industries to adopt what he calls the "30-40 now" plan. They offer prospective employees a normal forty-hour salary for a thirty-hour week. Increased employee productivity made the experiment successful for most.

THE "TAKE BACK YOUR TIME" CAMPAIGN

But to combat affluenza, we ought not fear trading income for free time. Beyond the reduction to 1,500 hours per year, legislation could ensure the right of workers to choose further reductions in working hours—instead of increased pay—when productivity rises, or further reductions in working hours at reduced pay, when productivity is stagnant.

In the short run, we need immediate legislation to provide time protections for American workers that resemble those that virtually every other industrial nation takes for granted:

- Paid childbirth leave for all parents. Today, only 40 percent of Americans are able to take advantage of the twelve weeks of unpaid leave provided by the Family and Medical Leave Act of 1993.
- At least one week of paid sick leave for all workers. Many Americans work while sick, lowering productivity and endangering other workers.
- At least three weeks of paid annual vacation for all workers. Studies show that 26 percent

of American workers receive no paid vacation at all.
- A limit on the amount of compulsory overtime work that an employer can impose, with the goal being to give employees the right to accept or refuse overtime work.
- Hourly wage parity and protection of promotions and prorated benefits for parttime workers.[2]

FALLING BEHIND THE REST OF THE WORLD

Back in July 2004, during an appearance on PBS's *NOW* with David Brancaccio, the Republican pollster and strategist Frank Luntz observed that a majority of "swing" voters were working women with young children. Luntz said his focus groups revealed that "lack of free time" is the number one issue with these voters. "The issue of time matters to them more than anything else in life," Luntz declared.

Yet President George W. Bush only paid lip-service to the issue, commenting about it in his speeches but offering no real solutions. And John Kerry, the Democratic candidate, failed to address it at all. The same was true of Barack Obama and his opponents. "Shut up and work overtime" seems to be the message from American politicians of both major parties.

American public policies protecting our family and personal time fall far short of those in other countries. A study released by the Harvard School of Public Health, covering 168 of the world's nations, concluded that "the United States lags dramatically behind all high-income countries, as well as many middle- and low-income countries when it comes to public policies designed to guarantee adequate working conditions for families."[3] The study found that:

- 163 of 168 countries guarantee paid leave for mothers in connection with childbirth. 45 countries offer such leave to fathers. The United States does neither.
- 139 countries guarantee paid sick leave. The US does not.
- 96 countries guarantee paid annual (vacation) leave. The US does not.
- 84 countries have laws that fix a maximum limit on the workweek. The US does not.
- 37 countries guarantee parents paid time off when children are sick. The US does not.

WORK SHARING AND WORK REDUCTION

Plans for spreading work around by shortening hours should begin now for another reason: When the next recession does come, will we simply say "tough luck" to those whose jobs are lost? There is a better way. Say a company needs to reduce production by 20 percent and believes it must lay off one-fifth of its workforce. What if, instead, it cut everybody's workweek by one day? We predict that most people would soon *love* the time off. We have some empirical evidence for this.

Public employees in Amador County, California, were outraged when their hours and pay were cut at the height of the Great Recession, but two years later, 71 percent of them voted to keep their shorter schedules despite the pay cut. With its timbered ridges and deep canyons extending to the snowy wilderness of the Sierra Nevada, Amador County, population 38,000, lies in the heart of California's "gold rush" country. It's decidedly conservative; no Democratic presidential candidate has carried the county since Jimmy Carter in 1976. John McCain won nearly 60 percent of the Amador vote in 2008.

Like the rest of California, Amador was hurting in 2009. The state, seeking to eliminate its $35 billion budget deficit, cut back on social service support for its counties, and Amador had to find a way to cope with less. Conservative county supervisors limited all but essential employees to a four-day week. Workers were to report Monday through Thursday for nine hours each day. County offices would be closed on Fridays. Salaries would be cut by 10 percent, commensurate with a 10 percent reduction in work hours.

When word of the change came down, the workers, and SEIU 1021, the union that represents them, were livid. Like other public employees, they had already made key concessions in recent years and, justifiably, felt their family budgets were severely strained. "The cut meant a lot of money for a lot of people," said one Amador County program manager, who asked to remain anonymous (the issue still generates animosity among some workers). "Then there were the questions like, 'How can we get the work done in four days?'"

But despite the workers' protests, the county argued that otherwise it would have to lay off workers, and county supervisors were adamant that they didn't want layoffs. Angry, but understanding the need to preserve jobs, union leaders agreed to the arrangement—but for only two years. So in 2011, county workers were given a choice of sticking with four-day shifts or returning to a five-day week with a pay increase and losing some of their colleagues to layoffs. Without directly consulting its members again, the union chose the five-day week. In June, the remaining employees started working Fridays again. Amador County cut 17 workers to balance its budget.

The remaining workers were glad to be getting higher pay again, but many soon had second thoughts. Quite a few were unhappy because they had been enjoying their four-day weeks. Some went fishing or camping over the long weekends; outdoor activities are popular in this rural county. "I was at first very concerned about losing the 10 percent," one worker told John, "but I found that I could make it work without a huge hardship. And I found that what I gained in time actually outweighed what I lost in money." Then too, many of the workers sympathized deeply with their union brothers and sisters who'd lost their jobs. They pressured SEIU for a vote that might restore the four-day week.

In August, the union polled its members. Of the 178 workers (nearly the entire work force) who voted, 71 percent (126) chose to return to the shorter week, *even with less pay.* Only 29 percent (52) wanted to keep the longer workweek. A month later, county employees returned to a four-day, 36-hour schedule. Sixteen of the seventeen laid-off workers were rehired. It's not perfect, one worker told John. The work must now be accomplished in less time. "A lot of folks still come in for a bit on Fridays," she reports. But she still believes that, on balance, most people feel the trade-off is worth it.[4]

With both parents in a majority of families working full time these days, weekends in America have become "workends" for most couples. For many Amador parents, the four-day week changed that. "The Fridays off gave me a chance to run errands and get chores done while my kids were at school, and that lets my weekend be a weekend," one observed. "Before, it felt like I had only one day off a week that was really for pleasure. Now I've got the whole weekend. It helps. It's nice to have this balance in terms of your family life and your sanity."

The Amador County story deserves closer attention from researchers. It's highly conceivable that the extra day off has relieved stress and improved family life for many workers. It may also be reflected in better health outcomes. We need studies to understand whether or not this is the case, since it might also be possible that nine-hour days and faster work schedules have negated any of these possible gains. It seems a valuable university research project. But in any case, we do know that the reduced schedule has been popular with many workers.

GOING DUTCH

It's unfortunate that the Amador case study involved a *compulsory* reduction of hours. But many agencies, nonprofits, and businesses might want to offer more opportunities for shorter hours with reduced pay (but job security and benefits), as in Europe. In the Netherlands, under the Hours Adjustment Act of 2000, workers are allowed to downsize their hours, while keeping the same hourly pay, full health care, and prorated benefits. Unless employers can prove a serious financial hardship for their firms, they must grant the request for shorter hours. More than 95 percent of requests are approved. Consequently, the Dutch now have the highest percentage of part-time workers and shortest working hours in the world. They also have among the highest levels of labor force participation, low unemployment, and among the highest levels of confidence among workers that they can find another job if they lose theirs.[5]

In the United States, a similar policy could allow those who want to work less to cut back, opening space for others who simply want to work. As early adapters experiment with these new schedules and find them to their liking, word will spread and other workers will follow. The Gallup daily happiness poll shows that Americans are 20 percent happier on weekends than on workdays. Finding ways to offer longer weekends for American workers, who work some of the longest hours in the industrial world, ought to be part of the progressive agenda. Happiness science shows that people don't always know what will make them happy; consequently, they tend to choose money over time. But an experience of more time and the life satisfaction that flows from it can change that attitude. It's a lesson that has been confirmed for many in Amador County. Amador is only a microcosm and a very small step up a big mountain of overwork and consumerist values. But mountains are conquered by single steps.

REMOVING THE BIG OBSTACLE TO WORK SHARING

Of course, one additional public policy change would help make work sharing possible. It is *single-payer health care,* which would relieve the cost of health care provision for American employers. Because health care is so expensive, businesses find it more cost-effective to hire fewer workers and work them longer rather than pay benefits for more employees. The cost of employer-financed health care is the single most important factor in reducing the international competitiveness of American firms.

With a single-payer system, Canada manages to cover all its citizens at a total cost per person that is far less than what we spend in the United States. Despite criticisms of the Canadian system by US politicians, Canadians are healthier and live longer than their neighbors. And Canadians are so fond of their health care system that a nationwide poll to determine "the greatest Canadian of all time," done by the Canadian Broadcasting Company, ended up bestowing the honor on Tommy Douglas. Douglas, the late Socialist premier of Saskatchewan, was chosen, according to those who voted for him, because he was the father of the Canadian health care system (he was also the grandfather of American actor Kiefer Sutherland, though that probably didn't affect the polling much).[6]

In any case, many Americans now work much longer than is healthy just to keep their health benefits, a problem that a public single-payer system would solve.

RETIRING STEP BY STEP

There are other ways of exchanging money for time. Many academics receive sabbaticals, anything from a quarter to a year off every several years, usually accepting a reduced salary during the period. Why not a system of sabbaticals every seven to ten years for all workers who are willing to take moderate salary reductions when they are on sabbatical? We all need to recharge our batteries every so often.

Or how about a system of graduated retirement? For many of us, self-esteem takes a hit and boredom a bounce when we suddenly go from forty-hour weeks to zero upon retiring. Instead, we could design a pension and social security system that would allow us to retire gradually. Let's say that at fifty years of age we cut 300 hours from our work year—nearly eight weeks. Then at fifty-five we cut 300 more. At sixty, 300 more. And at sixty-five, 300 more. Now, we're down to 800 (given no change in the present annual pattern). We might then have the option to stop paid labor entirely, or to keep working 800 hours a year for as long as we are capable.

What this would do is allow us to begin learning to appreciate leisure, volunteer more, and broaden our minds long before final retirement. It would allow more young workers to find positions and allow older workers to stay on longer to mentor them. It would allow older workers to both stay involved with their careers and also find time for more balance in their lives.

A variation on this idea is to allow workers to take some of their "early retirement" at different stages of their careers, perhaps when they need more parenting time, for example. The ultimate idea, promoted in some European countries, is that a certain number of hours would constitute a total *paid work life,* with considerable flexibility around when the hours are worked.

TAXES

A change in the tax system, similar to one already under way in parts of Europe, could also help contain affluenza. The first step toward a change could come through an idea called the progressive consumption tax. Proposed by the economist Robert Frank in his book *Luxury Fever*, the tax would replace the personal income tax. Instead, people would be taxed on what they consume, at a rate rising from 20 percent (on annual spending under $40,000) to 70 percent (on annual spending over $500,000). Basically the idea is to tax those with the most serious cases of "luxury fever" (which seems to be Frank's synonym for affluenza) at the highest rates, thus encouraging saving instead of spending.[7]

At the same time, we must make it possible for lower-income Americans to meet their basic needs without working several jobs. The old Catholic idea of a family, or living (we prefer the term *livable*), wage, championed by Pope Leo XIII in his 1891 Encyclical *Rerum Novarum*, could be accomplished by a negative income tax or tax credits that guarantee all citizens a simple but sufficient standard of living above the poverty line.

But the solution also includes a dramatic increase in a minimum wage that has languished in America and now buys less than it did in 1968. President Obama has talked of raising the minimum wage to $9 an hour. This would only be about half that in very successful Nordic economies and Australia, where minimum wages average $17 an hour. Given somewhat higher prices in these countries, that comes out to less—about $14 or $15—in actual buying power, but it allows minimum-wage workers to support themselves adequately without being mired in poverty. When John asked a McDonald's cashier in Melbourne, Australia, if she actually made the minimum wage of $17 an hour, she replied that she had started at that but was now up to about $18.50.

Granted, to avoid huge economic dislocations, this much higher minimum wage would need to be phased in, but not at the current glacial rate of change. Arguments by conservatives that raising the minimum wage decreases the number of jobs have been consistently shown to be false; indeed, as the multimillionaire Nick Hanauer points out, raises at the bottom of the economy keep it strong, not greater tax cuts for people like himself. Fighting affluenza is not just about the consuming less; it's also about fairness. Some Americans have called for a "maximum wage," an idea first broached by Saint Augustine many hundreds of years ago. We may or may not need that; strong consumption and luxury taxes could substitute. The point is to do all we can to make our economy fairer. Often, it is the poorest victims of affluenza who are accused of being spendthrifts and living beyond their means while the real luxury spenders get a pass.

Equally promising are so-called green taxes. Their proponents would replace a portion of taxes on "goods" such as income—and payroll taxes, which discourage increased employment—with taxes on "bads" such as pollution or waste of nonrenewable resources. The point would be to make the market reflect the true costs of our purchases. We'd pay much more to drive a gas guzzler, for example, and a little more for this book (to cover the true costs of paper), but no more for a music lesson or theater ticket.

Additional *carbon taxes* would discourage the burning of fossil fuels. *Pollution taxes* would discourage the contamination of water and air. The costs of cleaning up pollution would be added as a tax on goods whose production causes it. Such a tax could make organic foods as cheap as pesticide-laced produce. *Depletion taxes* would increase the price of nonrenewable resources and lower the comparative price of goods made to last.

While such a green tax system would be complicated, it could go a long way toward discouraging environmentally or socially harmful consumption, while encouraging benign alternatives. As things currently stand, we more often subsidize what we should be taxing—extractive industries like mining (as much as $3 billion in subsidies a year), and air and auto travel, for example.[8] We could, and should, turn that around, subsidizing clean technologies and activities like wind and solar power or organic family farms instead of oil and agribusiness.

CORPORATE RESPONSIBILITY

Another way to reduce the impact of consumption is to require corporations to take full responsibility for the entire life cycle of their products, an idea now gaining widespread acceptance in Europe. The concept is simple, and well-explained in the book *Natural Capitalism*, by Paul Hawken and Amory and Hunter Lovins.[9] In effect, companies would no longer sell us products but lease them. Then, when the products reach the end of their useful lives, the same companies would take them back to reuse and recycle them, saving precious resources.

STOPPING CHILD ABUSE

The consumer advocate Ralph Nader has called the recent upsurge in marketing that targets children a form of "corporate child abuse." It's as if marketers have set out knowingly to infect our children with affluenza by spreading the virus everywhere kids congregate. It's time to protect our kids. At a minimum, we can keep commercialism out of our schools. Second, we can begin to restrict television advertising to children. Already, places like Sweden and the province of Quebec don't allow it. If you're a parent, you probably long for relief from TV advertising's manipulation of your kids. Moreover, a stiff tax on all advertising would send a strong message to corporate America that curbing the spread of affluenza is serious business.

CAMPAIGN FINANCE REFORM

There are, of course, dozens of other good anti-affluenza legislative ideas out there and no space to mention them here, but none will come to fruition as long as those who profit most from affluenza pull the strings in our political system. The sheer cost of elections—a single New Jersey Senate race in 2000 resulted in $100 million in spending—leaves candidates beholden to those who pay, and those who pay are those who have money and want to keep it.

So anti-affluenza legislation has to include campaign finance reform (including an amendment overturning the disastrous *Citizens United* Supreme Court decision that allowed much greater corporate contributions to campaigns), taking the PACs out of politics, and offering competing candidates equal media time to present their ideas but no time for clever yet meaningless thirty-second commercials. Former Texas agriculture commissioner Jim Hightower has it right. "The water won't clear up," he says, "until you get the hogs out of the creek."[10]

BUT WON'T OUR ECONOMY COLLAPSE?

What if Americans started buying smaller, more fuel-efficient cars, driving them less and keeping them longer? What if we took fewer long-distance vacations? What if we simplified our lives, spent less money, bought less stuff, worked less, and enjoyed more leisure time? What if government began to reward thrift and punish waste, legislated shorter work hours, and taxed advertisers? What if we made consumers and corporations pay the real costs of their products? What would happen to our economy? Would it collapse, as some economists suggest?

Truthfully, we don't know exactly, since no major industrial nation has yet embarked on such a journey. But there's plenty of reason to suspect that the road will be passable if bumpy at first, and smoother later. If we continue on the current freeway, however, we'll find out it ends like Oakland's Interstate 880 during the 1989 earthquake—impassable and in ruins.

Surely we can't deny that if every American took up voluntary simplicity tomorrow, massive economic disruption would result. But that won't happen. A shift away from affluenza, if we're lucky enough to witness one, will come gradually, over a generation perhaps. Economic growth, as measured by the gross domestic product, will slow down and might even become negative. But as the economist Juliet Schor points out, there are many European countries (including Holland, Denmark, Sweden, and Norway) whose economies have grown far more slowly than ours, yet whose quality of life—measured by many of the indicators we say we want, including free time, citizen participation, lower crime, greater job security, income equality, and health—is higher than our own.[11] Gallup also finds that they are the world's happiest countries.

You might think of them as the world's first "postconsumer" societies. Their emphasis on balancing growth with sustainability is widely accepted across the political spectrum. As former Dutch prime minister Ruud Lubbers, a conservative, put it:

> It is true that the Dutch are not aiming to maximize gross national product per capita. Rather, we are seeking to attain a high quality of life, a just, participatory and sustainable society. While the Dutch economy is very efficient per working hour, the numbers of working hours per citizen are rather limited. We like it that way. Needless to say, there is more room for all those important aspects of our lives that are not part of our jobs, for which we are not paid and for which there is never enough time.[12]

These postconsumer economies show no sign of collapse—instead, the recent European economic crisis has been hardest on the very countries (Spain, Ireland, Greece, Iceland) that followed the US model of tax cutting, financial deregulation, longer working hours, housing speculation, and privatization to increase growth.

TIME FOR AN ATTITUDE ADJUSTMENT

If anti-affluenza legislation leads to slower rates of economic growth or a "steady state" economy that does not grow at all, so be it (as we argue in the next chapter, growth of GDP is a poor measure of social health anyway). Beating the affluenza bug will also lead to less stress, more leisure time, better health, and longer lives. It will offer more time for family, friends, and community. And it will lead to less traffic, less road rage, less noise, less pollution, and a kinder, gentler, more meaningful way of life.

In a '60s TV commercial, an actor claims that Kool cigarettes are "as cool and clean as a breath of fresh air." We watch that commercial today and can't keep a straight face, but when it first aired, nobody laughed. Since that time, we've come to understand that cigarettes are silent killers. We've banned TV ads for them. We tax them severely, limit smoking areas, and seek to make tobacco companies pay the full costs of the damage cigarettes cause. We once thought them sexy, but today most of us think they're gross.

Where smoking is concerned, our attitudes have certainly changed. Now, with growing evidence that affluenza is also hazardous, it's surely time for another attitude adjustment.

CHAPTER 24

Vital signs

> *The gross national product includes air pollution and advertising for cigarettes, and ambulances to clear our highways of carnage. It counts special locks for our doors, and jails for the people who break them.... It does not allow for the health of our families, the quality of their education, or the joy of their play.*
> —ROBERT KENNEDY, 1968

A patient in remission from cancer requires routine checkups to evaluate how things are going. It's the same with affluenza. Once we're on the road to recovery, annual checkups help prevent costly, energy-sapping relapses. Lingering germs like debt, susceptibility to advertising, and possession obsession can cause recurrences not only in individuals but in communities and national economies as well. Checkups help track these germs down where they hide, and wipe 'em out!

ENOUGH?

Too often, life's complexities get boiled down to a single nagging question: "Do we have enough money?" Vicki Robin, the coauthor of *Your Money or Your Life*, believes this question is far too narrow. Pointing out that money is really what we trade our life energy for, she asks,

> Do we receive fulfillment, satisfaction, and value in proportion to life energy spent?
>
> Is this expenditure of life energy in alignment with our values and life purpose?

You wouldn't expect weight alone to measure whether a person is sick or well. Nor would blood pressure, by itself, tell you if a person is healthy. Similarly, a grand total of expenditures (like GDP) blindly measures quantity but not quality. It can't distinguish thriving from surviving.

MAKING PERSONAL HISTORY

A very simple measurement of well-being, or gladness to be alive, is whether you're eager to get out of bed in the morning. But the cold, hard truth is, you may jump energetically out of bed one morning only to be laid off by midafternoon. Or worse, you could suddenly find out you have an illness even more critical than affluenza and only have a year to live. Are you really doing what's most important, such as making connections with people, ideas, and nature? What have you always wanted to do that you haven't done yet, because you've been too busy making and spending money? How can you do more of what you're most proud of accomplishing?

These are the kinds of questions that enable us to take stock, and take control, of our lives. Honest answers strip away illusions and worn-out patterns. They help get to the heart of what really matters. As Irvin Yalom observed, "Not to take possession of your life plan is to let your existence be an accident."[1]

A good first step in repossessing your life is to identify what you value most. Record the most significant events of your life in a notebook, including personal relationships, births and deaths, achievements, adventures, enlightenments, and disappointments. Recall the first house of your adult life, the first time you fell in love. Note the relative importance of material possessions. Have they satisfied as fully as the connections, emotions, and actions of your life?

Now, jot down a list of principles that are most important to you—things like fairness, trust, unconditional love, compassion, taking care of nature, financial security, fearlessness, maintenance of health. These are the principles to base your life decisions on, because they are your highest values. Apply these principles in your relationships, your career, and your plans for the future, and ask yourself whether the constant pursuit of wealth and stuff isn't more effort than it's worth.

When you perform your annual checkup, get out your notebook and review the memoir in progress. Do any events of the past year deserve inclusion in life's "greatest hits"? With another year behind you, are there events that now seem less important? Which people from the past year of your life do you most admire? Have you followed your personal code of ethics, with maybe a few forgivable exceptions?

WHAT REALLY MATTERS

Now comes the knockout punch—good night, affluenza! By cross-referencing your personal history and values with your annual expenditures, you can determine if you're living life on your terms. Every year when you file your taxes, also file your self-audit—but don't give yourself a deadline. (After all, the idea here is to give yourself a *life* line.) Are your consumption expenditures consistent with what really matters? Have you spent too much on housing, entertainment, or electronic gadgets? Did your expenditures cause you to work overtime, in turn reducing family time? Are you happy with the charitable contributions you made? Are you getting real value back from the money you spent?

COMMUNITY AND NATIONAL CHECKUPS

Newscasters, investment brokers, and lenders are among those who rely on the gross domestic product as an indicator of national prosperity.

But does GDP really tell us if our economy's vital signs are healthy? Back in 1999, one group of economists explained why they didn't think so.

> Imagine receiving an annual holiday letter from distant friends, reporting their best year, because more money was spent than ever before. It began during the rainy season when the roof sprang leaks and their yard in the East Bay hills started to slide. The many layers of roofing had to be stripped to the rafters before the roof could be reconstructed, and engineers were required to keep the yard from eroding away. Shortly after, Jane broke her leg in a car accident. A hospital stay, surgery, physical therapy, replacing the car, and hiring help at home took a bite out of their savings. Then they were robbed, and replaced a computer, two TVs, a VCR, and a video camera. They also bought a home security system, to keep these new purchases safe.[2]

These people spent more money than ever and contributed slightly to a rise in GDP, but were they happier? Not likely, in that year from hell. And what about a nation in which GDP continues to grow? Are its citizens happier? Clearly, that depends on *how the money is being spent.*

Politicians point to a swelling GDP as proof that their economic policies are working, and investors reassure themselves that with the overall expansion of the economy, their stocks will also expand. Yet even the chief architect of the GDP (then GNP), Simon Kuznets, believed that "the welfare of a nation can scarcely be inferred from a measurement like GNP."[3]

Here's why: Although the overall numbers continue to rise, many key variables have grown worse. As we have already mentioned, the gap between the rich and everyone else is expanding. In addition, the nation is borrowing more and more from abroad, a symptom of anemic savings and mountains of household debt. The economic and environmental costs of our addiction to fossil fuels continue to mount.

When a city cuts down shade trees to widen a street and homeowners have to buy air conditioning, the GDP goes up. It also goes up when families pay for daycare and divorce, when new prisons are built, and when doctors prescribe antidepressants. In fact, careful analysis reveals much of the economy as tracked by GDP is based on crime, waste, and environmental destruction!

In contrast to GDP—which lumps all monetary transactions together—a measurement of success called the Genuine Progress Indicator (GPI), first proposed in 1995, *evaluates* the expenses, adding in "invisible" assets such as housework, parenting, and volunteer work, but subtracting "bads," including the following from the national economy:[4]

- cost of crime
- cost of family breakdowns
- loss of leisure time
- cost of underemployment
- cost of commuting
- cost of household pollution abatement
- cost of automobile accidents
- cost of water pollution
- cost of air pollution
- cost of noise pollution
- depletion of nonrenewable resources
- cost of long-term environmental damage
- cost of ozone depletion
- loss of old-growth forests

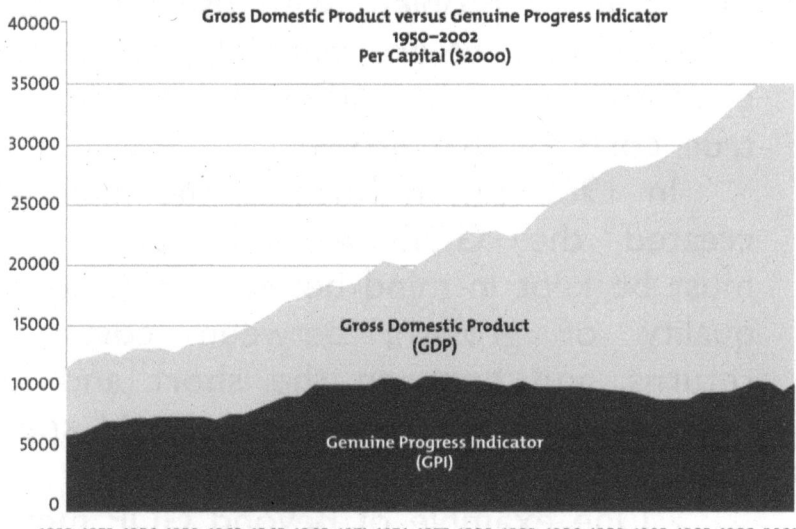

Source: Redefining Progress, Why Bigger Isn't Better: The Genuine Progress Indicator—2002 Update (San Francisco: Redefining Progress)

Using this metric as our measure of national progress, we find that although GDP has increased dramatically since the mid-1970s, GPI has remained flat or even fallen. GPI started out as an idea in a think tank, but it is gaining steam among policy makers. The states of Maryland and Vermont now officially measure their GPI, while Oregon and Utah have plans in the works, and leaders from some twenty states met recently at a conference called "Beyond GDP" to talk about how each could apply the idea.[5] Oregon's dynamic first lady, Cylvia Hayes, founder of a clean economy consulting group called 3EStrategies, set the tone:

> We tend to manage what we measure. The primary problem with using the GDP metric is that we are managing for constant economic growth, without measuring the true costs of that growth.
>
> In 1962 Simon Kuznets, the man who created the GDP, warned, "Distinctions must be kept in mind between quantity and quality of growth, between costs and returns, and between the short and long run. Goals for more growth should specify more growth of what and for what."
>
> ...One example of Beyond GDP metrics is the Genuine Progress Indicator. The goal of the Genuine Progress Indicator is to measure the actual societal well-being and health generated by economic activity. The Genuine Progress Indicator uses 26 metrics

and consolidates critical economic, environmental and social factors into a single framework in order to give a more accurate picture of the progress—and the setbacks—resulting from our economic activities.[6]

Maryland governor Martin O'Malley argued that it is not growth, but the kind of growth, that matters:

> In many ways, we Marylanders, think of ourselves as pro-growth Americans—but before you get "wiggy" about that term, let me explain: Like you, we believe in growing jobs and growing opportunity. Like you, we believe in children growing healthy, growing educated, and growing strong. We believe in grandparents growing old with dignity and with love. We believe in growing trees, growing sustainable Bay fisheries, growing food locally to feed our citizens. But not all growth is good.[7]

GPI is a step in the right direction, though as Ronald Colman, who first developed a GPI metrics for Atlantic Canada, has observed, most GPI models currently in use still start with consumption of goods and services as an unquestioned positive, then add and subtract assets and costs from that. In his view, a better GPI model would begin with security, fairness, and access to work. We agree.

Additional measures are needed to track our use of natural resources—what we have versus what we use. Measures like the ecological footprint (www.myfootprint.org) help us to see how our consumptive lifestyles are annually eating up resources faster than nature can regenerate them. A close look at our "footprint," the amount of productive land and water needed to produce our lifestyles, shows that we would need five planets if everyone on earth were to suddenly consume as Americans do. Like the spendthrift who goes on a shopping spree with a savings account, we won't have the steady supply of interest coming to us from nature in future years if we keep this up.

A number of years ago, the Swiss economist Mathis Wackernagel, cocreator of the footprint idea, told David, "The ecological footprint is gaining a foothold in the market analysis. Some banks have hired us to analyze the security of government bonds. They want to know, Do countries have ecological deficits? Are they overspending their natural wealth?"

The Genuine Progress Indicator and the ecological footprint are really common sense with an analytical, pragmatic edge. National vitality, like personal health and community health, is about real things like the health of people, places, natural capital, and future generations. At all levels of our society, it's time to schedule a holistic annual checkup. And the good news is that, led by a tiny and poor country in the Himalayas, the world is starting to take notice.

GROSS NATIONAL HAPPINESS

Coming Home is a sweet little children's book about a girl named Tashi Choden, who lives in the far-off city of Thimphu, the capital of Bhutan, a nation of seven hundred thousand tucked between two giant world powers, China and India. It's a country that could hardly be more unlike the United States, except ... Except that this story of the high school life of a fictional 15-year-old would not feel out of place to American teenagers. If the characters' names were not Tashi, Pema, Ugyen, Leki, Lhazom, and Tobden, you might think the story was set in suburban California. The lives of these young people revolve around popularity cliques, parties, sports, and the name-brand apparel they wear. They banter in American slang and proudly display their possessions:

Get SATISFIED

I was wearing my white Reeboks.... Tenzin was wearing an oversized Nike T-shirt.... Pema looked cute with red Superstars.... and Ugyen was in faded jeans with Converse high-tops.[8]

In Bhutan yet!

Here, even in one of the world's poorest countries, with a per capita income of $3,000, affluenza has clearly taken deep root. In the story, the teens discover the superficiality of their choices and the value of their friendships and their own traditions. But in reality, the fight against affluenza is not an easy one even in a place like this, whose Buddhist cultural traditions value moderation and simplicity.

But Bhutan is not accepting affluenza lying down.

Several decades ago, its King, Jigme Singye Wangchuck, challenged Western consumer culture by famously declaring that "Gross National Happiness is more important than Gross National Product." Since then, under the leadership of Dasho Karma Ura, a brilliant Bhutanese educator and artist, the former kingdom (now with a parliamentary government) has looked to international scholars in many fields to help create the Gross National Happiness Index (www.grossnationalhappiness.com), its national measure of progress. The index uses survey data to see how well Bhutanese are doing in a range of "domains" deemed essential to human well-being and happiness by experts in the field. While these domains include income, or "living standards," they also include eight other aspects of quality of life: health, psychological well-being, environment, cultural vitality, community vitality, government, time balance, and education.

In the past few years, Bhutan has been taking its ideas to the rest of the world, promoting the concept of "Equitable and Sustainable Well-Being and Happiness" in the United Nations. In April 2012 its prime minister, Jigmi Thinley, spoke to a gathering of 800 people at the UN:

> The time has come for global action to build a new world economic system that is no longer based on the illusion that limitless growth is possible on our precious and finite planet or that endless material gain promotes well-being. Instead, it will be a

system that promotes harmony and respect for nature and for each other; that respects our ancient wisdom traditions and protects our most vulnerable people as our own family, and that gives us time to live and enjoy our lives and to appreciate rather than destroy our world. It will be an economic system, in short, that is fully sustainable and that is rooted in true, abiding well-being and happiness.[9]

John has been part of a team of international advisers helping Bhutan's government as it promotes its "new world economic system," or New Development Paradigm, as it is now called. While in Bhutan, he watched as Enrico Giovannini, now Italy's minister of labor and social issues, first drew the diagram below with a stick in the sand, as a model of the paradigm.

The model starts with human needs, such as those described by Abraham Maslow (see chapter 10), and by a member of Bhutan's UN advisory group, the famed Chilean economist Manfred Max-Neef. The *development paradigm* is the economic system, modified in each society by market rules, policies, and cultural expectations that employ resources, known as *forms of capital*, to meet needs. *Capital*, until recently, referred to the factories, physical infrastructure, and finances that businesses used to provide employment and consumer goods, but its meaning has been expanded as part of the new discipline of ecological economics. Forms of capital now also include natural capital (the resources of nature, to which ecological economists now assign monetary value), human capital (the health, competence, and productivity of workers), and social capital (the value of social connection and nonmarket institutions such as government and the nonprofit sector).

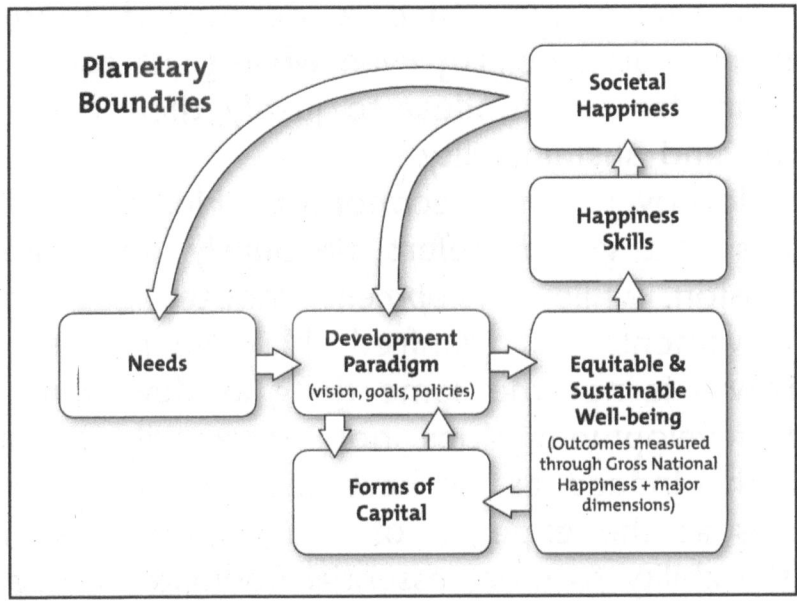

The new development paradigm promoted by Bhutan pays attention to all needs (and even extends that consideration to other species), and to the nine key domains of well-being, not just those so far counted by GDP. It is understood that such a system must be equitable, without large gaps between rich and poor, and that it must be sustainable; that is, it cannot grow beyond the planetary boundaries shown in the diagram. The new economy must fit within the earth's limits; indeed, the economy is a wholly owned subsidiary of the earth.

Despite denial from the political Right, modern analysis of well-being confirms the basic accuracy of the so-called Easterlin Paradox—income growth and GDP matter greatly for the happiness of very poor people, but their effects flatten out once a degree of modest comfort is attained.[10] Even while gains continue, they are far too modest to justify their costs in equity and sustainability.

Moreover, the economist Herman Daly argues that *growth* refers to purely quantitative expansion, while *development* denotes qualitative improvement. As Manfred Max-Neef puts it, "Growth is not the same thing as development, and development does not necessarily require growth." Indeed, as we have seen, if such growth comes at the expense of equality, sustainability, or the ability to meet essential nonmaterial needs, it may actually impede development and well-being.

In this model, the terms *happiness* and *well-being*, while often spoken of as just two ways to say the same thing, are not quite synonymous. Often, modern advocates of life satisfaction quarrel about this, with academics sometimes cringing over what they believe is the amorphousness of the word *happiness*, while ordinary people often find the term *well-being* overly wonky. But in this model, *equitable and sustainable well-being* is what can be measured through *objective* data—such things as income levels, life expectancy, literacy, pollution, voter participation, leisure hours, rates of depression, unemployment, poverty, and so on. In each domain, there are *levels of sufficiency* that are needed to be able to say that well-being has been achieved in a society and for a domain. The objective conditions of life are the goals of public policy.

But people may have sufficient conditions for a good life without being happy. Happiness in this model is the *subjective* sense of people's well-being, determined by survey questions such as: How do you *feel* about your health? your mental state? your access to nature? your finances? your time balance? your purpose in life? People are also asked to evaluate their overall life satisfaction, using several 1-to-10 scales. This happiness, more about long-term life satisfaction than hedonism, is akin to what Aristotle and the Greeks meant by the term *eudaimonia*.

The *United Nations Happiness Report* presents overall "happiness" scores for most of the world's countries. For 2012 Denmark, at 7.7, heads the list, while Togo, at 2.9 is at the bottom. The United States ranks seventeenth at 7.0, having dropped from eleventh (7.3) in 2007. Though most but not all (Costa Rica, for example, scores 7.3) of the world's happiest countries are quite wealthy, happiness levels in the richest are generally flat, while many poor nations have seen great improvement in recent years (Angola's score rose from 4.2 to 5.6), again illustrating that GDP growth is far more important for the poor than for the rich. Social insecurity has led to major drops in Greece, Spain, and Italy.[11]

The distribution of happiness within the population is equally important, if not more so. John Helliwell, a lead author of the *UN Happiness Report*, observes:

> Among those countries with high average scores, some have quite high degrees in the distribution of happiness (e.g., Denmark and The Netherlands), while in some other fairly high-ranking countries (e.g., Costa Rica and the United States) there is much dispersion, and a higher portion of the population has low life satisfaction.[12]

Between objective well-being and subjective happiness lie what the model calls *happiness skills*, and these are the tasks of *personal* change.

While conditions of life matter greatly for personal happiness, our great religions and wisdom traditions, as well as modern positive psychology and neuroscience, teach us that proper attitudes and behaviors are also essential, and in more comfortable nations, even more important—as we have seen earlier in this book, individuals with a "materialistic" outlook on life are often unhappy, even when they are rich.

The attitudes and behaviors that constitute "happiness skills" include such things as gratitude, altruism (it is, indeed, better for happiness to give than to receive), kindness, sociability, delayed gratification, empathy, compassion, cooperation, and many other virtues which education can play a part in cultivating.

The beauty of this model in our view is that it does not ignore either the importance of *policy* or of *personal behaviors* in achieving good lives for all. It does not force us to choose between happiness and well-being, but recognizes that they are different ways of measuring our success. And it excuses neither widespread inequality nor a cavalier attitude toward the ecological limits of our biosphere. But it is not a call for sacrifice; indeed, the research behind the model implies that we can have a better life with less consumption in wealthy countries while allowing economic growth where it really adds to well-being and, at the same time, protecting our planet. The sacrifice is now; "getting and spending," as Wordsworth put it, "we lay waste our powers." In the pursuit of affluenza and in the name of limitless growth, we decimate our only planet for which there is no spare.

THE HAPPINESS INITIATIVE

As we see, putting two and two together, objective indices such as GPI can help us measure well-being more effectively. Internationally, many such excellent indices are being developed; one of our favorites is the Canadian Index of Well-Being, which uses a set of domains closely aligned to that of Bhutan.[13] But for policy makers, such objective metrics are not enough. They must know not only if lives are improving objectively, but also whether people understand and appreciate the changes. If for instance, crime is falling, but people, fed a steady diet of TV crime shows, believe life is getting more dangerous, politicians may find themselves having achieved important successes but being cast out of office for their efforts. One of the solutions to this is to add a battery of subjective survey questions to measures like GPI, an idea which the state of Vermont calls "GPI Plus."

In our view, one of the best of these surveys is the joint creation of a Seattle-based nonprofit called the Happiness Initiative (HI) and psychologist Ryan Howell at San Francisco State University, who also developed the Beyond the Purchase project described in chapter 22. When you take that survey (www.happycounts.org) online—it takes about 15 minutes—you receive an immediate life-satisfaction score and scores for each of the ten domains the survey measures (it includes the nine Bhutan domains, and adds a tenth, work satisfaction, whose importance for wellbeing has been made clear by the Gallup organization). Howell and a team of his graduate students did extensive testing of hundreds of survey questions from around the world to find the ones with the highest correlations to reported subjective well-being for the HI survey.

The survey can be employed by collectivities of people ranging from cities to colleges to businesses to determine their aggregate levels of happiness. "We have been working with cities—from Seattle to Eau Claire, Wisconsin; Nevada City, California; and many others, to help them determine the happiness of their citizens, to engage those citizens in discussing the results, and to develop programs or policies that can improve well-being," says Laura Musikanski, the vibrant and articulate executive director of the Happiness Initiative. "We have also worked with more than a dozen colleges and universities to assess their student and staff happiness levels. On our website, we offer toolkits that allow all kinds of communities and organizations to use our survey effectively. Forty thousand people have already taken it."[14] (Their results are captured in easy-to-read graphs on the Happiness Initiative website.)

Measuring happiness and well-being will require us to draw from a plethora of good ideas and models out there in addition to GPI, and cull the best indicators from all of them. The ecological economists Robert Costanza and Ida Kubiszewski, both members of the International Expert Working Group advising Bhutan's government, believe the time has come to "embark on a new round of consensus-building" to develop new economic goals and better measures of success that can replace the famous Bretton Woods Agreement of 1944, which ushered in the age unlimited growth without limit, the Age of Affluenza. "You might call it Bhutan Woods," they say, suggesting that the nation that has championed the idea of a new development paradigm in the United Nations is the perfect place to hammer out the new plan. They've helped build a stunning new website and organization, the Alliance for Sustainability and Prosperity (www.asap4all.org), to promote the concept.

In due time, we believe, this widespread new interest in measuring what matters will help us take our affluenza temperature and record the most vital of our social and economic signs. You get what you measure, and we believe that if we start measuring the right things, we will use the information to make better lives.

A final caveat: Aggregate measures of subjective life satisfaction and contentment with conditions of life are important for societies, and together with objective data, can tell us how we are doing in meeting perceived human needs. But Prime Minister Thinley makes clear that what his country means by "happiness" is not merely a measurement of personal satisfaction, and certainly "not the fleeting, pleasurable 'feel good' moods so often associated with that term. We know that true abiding happiness cannot exist while others suffer and comes only from serving others."

CHAPTER 25

The glow of health

...one word to you and your children: stay together, learn the flowers, go light.
—GARY SNYDER, *Turtle Island*

For fast-acting relief, try slowing down.
—LILY TOMLIN

Everyone knows that feeling of waking up after a long illness and suddenly, miraculously, feeling full of life again! Good-bye, daytime TV. Hello, energy! How we love to dive back into our favorite activities when we don't feel isolated, powerless, or estranged anymore! That's what happens when we beat affluenza—we realize at last how stressful it was to keep up with the Joneses; to stay at a job we hated just for the money and benefits; to write endless checks to credit card companies and always be worried about the next house payment ... What a relief, when we discover there's a way out!

In the course of writing and then updating this book, we discovered that many other Americans feel the way we do. Their comments and ideas became part of our own thought processes. One early reader of the manuscript saw similarities between victims of affluenza and prisoners of war. "Except we're prisoners of an economy that destroys our environment, our communities, and our peace of mind," he said. "Imagine what it must feel like when the war is over, and we're liberated. Or when affluenza is purged from our lives. We'll feel such a sense of freedom and such a sense of lightness."

After reading about historically low savings rates in the United States, another reader whimsically imagined fifty million people retiring all at once with virtually no savings and slamming on the brakes. "There's gonna be one huge garage sale," he said, shaking his head. "I can see the Craigslist entries now: Ford Expedition, near-new, $400. Big-screen TV (59-inch), free. Hot tub, free."

A third reader commented that each of our homes seems to have an elephant in the living room that we try desperately to ignore: the unshakable feeling that something is fundamentally wrong. "We can't figure out how to chase it out, so we learn to just live with it," he said. But maybe we don't have to. Maybe we can change our way of life, together, as we have so many times before. (Look, if we can't make massive changes in our collective value system, where did all these suburbs, airports, and computers come from?) A recent poll conducted by professional homebuilders found that energy efficiency has in recent years become one of the top considerations for homebuyers. Healthy habits like exercising and yoga are becoming more popular. Basic changes are occurring in our diet, in the way we generate energy, and even the way we consume products; from Netflix to Zipcar, access via leasing is substituting for ownership. Our civic focus is shifting to the local scale, where we can have a voice in decision making. Clearly, our culture is in transition.

THIS WAY OUT

A common thread in the recovery process is admitting we have a problem. A string of events including 9/11, megastorms like Katrina and Sandy, and the Great Recession has convinced many of us that affluenza will knock us out unless we take action, now. These changes need to happen deep in our value system, in a basic redefinition of the word *success*. Mahatma Gandhi's words should be a beacon: "Speed is irrelevant if you're traveling in the wrong direction," he warned, calling for economic balance as the world's industrial pace began to exceed what nature could provide and culture could moderate. We may be playing the game expertly, he was saying, but it's the wrong game. "No matter how far you've gone down the wrong road, turn back," echoes an old Turkish proverb.

The systems thinker Joanna Macy urges our civilization to take a deep breath, admit we do have a major problem, and collectively go cold turkey. Throughout history, we've done this whenever we had to. In the past, as she discusses in the book *Coming Back to Life*, we've looked at the world as a collection of parts and pieces, but now we're ready for a more holistic Great Turning, a new way of understanding. Donella Meadows calls it a paradigm shift: "There's nothing physical or expensive or even slow about paradigm change," she writes. "In a single individual it can happen in a millisecond. All it takes is a click in the mind, a new way of seeing. It is in the space of mastery over paradigms that people throw off addictions, bring down empires, and have impacts that last for millennia."[1]

The earth's systems use feedback just as a thermostat does, to maintain resilience and balance. But Macy and Meadows believe human feedback signals are being jammed by an economy with a one-track mind. "It's natural for us to be distressed over the state of the world," says Macy. "We are integral components of it, like cells in a larger body. When that body is traumatized, we feel it.... However, our culture conditions us to view pain as dysfunction. A successful person, as we conclude from commercials and electoral campaigns, brims with optimism.... 'Keep smiling,' 'If you can't say something nice, don't say anything at all.'"[2] But until we acknowledge that our environment and many aspects of our culture are sick, how can we take focused action to heal it? Denial is an obstacle to effective action, says Macy. Saving the world will require being outside our comfort zones, and adopting sustainable, equitable solutions even if they feel unfamiliar.

The ecopsychologist Terrance O'Connor believes "saving the world" is really about enlightened self-interest. "If this is not my planet," he asks, "whose is it? I am the cause, and I am the cure. When I act out of this realization, I act not out of guilt but out of self-love. I break through my denial and see that humankind is facing an absolutely unprecedented crisis. I act not out of obligation or idealism, but because I live in a straw house and I smell smoke."[3]

One of the most time-worn slogans of the old way of thinking is "The show must go on." But those who have successfully kicked affluenza ask, "Why?" If the buyer must always beware, and if our economy often resembles a pyramid scheme in which risks are pushed onto the poor and the environment, why don't we just change the script? Why don't we look, together, at what it will take to be truly successful?

DESIGNING A NEW LIFESTYLE

Writes the change agent Paul Hawken, "Join a diverse group of people in a room—different genders, races, ages, occupations, and levels of education—and ask them to describe a world they want to live in fifty years from now. "Do we want to drive two hours to work? No. Do we want to be healthy? Yes. Do we want to live in places that are safe? Do we want our children to grow up in a world where they are hopeful? Do we want to be able to worship without fear of persecution? Do we want to live in a world where nature is rebounding and not receding? No one disagrees; our vision is the same. What we need to do is identify, together, the design criteria for how we get there."[4] Dave has been thinking about these criteria for years, and has compiled a list of them:

OLD, WORN-OUT WAY OF THINKING	NEW WAY OF THINKING
The old paradigm	The new paradigm
• has the growth of capital as its goal.	• has as its goals sustainable yield, the preservation of systems, and a good quality of life.
• considers outputs to be products and profit.	• considers outputs to be people, culture, and natural restoration.
• emphasizes quantity, appearance, force.	• emphasizes quality, durability, precision, flexibility.
• has a throwaway mentality: products are used once and are not repairable.	• has a closed-loop, continuous recycling mentality; products are easily repaired.
• regards a disruption of the natural balance acceptable if profit justifies it.	• believes that natural systems must remain intact and functional.
• is biologically oblivious.	• believes that function and value are enriched by an understanding of nature.
• is understandable only by experts.	• is easily understood by anyone.

• generates hazards and requires protective equipment, guards, or defensive spending.	• increases security and safety, doesn't require vigilance or monitoring.
• operates with inflexible standard procedures.	• offers innovative, diverse solutions to both technical and social problems.
• centralizes authority, limits access.	• empowers individuals and communities, broadens and decentralizes authority.
• uses nonrenewable energy and materials from different sources	• uses renewable energy sources and recycled materials obtained locally.
• extends supply lines and process steps to deliver goods and services.	• shortens supply lines and process steps, saving energy and preserving culture.
• causes unforeseen health effects, limits wellness, and dominates nature.	• is compatible with nature, proven over the course of billions of years.
• sees nature as a warehouse of resources to be extracted and exploited.	• believes that nature has intrinsic, quantifiable values when left in place.
• promotes and fosters exclusiveness and the isolation of people from what they need.	• meets needs precisely and inclusively with rich local networks that enable accountability and participation.

What if we systematically apply these criteria to our designs, policies, and daily decisions? Let's look at a lifestyle—and a civilization—that could deliver twice the satisfaction for half the cost and half the resources we now use. A lifestyle of health and wellness rather than the same old wealth and "hellness." A lifestyle in which nonmonetary forms of real wealth begin to overpower the epidemic of affluenza.

It's important to note that we're not talking about "add-ons" that lengthen our to-do lists and add stress to our lives, but substitutions that give us more time and less stress. Real wealth is the contentedness that comes with feeling good, physically; a regenerative sense of well-being that makes *anything* seem like an event. When we gain an understanding of how the world works, we can substitute information, convictions, and brilliant design for wasted resources, including our time and money. When we choose real wealth in our everyday lives, we can have healthful, great-tasting food; exciting hobbies and adventures; work that challenges and stimulates us; and spiritual connection with a universe that's infinitely larger than our stock portfolio.

Instead of more stuff in our already-stuffed lives, we can have fewer things but better, higher-quality things; fewer visits to the doctor and more visits to museums and friends' houses. More joyful intimacy, more restful sleep, and more brilliantly sunny mornings in campsites on the beach—bacon and eggs sizzling in the skillet and coffee brewing in the pot. Greater use of our hands and minds in creative activities like playing a flute, building a table, knitting a sweater, or harvesting the season's first juicy heirloom tomato. These are the things that matter, and we can choose them, if we spend less time, money, and energy being such obediently desperate consumers.

Because real wealth makes us feel content, the marketers have learned how to ridicule it and portray it as "boring." You don't see a lot of ads for small, well-designed houses, backpacking adventures, potluck dinners, or other experiences and products that reduce the GDP yet elevate our gladness to be alive.[5]

Readers of *Affluenza* have often agreed with this book's message but many let their cynicism or their politics stand in the way. "These changes can never happen in my life, because I don't have the time, and besides, I need the money to live the way I want." But what if a different way of thinking and being generates its own income, by avoiding expenses and substituting real wealth? What if these folks spend more for healthful food but less for clothes, consumer trinkets, and housing? More for exercise and preventive health care and less for prescription drugs? We're really just talking about changes in priorities to match our values.

CREATING AN AFFORDABLE ECONOMY

To create a healthy, germ-free economy we'll need to slow the metabolism of human civilization itself, by improving the usefulness and also questioning the necessity of certain habits and products. Beverage containers are one small example. Writes Lester Brown, "A refillable glass bottle used over and over requires about 10 percent as much energy per use as an aluminum can that's recycled. Banning nonrefillable containers is a win-win-win option—cutting material and energy use, garbage flow, and air and water pollution."[6] With inspired designs and policies, we can create architecture that lasts a thousand years, products that mimic nature the way Velcro mimics burrs, and energy that lasts as long as the earth itself.

THE SHAPE OF AN AFFORDABLE ECONOMY

- As our collective demand for products falls, so will prices, as we've seen recently with gasoline after the recession hit.
- When we design communities to fit human needs rather than developer or automobile needs, our whole lifestyle requires less money. Public transit will be far less expensive per capita than America's current inefficient fleet of cars.
- Protecting and restoring nature delivers free services like water purification, pollination, and recreation that we now pay for. For example, restoring wetlands in New Orleans, along the Mississippi River, and elsewhere will

potentially save hundreds of billions of dollars by preventing floods.

- Getting rid of packaging, glossy green lawns, and food waste also takes a huge chunk out of the collective cost of our lifestyle. So does advertising; we currently spend $900 per capita to be shelled with unsolicited information, which of course is embedded in the cost of products and services. Less consumption means less advertising as well as less debt. And less debt means less interest on the debt.
- Reasonable reductions in meat consumption, air travel, and energy-intensive materials like cement, aluminum, paper, and synthetic chemicals increase personal and national income because producing them uses a lot of expensive energy.
- Green chemistry, which shortens the steps and softens the environmental cost of making chemicals, in turn lowers the cost of everything manufactured.
- Credit unions can lend capital at lower interest rates and already save borrowers $8 billion a year in interest on loans.
- Preventive health approaches and more empathetic, service-oriented doctors and nurses lower the cost of maintaining our

health, and better industrial design prevents unhealthy pollution.
- Eliminating subsidies that result in the destruction of ecosystems will save the world about $700 billion annually, about a third of that in the United States. Rather than drawing down aquifers, letting soil erode, clear-cutting forests, and overfishing the world's fish species, we will learn how to make best use of each resource and how to harvest only a sustainable yield.
- In the new economy, recycling will become a ritualized, standard practice, embedded in design and policy, so less costly extraction is required.
- In a world with fewer materialistic goals and priorities, there is less need for crime control, lawsuits, and security systems. An emphasis on social support as well as greater equality nurtures a society that is more trusting and less fearful and has less "status anxiety," a direct cause of crime.
- When we avoid designing for the "worst-case scenario," we save huge amounts of money. For example, why spend a third more for an office building's oversized air conditioning system to handle the hottest day of the year? Why not instead let employees work at home on that day?

Source: David Wann, *The New Normal* (New York: St. Martin's Press), 38–39.

SURVIVAL OF THE KINDEST

Do we have the right stuff to shift our civilization in the right direction—away from runaway individualism and back toward generosity and collective well-being? Of course we do: it's in our genes to be generous and kind. The University of California, Berkeley, psychologist Dacher Keltner challenges the familiar dog-eat-dog interpretation of natural selection, arguing that humans are successful as a species because of our nurturing, altruistic, and compassionate traits. His own interpretation of evolution? "Survival of the kindest."[7] We thrive because we take care of each other. We find ways to share the wealth and help each other meet needs. For example, the entrepreneur David Green started a company, Aurolab, which has helped eighteen million people, mostly in India, regain their eyesight by replacing lenses damaged by cataracts with synthetic ones. Lenses that used to cost hundreds of dollars now cost $2. He could be making millions or billions of dollars, but he's content with $150,000 or so a year, and the real wealth of having a purpose: empathetic capitalism. "How do we make sight and hearing or even life itself affordable to poor people?" he asks. "My competitive juices get flowing when I start to think about a big, $4 billion medical-device company and how I'm going to beat them," Green says.[8]

Susan Riederer of Boulder, Colorado, is generous with her time, recently traveling to Washington, DC, with 368 other members of a group called Citizen Climate Lobbyist to meet with members of Congress. Says Riederer, "I was intimidated initially by the challenge of talking to my representatives. But I was driven to push through my fear because of the magnitude of the situation we are currently facing."[9] Researchers are discovering that having information on a given issue won't create change unless other factors are present, like motivation, conviction, and a sense of responsibility. Emotions are often a driving force: the sense that something is shameful, dangerous, or unfair. We'll do something for our kids that we wouldn't do for ourselves, and we'll more readily create change when we see others doing it.

Shortly after giving a billion dollars to the United Nations, the media mogul Ted Turner came up with a stimulant to get more charitable donations out of fellow billionaires: each year, post how much each of them gave away. "I figured this would not only motivate people to get to the top of the list, it would also shame some whose names didn't show up." The following year, philanthropic donations began to rise. In 2010, Warren Buffett and Bill and Melinda Gates launched the Giving Pledge, challenging the super-rich to give away more than half of their wealth by the time they die. Three years later, 114 individuals and families had signed.[10]

THE LAST PICTURE SHOW

As individuals, we don't need to be billionaires to eat well, sleep soundly, or feel like our life has a purpose. The fact is, we *do* need to consume less per person, because we're running out of affordable resources as well as tolerable places to dump our wastes. But the core issue of this book goes beyond consuming less to *wanting* less and *needing* less. Think about all the money we spend to fight various diseases, many of which (like allergies, cancer, diabetes, and heart disease) can be caused or aggravated by affluent lifestyles. Then remember that affluenza is one disease that we can cure by spending *less* money, not more.

The bottom line is this: When your time comes and your whole life flashes before you, will it hold your interest? How much of the story will be about moments of clarity and grace, kindness, and caring? Will the main character—you—appear as large and noble as life itself, or as tiny and absurd as a cartoon figure, darting frantically among mountains of stuff? It's up to you, and indeed, it's up to all of us!

ACKNOWLEDGMENTS

The authors wish to thank
  Vivia Boe
  Vicki Robin
  Scott Simon
  David Horsey
  Chris de Boer
  Paula Wissel
  David de Graaf
  Francine Strickwerda
  Hope Marston
  Carol Holst
  Mike Swofford
  Stephen Piersanti
  Neal Maillet
  Karen Seriguchi
  Laura Musikanski
  Annie Leonard
  John Lindsay
  Cecile Andrews
  Wanda Urbanska
  Monique Tilford
  Todd Keithley
  Pamela Rands
  Berrett-Koehler staff
  Seventeenth Street Studios
  Simplicity Forum

Take Back Your Time
Postconsumers.com
Mesa Refuge
Bullfrog Films
KCTS Television
Oregon Public Broadcasting
New Road Map Foundation
Merck Family Fund
True North Foundation
Threshold Foundation
Weeden Foundation
Fred Gellert Foundation
Center for a New American Dream
Redefining Progress

NOTES

INTRODUCTION

[1] Center for a New American Dream, *New American Dream Survey Report* (Charlottesville, VA: September 2004), http://newdream.s3.amazonaws.com/19/e3/b/2268/ND2004Finalpollreport.pdf.

CHAPTER I

[1] For an example, see the version in John McPhee, *Encounters with the Archdruid* (New York: Farrar, Straus, and Giroux, 1971).

[2] US Census Bureau, *Statistical Abstract of the United States: 2004–2005* (Washington, DC: US Census Bureau, 2004), 431, http://www.census.gov/prod/2004pubs/04statab/income.pdf.

[3] New Road Map Foundation in partnership with Northwest Environment Watch, *All-Consuming Passion: Waking Up from the American Dream* (Seattle: New Road Map Foundation, 1998), 6.

[4] Interviews broadcast on KCTS Seattle, October 1995.

[5] Michael Jacobson, interview by John de Graaf, *Affluenza*, produced by KCTS Seattle

and Oregon Public Broadcasting (1997; Oley, PA: Bullfrog Films), DVD/VHS.

[6] New Road Map Foundation, *All-Consuming Passion*, 6.

[7] "List of Largest Shopping Malls in the World," *Wikipedia*, last modified August 14, 2013, http://en.wikipedia.org/wiki/List_of_largest_shopping_malls_in_the_world.

[8] "2013 Protests in Turkey," *Wikipedia*, last modified August 17, 2013, http://en.wikipedia.org/wiki/2013_protests_in_Turkey.

[9] David Sharp, "Online Sales Fail to Slow Onslaught of Catalog Mailings," Associated Press, December 25, 2004, http://www.utsandiego.com/uniontrib/20041225/news_1b25catalogs.html.

[10] "E-Commerce Sales Top $50 Billion in First Quarter," *Balboa Capital*, May 30, 2012, http://www.balboacapital.com/e-commerce-sales-top-50-billion-infirst-quarter.

[11] Bonnie Kavoussi, "Average Home Size Rose 4 Percent in 2011," *Huffington Post*, June 7, 2012, http://www.huffingtonpost.com/2012/06/06/average-home-size-2011_n_1575617.html.

[12] Keith Bradsher, "G.M. Has High Hopes for Vehicle Truly Meant for Road Warriors," *New York Times*, August 6,

	2000, http://www.nytimes.com/2000/08/06/business/gm-has-high-hopes-for-vehicle-truly-meant-for-road-warriors.html?pagewanted=all&src=pm.
[13]	Paul Andrews, "Compaq's New iPaq May Be the PC for Your Pocket," *Seattle Times*, November 5, 2000, http://community.seattletimes.nwsource.com/archive/?date=20001105&slug=4051350.
[14]	Monica Guzman, "Is This the End of Waiting?" *Seattle Times*, May 11, 2013, http://mobile.seattletimes.com/story/today/2020969786.
[15]	New Road Map Foundation, *All-Consuming Passion*, 4.
[16]	Juliet Schor in discussion with John de Graaf, May 1997.
[17]	Sheldon Garon, *Beyond Our Means* (Princeton, NJ: Princeton University Press, 2011), 4.
[18]	Stefano Bartolini, *Manifesto per la Felicità: Come Passare dalla Società del Ben-avere a quella del Ben-essere* [Manifesto for Happiness: Shifting Society from Money to Well-Being] (Rome: Donzelli, 2010); English translation to be published by University of Pennsylvania Press in 2013.
[19]	National Institute on Drug Abuse, North Bethesda, Maryland.

[20] Scott Cohen, "Shopaholics Anonymous," *Elle*, May 1996, 120.

[21] "News and Trends," *Psychology Today*, January/February 1995, 8.

[22] David G. Myers, "Wealth, Well-Being, and the New American Dream," *Enough!* 12 (Summer 2000): 5, http://community-wealth.org/sites/clone.community-wealth.org/files/downloads/article-myers.pdf.

[23] Ronald J. Faber, "Money Changes Everything: Compulsive Buying from a Biopsychosocial Perspective," *American Behavioral Scientist* 35 (1992), 809–819.

[24] Ibid.

[25] James Lardner and Elise Ackerman, "The Urge to Splurge," *US News & World Report*, May 24, 1999, http://www.usnews.com/usnews/biztech/articles/990524/archive_001070.htm.

CHAPTER 2

[1] La Nita Wacker, interview by Vivia Boe, September 1996.

[2] Beth Johnson, interview by David Wann, February 2000.

[3] Self Storage Association fact sheet, http://www.self-storage.org/ssa/content/navigationmenu/aboutssa/factsheet.

[4] Tim Lomax, Texas A&M Transportation Institute, interview by David Wann, May 1, 2013.

[5] "New York Times Energy for Tomorrow Conference: Building Sustainable Cities" (conference, The TimesCenter, New York City, NY, April 25, 2013).

[6] "Table 1-45: Air Passenger Travel Arrivals in the United States from Selected Foreign Countries by Flag of Carriers," US Department of Transportation, http://www.rita.dot.gov/bts/sites/rita.dot.gov.bts/files/publications/national_transportation_statistics/html/table_01_45.html.

[7] Ellen Goodman, as quoted in New Road Map Foundation, *All-Consuming Passion* (see chap.1, n.3).

[8] John Naisbitt, *High Tech/High Touch: Technology and Our Accelerated Search for Meaning* (London: Nicholas Brealey, 2001), 57.

CHAPTER 3

[1] Ray B. Williams, "Workaholism and the Myth of Hard Work," *Psychology Today*, March 15, 2012, http://www.psychologytoday.com/blog/wired-success/201203/workaholism-and-the-myth-hard-work.

[2] Staffan Linder, *The Harried Leisure Class* (New York: Columbia University Press, 1970), 4.

[3] Juliet Schor in discussion with John de Graaf, October 1992.

[4] Wayne Parker, "Work Life Balance Statistics," *About.com*, http://fatherhood.about.com/od/workingfathers/a/Work-Life-Balance-Statistics.htm.

[5] Wendy Wang, Kim Parker, and Paul Taylor, "Breadwinner Moms," Pew Research Center, May 29, 2013, http://www.pewsocialtrends.org/2013/05/29/breadwinner-moms.

[6] Karen Nussbaum in discussion with John de Graaf, September 1993.

[7] "Work Stress on the Rise: 8 in 10 American Are Stressed about Their Jobs, Survey Finds," *Huffington Post*, last modified April 12, 2013, http://www.huffingtonpost.com/2013/04/10/work-stress-jobs-americans_n_3053428.html.

[8] Jessica Dickler, "$67 Billion in Vacation Days, Out the Window," *CNNMoney*, May 25, 2011, http://money.cnn.com/2011/05/25/pf/unused_vacation_days/index.htm.

[9] Jody Heymann and Alison Earle, *Raising the Global Floor: Dismantling the Myth That We Can't Afford Good Working Conditions*

for Everyone (Stanford, CA: Stanford University Press, 2010), 105.

[10] Sarah Speck, interview by John de Graaf, April 2013.

[11] Vatsal Chikani et al., "Vacations Improve Mental Health among Rural Women: The Wisconsin Rural Women's Health Study," *Wisconsin Medical Journal* 104 (2005): 20–23, https://www.wisconsinmedicalsociety.org/_WMS/publications/wmj/pdf/104/6/20.pdf.

[12] David Friedman, "How Long Should a Man's Vacation Be?" SundayMagazine.org, July 30, 2010, http://sundaymagazine.org/2010/07/how-long-should-a-mans-vacation-be.

[13] Schor, October 1992.

[14] Michelle Castillo, "Report: U.S. Life Expectancy Lowest among Wealthy Nations Due to Disease, Violence," *CBSNews.com,* January 10, 2013, http://www.cbsnews.com/8301-204_162-57563279/report-u.s-life-expectancy-lowest-among-wealthy-nations-due-to-disease-violence; see also Damien Gayle, "How Long Will YOU Live?" *MailOnline,* November 30, 2012, http://www.dailymail.co.uk/news/article-2240855/How-does-nation-rank-world-map-life-expectancy.html.

CHAPTER 4

[1] William J. Bennett, *The Index of Leading Cultural Indicators: American Society at the End of the Twentieth Century* (New York: Touchstone, 1994), 68.

[2] William Doherty, interview by John de Graaf, 2003.

[3] Jacqueline Olds and Richard S. Schwartz, *The Lonely American* (Boston: Beacon, 2009), 102.

[4] "Television Viewing (Most Recent) by Country," NationMaster.com, http://www.nationmaster.com/graph/med_tel_vie-media-television-viewing.

[5] Olds and Schwartz, *Lonely American*, 185.

[6] Ibid., 118.

[7] Ibid., 92.

[8] Brad Edmondson, "All the Lonely People," *AARP: The Magazine*, November/December 2010, http://www.aarp.org/personal-growth/transitions/info-09-2010/all_the_lonely_people.html.

[9] Katie McDonough, "U.S. Ranks Near Bottom of UNICEF Report on Child Well-Being," *Salon*, April 12, 2013, http://www.salon.com/2013/04/12/us_ranks_near_bottom_of_unicef_report_on_child_well_being.

[10] See Juliet B. Schor, *Born to Buy: The Commercialized Child and the New Consumer Culture* (New York: Simon & Schuster, 2004).

[11] Joan Chiaramonte, interview by Vivia Boe, 1996.

[12] Susan Linn, *Consuming Kids: The Hostile Takeover of Childhood* (New York: New Press, 2004).

[13] "Yearning for Balance," The Harwood Group, July 1995, http://www.iisd.ca/consume/harwood.html.

[14] David Walsh, interview by John de Graaf, 2000.

[15] Alex Molnar, "Virtually Everywhere: Marketing to Children in America's Schools," National Education Policy Center, September 2004, http://nepc.colorado.edu/files/EPSL-0409-103-CERU.pdf.

[16] "CDC: Teen Suicide Attempts on the Rise," FoxNews.com, June 8, 2012, http://www.foxnews.com/health/2012/06/08/cdc-teen-suicide-attempts-on-rise.

[17] David Korten, *The Post-Corporate World: Life after Capitalism* (San Francisco: Kumarian/Berrett-Koehler, 2000), 33.

[18] Olds and Schwartz, *Lonely American*, 86.

[19] Edward Luttwak, interview by John de Graaf, 1996.

[20]   Ibid.

CHAPTER 5

[1]   James Kunstler, interview by David Wann, March 1997.

[2]   Robert D. Putnam, *Bowling Alone: The Collapse and Revival of American Community* (New York: Simon & Schuster, 2000), 49.

[3]   Sage Stossel, "Lonely in America," *Atlantic Unbound*, September 21, 2000, http://www.theatlantic.com/past/docs/unbound/interviews/ba2000-09-21.htm.

[4]   Sherry Turkle, *Alone Together: Why We Expect More from Technology and Less from Each Other* (Philadelphia: Basic Books, 2011), 161.

[5]   "Top 100 Chains: U.S. Sales," *Nation's Restaurant News*, http://nrn.com/us-top-100/top-100-chains-us-sales.

[6]   Gregory Heires, "The Low-Wage Wal-Mart Business Model Has Ruined the Economy for Working Families," *Reader Supported News*, June 23, 2013, http://readersupportednews.org/pm-section/84-84/18080-the-low-wage-wal-mart-business-model-has-ruined-the-economy-for-working-families.

[7] Al Norman, interview by David Wann, November 2004.

[8] Sudhir Venkatesh, "Adventures in Ideas: Conversation with Al Norman, Author of *Occupy Walmart*," Freakonomics, LLC, August 8, 2012, http://www.freakonomics.com/2012/08/10/adventures-in-ideas-conversation-with-al-norman-author-of-occupy-walmart.

[9] Ibid.

[10] Edward J. Blakely and Mary Gail Snyder, *Fortress America: Gated Communities in the United States* (Washington, DC: Brookings Institution Press, 1997).

[11] Robert B. Reich, "Secession of the Successful," *New York Times*, January 20, 1991, http://www.nytimes.com/1991/01/20/magazine/secession-of-the-successful.html.

[12] Putnam, *Bowling Alone*, 325.

[13] Nicole A. Flotteron, "New Gun Laws Could Mean Economic Woes for Booming Gun Industry," *Daily Caller*, March 29, 2013, http://dailycaller.com/2013/03/29/new-gun-laws-could-mean-economic-woes-for-booming-gun-industry.

[14] Diane Mapes, "Bury Me with My Cell Phone," *MSNBC.com*, December 16, 2008, http://www.nbcnews.com/id/28182292/ns

/technology_and_sciencetech_and_gadgets/t/bury-me-my-cell-phone.

[15] Alice Waters, "Slow Food Nation," *The Nation*, September 11, 2006, http://www.thenation.com/article/slow-food-nation.

CHAPTER 6

[1] Harry Boyte, interview by John de Graaf, October 1999.

[2] Robert Seiple, interview by John de Graaf, September 1996.

[3] Lee Atwater and T. Brewster, "Lee Atwater's Last Campaign," *Life*, February 1991.

[4] Cindy Wooden, "Pope Francis Warns of the Dangers of 'Unbridled Capitalism,'" *Catholic Herald*, May 22, 2013, http://www.catholicherald.co.uk/news/2013/05/22/pope-francis-warns-of-the-dangers-of-unbridled-capitalism.

[5] Michael Lerner, *The Politics of Meaning: Restoring Hope and Possibility in an Age of Cynicism* (Reading, MA: Addison-Wesley, 1996), 5–8.

[6] Daniel Goleman, "A Rising Cost of Modernity: Depression," *New York Times*, December 8, 1992, http://www.nytimes.co

m/1992/12/08/science/a-rising-cost-of-modernity-depression.html.

[7] Tim Kasser and Richard M. Ryan, "A Dark Side of the American Dream: Correlates of Financial Success as a Central Life Aspiration," *Journal of Personality and Social Psychology* 65 (1993): 410–412.

[8] Tom Hayden, *Reunion: A Memoir* (New York: Random House, 1988), 82.

[9] Wilhelm Röpke, *A Humane Economy: The Social Framework of the Free Market* (Indianapolis: Liberty Fund, 1971), 102.

[10] Ibid., 113.

[11] Ibid., 114.

[12] Ernest van den Haag, "Of Happiness and of Despair We Have No Measure," in *Man Alone: Alienation in Modern Society*, ed. Eric Josephson and Mary Josephson (New York: Dell, 1970), 184.

[13] Ibid., 197.

CHAPTER 7

[1] Julia Philips, "Bangladesh Building Collapse: Why It Should Scare Americans," *PolicyMic*, n.d., http://www.policymic.com/articles/39931/bangladesh-building-collapse-why-it-should-scare-americans.

[2] "Bangladesh Ends Search for Collapse Victims; Final Toll 1,127," The Associated Press, May 13, 2013, http://www.usatoday.com/story/news/world/2013/05/13/bangladesh-to-end-search-for-collapse-victims/2154753.

[3] "List of Countries by Income Equality," *Wikipedia*, last modified August 9, 2013, http://en.wikipedia.org/wiki/List_of_countries_by_income_equality.

[4] For a wide range of data documenting inequality trends in the United States, see Emmanuel Saez, "Striking It Richer: The Evolution of Top Incomes in the United States," University of California, Berkeley, January 23, 2013, http://elsa.berkeley.edu/~saez/saez-UStopincomes-2011.pdf.

[5] Felicity Barringer, "Giving by the Rich Declines, on Average," *New York Times*, May 24, 1992.

[6] Isaac Shapiro and Robert Greenstein, "The Widening Income Gulf," Center on Budget and Policy Priorities, September 5, 1999, http://www.cbpp.org/cms/index.cfm?fa=view&id=2204.

[7] For a range of hunger data, see "Hunger in America," Feeding America, http://feedingamerica.org/hunger-in-america.aspx.

[8] Timothy Pilgrim, "America's Rich Get Richer," posted on Pilgrim's personal webpage, http://hope.journ.wwu.edu/tpilgrim/j190/richgetricher.html.

[9] Chuck Marr and Nathaniel Frentz, "Federal Income Taxes on Middle-Income Families Remain near Historic Lows," Center on Budget and Policy Priorities, last modified April 11, 2013, http://www.cbpp.org/cms/?fa=view&id=3151.

[10] "Poverty in the United States," *Wikipedia*, last modified August 18, 2013, http://en.wikipedia.org/wiki/Poverty_in_the_United_States.

[11] Sanjay Bhatt, "Cashing In," *Seattle Times*, June 23, 2013.

[12] David Broder, "To Those Who Toil Invisibly amid Billionaires," *Seattle Times*, April 16, 2000.

[13] Barbara Ehrenreich, "Maid to Order: The Politics of Other Women's Work," *Harper's Magazine*, April 2000, 59–70.

[14] For prison data, see "Rough Justice," *The Economist*, July 24, 2010, http://www.economist.com/node/16640389.

[15] Richard Wilkinson and Kate Pickett, *The Spirit Level* (New York: Bloomsbury, 2009); see also "Poverty," The World

Bank Group, last modified April 2013, http://go.worldbank.org/VL7N3V6F20.
[16] David Korten, inteview by John de Graaf, October 1996.
[17] "Poverty," World Bank Group.

CHAPTER 8

[1] Jim Meyer, "How to Make Gasoline from Tar Sands, in Six Simple Steps," *Grist*, January 23, 2013, http://grist.org/basics/how-to-make-gasoline-from-tar-sands-in-six-simple-steps.
[2] Ibid.
[3] Donella H. Meadows, Dennis L. Meadows, and Jørgen Randers, *Beyond the Limits: Confronting Global Collapse, Envisioning a Sustainable Future* (Post Mills, VT: Chelsea Green, 1992), 53.
[4] Daryll E. Ray and Harwood D. Schaffer, "Drought's Winners and Losers," *Daily Yonder*, September 14, 2012, http://www.dailyyonder.com/droughts-winners-and-losers/2012/09/13/4429.
[5] Paul Hawken, Amory Lovins, and L. Hunter Lovins, *Natural Capitalism: Creating the Next Industrial Revolution* (Boston: Little, Brown, 1999), 51–52.

[6] Mathis Wackernagel, interview by David Wann, August 2000.

[7] Vince Matthews, interview by David Wann, May 2013.

[8] Judy Fahys, "U. Scientist: Kennecott Landslide Is One for the Record Books," *Salt Lake Tribune*, last modified May 23, 2013, http://www.sltrib.com/sltrib/news/56317801-78/kennecott-slide-landslide-moore.html.csp. 8. Matthews, interview.

[9] Ibid.

[10] Ibid.

[11] Bernice Napach, "Food Is the New Oil and Land the New Gold: Lester Brown," *Daily Ticker*, October 5, 2012, http://www.cnbc.com/id/49301763.

[12] Lester Brown, "Chapter 1. Food: The Week Link," *Grist*, April 9, 2013, http://grist.org/article/chapter-1-food-the-weak-link/.

[13] Ibid.

[14] Stephanie Pappas, "Earth's Ecosystems Nearing Catastrophic 'Tipping Point,' Warn Scientists," *Christian Science Monitor*, June 7, 2012, http://www.csmonitor.com/Science/2012/0607/Earth-s-ecosystems-nearing-catastrophic-tipping-point-warn-scientists-video.

[15] Melanie Jae Martin, "Newly Released Tim DeChristopher Finds a Movement Transformed by His Courage," *Yes!*, April 22, 2013, http://www.yesmagazine.org/planet/tim-dechristopher-peaceful-uprising-movement-transformed-courage.

[16] "Do the Math," 350.org, http://math.350.org.

[17] "Exxon Mobil CEO pivots on climate, slams 'manufactured fear' on fracking," *Muck Rack*, June 28, 2012, http://muckrack.com/link/xFUJ/exxon-mobil-ceo-pivots-on-climate-slams-manufactured-fear-on-fracking.

[18] Martin, "Newly Released Tim DeChristopher."

CHAPTER 9

[1] Suzanne Wuerthele, interview by David Wann, March 2000.

[2] "Chemical Testing & Data Collection," US Environmental Protection Agency, last modified August 8, 2013, http://www.epa.gov/opptintr/chemtest.

[3] Sandra Steingraber, *Living Downstream: An Ecologist Looks at Cancer and the Environment* (Reading, MA: Addison-Wesley, 1997), 99.

[4] Quoted in Natural Solutions, "How Much Impact Do Toxic Chemicals Have on Society? Read the Statistics," accessed September 16, 2013, http://www.non-toxic.info/Health_Statistics.htm.

[5] Dan Fagin, Marianne Lavelle, and the Center for Public Integrity, *Toxic Deception: How the Chemical Industry Manipulates Science, Bends the Law and Endangers Your Health* (Monroe, ME: Common Courage, 1999), 43.

[6] Trish Riley, "How Healthy Is Your Home?" *South Florida Parenting*, 2004.

[7] Anne Platt McGinn, "Phasing Out Persistent Organic Pollutants," in *State of the World 2000: A Worldwatch Institute Report on Progress Toward a Sustainable Society*, ed. Linda Starke (New York: W.W. Norton, 2000), 86, http://www.worldwatch.org/system/files/ESW020.pdf.

[8] "Body Burden: Methodology," Environmental Working Group, http://www.ewg.org/sites/bodyburden1/methodology.php.

[9] Edward Furlough and Chris Bowman, "Medicines, Chemicals Taint Water: Contaminants Pass Through Sewage Plants," *Sacramento Bee*, March 28, 2000.

[10] Natural Resources Defense Council, "Bottled Water," last modified July 15, 2013, http://www.nrdc.org/water/drinking/bw/chap2.asp.

[11] Ibid.

[12] Theo Colborn, Dianne Dumanoski, and John Peterson Myers, *Our Stolen Future: Are We Threatening Our Fertility, Intelligence, and Survival? A Scientific Detective Story* (New York: Plume, 1997), 137.

[13] Tom Philpott, "How GMOs Unleashed a Pesticide Gusher," *Mother Jones*, October 3, 2012, http://www.motherjones.com/tom-philpott/2012/10/how-gmos-ramped-us-pesticide-use.

[14] Jeffrey M. Smith, *Genetic Roulette: The Documented Health Risks of Genetically Engineered Foods* (Fairfield, IA: Yes! Books, 2007).

[15] Ibid., 59.

[16] Donovan Webster, "The Stink about Pork," *George* 4 (1999), 94.

CHAPTER 10

[1] Robert J. Samuelson, "Health Care's Heap of Wasteful Spending," *Washington Post*, September 13, 2012, http://articles.washin

gtonpost.com/2012-09-13/opinions/35495674_1_health-care-insurance-premiums-runaway-health.

[2] Joseph Mercola, "Americans Are Less Healthy, and Die Sooner than People in Other Developed Nations," Mercola.com, January 23, 2013, http://articles.mercola.com/sites/articles/archive/2013/01/23/united-states-health-ranking.aspx.

[3] "OECD Factbook 2013," Organization for Economic Cooperation and Development, http://www.oecd-ilibrary.org/economics/oecd-factbook-2013_factbook-2013-en.

[4] Steven H. Woolf and Laudan Aron, eds., *U.S. Health in International Perspective: Shorter Lives, Poorer Health* (Washington, DC: The National Academies Press, 2013), 2–3, http://www.nap.edu/catalog.php?record_id=13497.

[5] David Korten, "Living Wealth: Better than Money," *Yes!* (Fall 2007): 37–41, http://www.yesmagazine.org/issues/stand-up-to-corporate-power/living-wealth-better-than-money.

[6] Richard Ryan, interview by David Wann, June 2000.

[7] Meadows, Meadows, and Randers, *Beyond the Limits,* 216 (see chap.8, n.3).

[8] David Wann, *Simple Prosperity: Finding Real Wealth in a Sustainable Lifestyle* (New York: St. Martin's, 2007), 135.

[9] Mihaly Csikszentmihalyi, *Flow: The Psychology of Optimal Experience* (New York: Harper Perennial, 1991), 54.

[10] Ibid., 99.

[11] Alan Durning, "How Much Is Enough?" *The Social Contract* (Spring 1993): 179, http://www.thesocialcontract.com/pdf/three-three/Durning.pdf; originally published in Alan Durning, *How Much Is Enough?* (New York: W.W. Norton, 1992).

[12] Tanja C. Adam and Elissa S. Epel, "Stress, Eating and the Reward System, *Physiology & Behavior* 91 (2007), 449–458, http://www.foodaddictionsummit.org/documents/StressEatingandtheRewardSystem.pdf.

[13] Jerry Mander, *Four Arguments for the Elimination of Television* (New York: William Morrow, 1978), 118.

CHAPTER 11

[1] "Original Affluent Society," *Wikipedia*, last modified February 16, 2013, http://en.wikipedia.org/wiki/Original_affluent_society.

[2] Allen Johnson, interview by John de Graaf, May 1993

[3] James M. Childs Jr., *Greed: Economics and Ethics in Conflict* (Minneapolis: Fortress, 2000), 1.

[4] Quoted in Jerome M. Segal, *Graceful Simplicity: The Philosophy and Politics of the Alternative American Dream* (New York: Henry Holt, 1999), 167.

[5] Ibid., 189.

[6] Matthew 19:22 (New International Version).

[7] T.C. McLuhan, *Touch the Earth: A Self-Portrait of Indian Existence* (New York: Touchstone, 1976), 90.

CHAPTER 12

[1] Segal, *Graceful Simplicity*, 13 (see chap. 11, n.4).

[2] Ibid.

[3] Ibid., 14.

[4] Juliet B. Schor, *The Overworked American: The Unexpected Decline of Leisure* (New York: Basic Books, 1992).

[5] Rodney Clapp, ed. *The Consuming Passion: Christianity and the Consumer Culture* (Downer's Grove, IL: Intervarsity, 1998), 173.

[6] Karl Marx and Friedrich Engels, "The Communist Manifesto," in *Basic Writings in Politics and Philosophy*, ed. Lewis S. Feuer (Garden City, NY: Anchor Books, 1959), 1–41.

[7] Karl Marx, "The Economic and Philosophic Manuscripts of 1844," in *Marx's Concept of Man*, ed. Erich Fromm (New York: Frederick Ungar, 1971), 55.

[8] Ibid., 107.

[9] Ibid., 37.

[10] Karl Marx, *Capital: A Critique of Political Economy, Volume III*, ed. Friedrich Engels (New York: Modern Library, 1906), 954.

[11] Philip B. Smith and Manfred Max-Neef, *Economics Unmasked: From Power and Greed to Compassion and the Common Good* (Totnes, UK: Green Books, 2012), 120.

[12] Perry Miller, ed., *The American Transcendentalists: Their Prose and Poetry* (Garden City, NY: Anchor Books, 1957), 313.

[13] Ibid., 309.

[14] Ibid., 310.

CHAPTER 13

[1] Paul Lafargue, *The Right to Be Lazy* (Chicago: Charles Kerr, 1989), 40.

[2] A.L. Morton, ed., *Political Writings of William Morris* (New York: International Publishers, 1973), 112.

[3] Ibid.,

[4] "James Oppenheim," *Wikipedia*, last modified April 13, 2013, http://en.wikipedia.org/wiki/James_Oppenheim.

[5] James Oppenheim, *The Nine-Tenths: A Novel* (New York: Harper & Brothers, 1911), 319, http://books.google.com/books?id=2qwcAAAAMAAJ&pg=PA319&lpg=PA319&dq=The+Nine-Tenths+Oppenheim.

[6] Meredith Tax, *The Rising of Women: Feminist Solidarity and Class Conflict, 1880–1917* (Champaign, IL: University of Illinois Press, 2001), 241, http://www.amazon.com/The-Rising-Women-Solidarity-1880-1917/dp/0252070070.

[7] Benjamin Kline Hunnicutt, *Work without End: Abandoning Shorter Hours for the Right to Work* (Philadelphia: Temple, 1988), 82.

[8] Ibid., 75.

[9] Ibid., 88–97.

[10] Ibid., 99.

[11] Ibid., 53.

[12] James Twitchell, "Two Cheers for Materialism," *The Wilson Quarterly* 23 (Spring 1999).

[13] Ralph Borsodi, *This Ugly Civilization* (New York: Simon & Schuster, 1929), http://www.soilandhealth.org/03sov/0303critic/030302borsodi.ugly/030302borsodi.ch16.html.

[14] John de Graaf, "When America Came 'This Close' to Establishing a 30-Hour Workweek," *AlterNet*, April 2, 2013, http://www.alternet.org/labor/when-america-came-close-establishing-30-hour-workweek. 15. Ibid.

CHAPTER 14

[1] Susan Strasser, interview by John de Graaf, April 1996.

[2] For excerpts from this film and TV ad, see *Affluenza*, produced by KCTS Seattle and Oregon Public Broadcasting (1997; Oley, PA: Bullfrog Films), DVD/VHS.

[3] Gary Cross, *An All-Consuming Century: Why Commercialism Won in Modern America* (New York: Columbia University Press, 2000), 169.

[4] Röpke, *Humane Economy*, 109 (see chap.6, n.9).

[5] John Kenneth Galbraith, *The Affluent Society* (Boston: Houghton Mifflin, 1998), 258.

[6] Ibid., 266.

[7] "Johnson Introduces 'Great Society,'" audio recording, 2:54, from Lyndon B. Johnson's commencement speech at the University of Michigan on March 22, 1964, http://www.history.com/speeches/johnson-introduces-great-society.

[8] "Robert F. Kennedy Challenges Gross Domestic Product," YouTube video, 2:12, audio recording from his speech at the University of Kansas on March 18, 1968, posted by "colinatpyramid," September 11, 2008, http://www.youtube.com/watch?v=77IdKFqXbUY&noredirect=1.

[9] Cross, *All-Consuming Century*, 261.

[10] "President Jimmy Carter—'Crisis of Confidence' Speech," YouTube video, 5:17, from a national television broadcast from the White House on July 15, 1979, posted by "MCamericanpresident," March 28, 2008, http://www.youtube.com/watch?v=1IIRVy7oZ58.

CHAPTER 15

[1] Pierre Martineau, *Motivation in Advertising: Motives That Make People Buy* (New York: McGraw Hill, 1971), 190.

[2] New Road Map Foundation, *All-Consuming Passion* 6 (see chap.1, n.3).

[3] Alex Konrad, "Even with Record Prices, Expect a $10 Million Super Bowl Ad Soon," *Forbes*, February 2, 2013, http://www.forbes.com/sites/alexkonrad/2013/02/02/even-with-record-prices-10-million-spot.

[4] Christina Austin, "The Billionaires' Club: Only 36 Companies Have $1,000 Million-Plus Ad Budgets," *Business Insider*, November 11, 2012, http://www.businessinsider.com/the-35-companies-that-spent-1-billion-on-ads-in-2011-2012-11?op=1.

[5] Kevin Armitage, "What Studying Nature Has Taught Us," Solutions, December 2010, http://www.thesolutionsjournal.com/node/814.

[6] Michael F. Jacobson and Laurie Mazur, *Marketing Madness: A Survival Guide for a Consumer Society* (Boulder, CO: Westview, 1995), 31.

[7] Michael Jacobson, interview by John de Graaf, April 1996.

[8] Robert Hof, "Online Ad Spending Tops $100 Billion in 2012," *Forbes*, January 9, 2013, http://www.forbes.com/sites/roberthof/2013/01/09/online-ad-spending-tops-100-billion-in-2012.

[9] Laurie Mazur, interview by John de Graaf, April 1996

[10] Röpke, *Humane Economy*, 128 (see chap.6, n.9).

[11] Stephen Foley, "Whoops!, by John Lanchester," review of *Whoops! Why Everyone Owes Everyone and No One Can Pay*, by John Lanchester, *The Independent*, January 29, 2010, http://www.independent.co.uk/arts-entertainment/books/reviews/whoops-by-john-lanchester-1882280.html.

CHAPTER 16

[1] Kalle Lasn, *Culture Jam: The Uncooling of America* (New York: Eagle Brook, 1999), 27.

[2] John Stauber and Sheldon Rampton, *Toxic Sludge Is Good for You: Lies, Damn Lies and the Public Relations Industry* (Monroe, ME: Common Courage, 2002), 28.

[3] David Knowles, "Senator Seeks to Overturn So-Called Monsanto Protection

Act," *New York Daily News*, May 22, 2013, http://www.nydailynews.com/news/politics/push-overturn-monsanto-protection-act-article-1.1352178#ixzz2YNrWFqID.

[4] Al Gore, *The Future: Six Drivers of Global Change* (New York: Random House, 2013), 104–105.

[5] Ibid.

[6] Myron Ebell, "Love Global Warming: What's Wrong with Mild Winters, Anyway?" *Forbes*, December 8, 2006, http://www.forbes.com/forbes/2006/1225/038.html.

[7] Jill Fitzsimmons, "Meet the Climate Denial Machine," Media Matters for America, November 28, 2012, http://mediamatters.org/blog/2012/11/28/meet-the-climate-denial-machine.

[8] George Orwell, "The Principles of Newspeak," written in 1948 as an appendix to George Orwell, *1984* (London: Secker and Warburg, 1949), http://www.newspeakdictionary.com/ns-prin.html.

[9] John Sullivan, "PR Industry Fills Vacuum Left by Shrinking Newsrooms," *ProPublica*, May 1, 2011, http://www.propublica.org/article/pr-industry-fills-vacuum-left-by-shrinking-newsrooms.

[10] Craig Fehrman, "The Incredible Shrinking Sound Bite," *Boston.com*, January 2, 2011, http://www.boston.com/bostonglobe/ideas/articles/2011/01/02/the_incredible_shrinking_sound_bite/.

[11] Miranda Spencer, "Natural Gas and the News," Fairness & Accuracy in Reporting, February 1, 2012, http://fair.org/extra-online-articles/natural-gas-and-the-news.

[12] "How Much Land Do All the Fracking Wells in the United States Take Up?" *Artists against Fracking*, accessed August 20, 2013, http://www.causes.com/actions/1712550-how-much-land-do-all-the-fracking-wells-in-the-united-states-take-up.

[13] Elizabeth Royte, "Fracking Our Food Supply," *The Nation*, November 28, 2012, http://www.thenation.com/article/171504/fracking-our-food-supply.

[14] Meadows, Meadows, and Randers, *Beyond the Limits*, 1 (see chap.8, n.3).

CHAPTER 18

[1] Joe Dominguez and Vicki Robin, *Your Money or Your Life: Transforming Your Relationship with Money and Achieving*

Financial Independence (New York: Viking, 1992).

[2] Dominic Holden, "The Fight against Small Apartments," *The Stranger*, May 8, 2013, http://www.thestranger.com/seattle/the-fight-against-small-apartments/Content?oid=16701155.

[3] William Powers, "What's Your 12 x 12? An Article by William Powers," New World Library, https://www.newworldlibrary.com/ArticleDetails/tabid/230/ArticleID/177/Default.aspx#.UhOuQW28CSo, based on an excerpt from William Powers, *Twelve by Twelve: A One-Room Cabin Off the Grid & Beyond the American Dream* (Novato, CA: New World Library, 2010), 28–29.

[4] Taken from the official book description for Colin Beavan, *No Impact Man: The Adventures of a Guilty Liberal Who Attempts to Save the Planet, and the Discoveries He Makes About Himself and Our Way of Life in the Process* (New York: Farrar, Straus, and Giroux, 2009).

[5] The Harwood Group, *Yearning for Balance* (Takoma Park, MD: Center for a New American Dream, 1995).

[6] Rick Heller, "Slowing Down the Consumer Treadmill," *The Humanist*, July–August 2011,

http://thehumanist.org/july-august-2011/slowing-down-the-consumer-treadmill/.

[7] Kirk Warren Brown and Richard M. Ryan, "The Benefits of Being Present: Mindfulness and Its Role in Psychological Well-Being," *Journal of Personality and Social Psychology* 84 (2003): 822–848, doi:10.1037/0022-3514.84.4.822.

CHAPTER 20

[1] John Upton, "Buzzkill: Huge Bee Die-Off in Oregon Parking Lot Blamed on Insecticide Spraying," *Grist,* June 20, 2013, http://grist.org/news/huge-bee-die-off-in-oregon-parking-lot-blamed-on-insecticide-spraying.

[2] Kaveri Subrahmanyam et al., "The Impact of Home Computer Use on Children's Activities and Development," *The Future of Children* 10 (Fall/Winter 2000): 123–144, https://www.princeton.edu/futureofchildren/publications/docs/10_02_05.pdf.

[3] Fred First, "The Wisdom of One Place: Why We Need to Know Where We Are," *The New Nature Movement,* June 6, 2013, http://blog.childrenandnature.org/2013/06/06/the-wisdom-of-one-place-why-we-need-to-know-where-we-are.

[4] "Leaf Litter Talks with Richard Louv," *Leaf Litter* 10 (2012), http://www.biohabitats.com/newsletters/giving-children-the-gift-of-nature/#leaf-litter-talks-with-richard-louv.

[5] As quoted in Wann, *Simple Prosperity*, 112 (see chap.10, n.8).

[6] Gretchen C. Daily et al., "Ecosystem Services: Benefits Supplied to Human Societies by Natural Ecosystems," *Issues in Ecology* 2 (1997): 1–18, http://www.esa.org/science_resources/issues/TextIssues/issue2.php.

[7] Barbara J. Huelat, "The Wisdom of Biophilia: Nature in Healing Environments," *Journal of Green Building* 3 (September 25, 2008), 1–13, http://www.aahid.org/assets-files/JGB_V3N3_a03_heulat.pdf.

[8] Bill McKibben, *The Age of Missing Information* (New York: Random House, 1992), 70.

[9] David Sobel, *Beyond Ecophobia: Reclaiming the Heart in Nature Education* (Great Barrington, MA: The Orion Society and The Myrin Institute, 1996),34.

[10] Robert Greenway, "The Wilderness Effect and Ecopsychology," in *Ecopsychology: Restoring the Earth, Healing the Mind*, ed. Theodore Roszak, Mary E.

Gomes, and Allen D. Kanner (New York: Sierra Club Books, 1995), 128–9.

[11]   Lana Porter, interview by David Wann, July 2012.

CHAPTER 21

[1]   Marianne Williamson, *The Healing of America* (New York: Simon & Schuster, 1997), 50.

[2]   Bruce Upbin, "The 147 Companies That Control Everything," *Forbes*, October 22, 2011, http://www.forbes.com/sites/bruceupbin/2011/10/22/the-147-companies-that-control-everything/.

[3]   Marjorie Kelly, *Owning Our Future: The Emerging Ownership Revolution* (San Francisco: Berrett-Koehler, 2012), 111.

[4]   Ibid., 42.

[5]   Ibid., 59.

[6]   John Maynard Keynes, "National Self-Sufficiency," *The Yale Review* 22 (June 1933), 755–769.

[7]   Judy Wicks, interview by David Wann, July 25, 2009.

[8]   Van Jones, "Crowdsourcing Our Economic Recovery," *CNN*, last modified March 7, 2013, http://www.cnn.com/2013/01/08/opinion/jones-share-economy.

[9] "Solar Industry Data," Solar Energy Industries Association, http://www.seia.org/research-resources/solar-industry-data.

[10] Janet Larsen, "Bike-Sharing Programs Hit the Streets in Over 500 Cities Worldwide," Earth Policy Institute, April 25, 2013, http://www.earth-policy.org/plan_b_updates/2013/update112.

CHAPTER 22

[1] "Buy Nothing Day," *Wikipedia*, last modified May 12, 2013, http://en.wikipedia.org/wiki/Buy_Nothing_Day.

[2] *The Story of Stuff*, directed by Louis Fox (2007; Washington, DC: Free Range Studios), online video, http://www.storyofstuff.org/movies-all/story-of-stuff; see also Leslie Kaufman, "Video Warning of Pitfalls of Consumption Is a Hit in Schools," *New York Times*, May 10, 2009, http://www.nytimes.com/2009/05/11/education/11stuff.html?pagewanted=all&_r=0.

[3] Jeffrey Kluger, "The Happiness of Pursuit," *Time*, June 27, 2013, http://www.time.com/time/magazine/article/0,9171,2146449-6,00.html.

[4] Greg Norris, interview by John de Graaf, June 2013.

CHAPTER 23

[1] New Road Map Foundation, *All-Consuming Passion* 16 (see chap.1, n.3).

[2] "Time to Care Public Policy Agenda," Take Back Your Time, http://www.timeday.org.

[3] Jody Heymann et al., *The Work, Family, and Equity Index: Where Does the United States Stand Globally?* (Cambridge, MA: Harvard School of Public Health, 2004).

[4] John de Graaf, "Life Away from the Rat-Race: Why One Group of Workers Decided to Cut Their Own Hours and Pay," *AlterNet,* July 2, 2012, http://www.alternet.org/story/156126/life_away_from_the_rat-race:_why_one_group_of_workers_decided_to_cut_their_own_hours_and_pay.

[5] John de Graaf and David K. Batker, "Americans Work Too Much for Their Own Good," *Bloomberg,* November 3, 2011, http://www.bloomberg.com/news/2011-11-03/americans-work-too-much-for-their-own-good-de-graaf-and-batker.html; see also Hanne Groenendijk and Saskia Keuzenkamp, "The Netherlands," International Network on Leave Policies & Research, October 2010, http://www.le

avenetwork.org/fileadmin/Leavenetwork/Country_notes/The_Netherlands.published.oct_2010.pdf.

[6] "Tommy Douglas: 'Greatest Canadian' Brought Universal Healthcare to His Nation," *Alter+Care*, August 20, 2009, http://www.altergroup.com/alter-care-blog/index.php/healthcare/tommy-douglas-greatest-canadian-brought-universal-healthcare-to-his-nation.

[7] Robert Frank, "Progressive Consumption Tax," *Democracy* 8 (2008), http://www.democracyjournal.org/8/6591.php.

[8] "Mining Subsidies: $3.5 Billion a Year," *Third World Traveler*, excerpt from Mark Zepezauer and Arthur Naiman, *Take the Rich off Welfare* (Boston: South End Press, 1996), http://www.thirdworldtraveler.com/Corporate_Welfare/Mining_Subsidies.html.

[9] Hawken, Lovins, and Lovins, *Natural Capitalism* (see chap.8, n.5).

[10] Speech by Jim Hightower at Santa Barbara, California, May 13, 2000.

[11] Juliet Schor, "Video: New Dream Mini-Views: Visualizing a Plenitude Economy," *Plenitude: The Blog*, August 16, 2011, http://www.julietschor.org/2011/08/video-new-dream-mini-views-visualizing-a-plenitude-economy.

[12] Anders Hayden, *Sharing the Work, Sparing the Planet: Work, Time, Consumption, and Ecology* (London: Zed Books, 1999), 36.

CHAPTER 24

[1] Irvin D. Yalom, *Existential Psychotherapy* (New York: Basic Books, 1980), 12.

[2] Clifford Cobb, Gary Sue Goodman, and Mathis Wackernagel, *Why Bigger Isn't Better: The Genuine Progress Indicator—1999 Update*, (San Francisco: Redefining Progress), 1, http://users.nber.org/~rosenbla/econ302/lecture/GPI-GDP/gpi1999.pdf.

[3] Simon Kuznets, "National Income, 1929–1932," National Bureau of Economic Research, S. Doc. No.124, at 7 (1934).

[4] "Genuine Progress Indicator," *Wikipedia*, last modified August 15, 2013, http://en.wikipedia.org/wiki/Genuine_progress_indicator.

[5] "Governor O'Malley Hosts GPI Summit," Maryland Department of Natural Resources, June 17, 2013, http://news.maryland.gov/dnr/2013/06/17/governor-omalley-hosts-gpi-summit.

[6] "Cylvia Hayes, Governor Martin O'Malley and Jeffrey Sachs Discuss a More Prosperous and Beneficial Economy," *Clean*

Economy Bulletin, June 2013, http://myemail.constantcontact.com/Clean-Economy-Bulletin.html?soid=1101847878821&aid=E77ZPdv_5Pw.

[7] Speech by Martin O'Malley at the Genuine Progress Indicators Conference, June 14, 2013, Baltimore, MD, http://www.governor.maryland.gov/blog/?p=8837.

[8] Pema Euden, *Coming Home* (Thimphu, Bhutan: Peden Press, 2008).

[9] Laura Musikanski, "The UN Embraces the Economics of Happiness," *Yes!,* April 12, 2012, http://www.yesmagazine.org/happiness/the-un-embraces-the-economics-of-happiness.

[10] Alok Jha, "Happiness Doesn't Increase with Growing Wealth of Nations, Finds Study," *Guardian,* December 13, 2010, http://www.guardian.co.uk/science/2010/dec/13/happiness-growing-wealth-nations-study.

[11] Updates (not yet published) to John Helliwell, Richard Layard, and Jeffrey Sachs, *World Happiness Report* (New York: The Earth Institute, 2012), http://www.earth.columbia.edu/sitefiles/file/Sachs Writing/2012/World Happiness Report.pdf.

[12] Ibid. (original report).

[13] "Canadian Index of Well-being," University of Waterloo, https://uwaterloo.ca/canadian-index-wellbeing.

[14] Laura Musikanski and John de Graaf, "The Happiness Initiative: The Serious Business of Well-Being," *Solutions* 4 (2013), http://happycounts.blogspot.com/2013/02/re-post-article-from-solutions-journal.html.

CHAPTER 25

[1] Donella Meadows, "Leverage Points: Places to Intervene in a System," *Solutions* 1 (2009), 41–49, http://www.thesolutionsjournal.com/node/419.

[2] Joanna Macy and Molly Young Brown, *Coming Back to Life: Practices to Reconnect Our Lives, Our World* (Gabriola Island, BC, Canada: New Society, 1998), 27.

[3] Terrance O'Connor, "Therapy for a Dying Earth," in *Ecopsychology: Restoring the Earth, Healing the Mind*, ed. Theodore Roszak, Mary E. Gomes, and Allen D. Kanner (New York: Sierra Club Books, 1995), 153.

[4] Allan Hunt Badiner, "Paul Hawken, an Interview on Natural Capitalism," *Yoga Journal* 118 (1994), 68, 70.

[5] Wann, *Simple Prosperity*, 6 (see chap. 10, n.8).

[6] Lester Brown, *Plan B 2.0: Rescuing a Planet under Stress and a Civilization in Trouble* (New York: W.W. Norton, 2006), 49.

[7] Dacher Keltner, *Born to Be Good: The Science of a Meaningful Life* (New York: W.W. Norton, 2009), 8.

[8] John Ydstie, "One Man's Quest to Make Medical Technology Affordable to All," *National Public Radio*, July 3, 2013, http://www.npr.org/blogs/health/2013/07/03/198065436/one-mans-quest-to-make-health-care-accessible-and-affordable.

[9] Susan Riederer, "Carbon Tax Is the Best Market-Based Solution," Boulder Daily Camera, July 3, 2013, http://www.dailycamera.com/guest-opinions/ci_23585394/carbon-tax-is-best-market-based-solution.

[10] The Giving Pledge website, http://givingpledge.org.

BIBLIOGRAPHY

Acuff, Dan. *What Kids Buy and Why: The Psychology of Marketing to Kids.* New York: Free Press, 1997.

Andrews, Cecile. *The Circle of Simplicity: Return to the Good Life.* New York: HarperCollins, 1997.

_____. *Living Room Revolution: A Handbook for Conversation, the Community and the Common Good.* Gabriola Island, BC: New Society, 2013.

_____. *Slow Is Beautiful: New Visions of Community, Leisure and Joie de Vivre.* Gabriola Island, BC: New Society, 2006.

Andrews, Cecile, and Wanda Urbanska. *Less Is More: Embracing Simplicity for a Healthy Planet, a Caring Economy and Lasting Happiness.* Gabriola Island, BC: New Society, 2009.

Anielski, Mark. *The Economics of Happiness: Building Genuine Wealth.* Gabriola Island, BC: New Society, 2007.

AtKisson, Alan. *Believing Cassandra: An Optimist Looks at a Pessimist's World.* White River Juction, VT.: Chelsea Green, 1999.

Baker, Dean. *The United States Since 1980.* New York: Cambridge, 2007.

Barber, Benjamin R. *Consumed: How Markets Corrupt Children, Infantilize Adults, and Swallow Citizens Whole.* New York: W.W. Norton, 2007.

_____. *A Place for Us: How to Make Society Civil and Democracy Strong.* New York: Hill and Wang, 1998.

Barnes, Peter. *Capitalism 3.0: A Guide to Reclaiming the Commons.* San Francisco: Berrett-Koehler, 2006.

Bartlett, Bruce. *The New American Economy: The Failure of Reaganomics and a New Way Forward.* New York: Palgrave Macmillan, 2009.

Bartlett, Donald L., and James B. Steele. *America: What Went Wrong?* Kansas City: Andrews and McNeal, 1992.

Beder, Sharon. *Global Spin: The Corporate Assault on Environmentalism.* White River Junction, VT: Chelsea Green, 1997.

Bellah, Robert N., Richard Madsen, William M. Sullivan, Anne Swidler, and Steven M. Tipton. *The Good Society.* New York: Alfred A. Knopf, 1991.

_____. *Habits of the Heart: Individualism and Commitment in American Life.* Berkeley, CA: University of California Press, 1985.

Berman, Morris. *Why America Failed: The Roots of Imperial Decline.* New York: Wiley, 2012.

Blades, Joan, and Kristin Rowe-Finkbeiner. *The Motherhood Manifesto: What America's Moms Want—and What to Do about It.* New York: Nation Books, 2006.

Blakely, Edward J., and Mary Gail Snyder. *Fortress America: Gated Communities in the United States.* Washington, DC: Brookings Institution, 1997.

Bok, Derek. *The Politics of Happiness: What Government Can Learn from the New Research on Well-Being.* Princeton, NJ: Princeton University Press, 2010.

Boyte, Harry C., and Nancy N. Kari. *Building America: The Democratic Promise of Public Work.* Philadelphia: Temple, 1996.

Brower, Michael, and Warren Leon. *The Consumer's Guide to Effective Environmental Choices: Practical Advice from the Union of Concerned Scientists.* New York: Three Rivers, 1999.

Buettner, Dan. Thrive: *Finding Happiness the Blue Zones Way.* Washington DC: National Geographic, 2010.

Bunting, Madeleine. *Willing Slaves: How the Overwork Culture Is Ruling Our Lives.* London: HarperCollins, 2004.

Celente, Gerald. Trends 2000: *How to Prepare for and Profit from the Changes of the 21st Century.* New York: Warner, 1997.

Chang, Ha-Joon. *23 Things They Don't Tell You about Capitalism.* New York: Bloomsbury, 2010.

Chappell, Tom. *The Soul of a Business: Managing for Profit and the Common Good.* New York: Bantam, 1993.

Childs Jr., James M. *Greed: Economics and Ethics in Conflict.* Minneapolis: Fortress, 2000.

Clapp, Rodney, ed. *The Consuming Passion: Christianity and the Consumer Culture.* Downer's Grove, IL.: Intervarsity, 1998.

Cobb, Clifford, Mark Glickman, and Craig Cheslog. *The Genuine Progress Indicator, 2000 Update.* Oakland, CA: Redefining Progress, 2001.

Cohen, Joel E. *How Many People Can the Earth Support?* New York: W.W. Norton, 1995.

Colburn, Theo, Diane Dumanoski, and John Peterson Myers. *Our Stolen Future: Are We Threatening Our Fertility, Intelligence, and Survival? A Scientific Detective Story.* New York: Dutton, 1996.

Collins, Chuck, and Mary Wright. *The Moral Measure of the Economy.* Maryknoll, NY: Orbis, 2007.

Collins, Robert M. *More: The Politics of Growth in Postwar America.* New York: Oxford, 2000.

Costanza, Robert, John Cumberland, Herman Daly, Robert Goodland, and Richard Norgaard.

An Introduction to Ecological Economics. Boca Raton, FL: St. Lucie, 1997.

Crittenden, Ann. *The Price of Motherhood: Why the Most Important Job in the World Is Still the Least Valued.* New York: Picador, 2010.

Cross, Gary. *An All-Consuming Century: Why Commercialism Won in Modern America.* New York: Columbia University Press, 2000.

Cunningham, Storm. *ReWealth! Stake Your Claim in the $2 Trillion Redevelopment Trend That's Renewing the World.* New York: McGraw-Hill, 2008.

Daly, Herman E. *Steady-State Economics.* Washington, DC: Island Press, 1991.

Daly, Herman, and John B. Cobb Jr. *For the Common Good: Redirecting the Economy toward Community, the Environment, and a Sustainable Future.* Boston: Beacon, 1994.

De Graaf, John. *Take Back Your Time: Fighting Overwork and Time Poverty in America.* San Francisco: Berrett-Koehler, 2003.

De Graaf, John, and David K. Batker. *What's the Economy for, Anyway? Why It's Time to Stop Chasing Growth and Start Pursuing Happiness.* New York: Bloomsbury, 2011.

Devall, Bill. *Living Richly in an Age of Limits: Using Deep Ecology for an Abundant Life.* Salt Lake City: Gibbs Smith, 1993.

DeWitt, Calvin B. *Earth-Wise: A Biblical Response to Environmental Issues.* Grand Rapids, MI: CRC Publications, 1994.

Diener, Ed, Richard Lucas, Ulrich Schimmack, and John Helliwell. *Well-Being for Public Policy.* New York: Oxford University Press, 2009.

Dietz, Rob, and Dan O'Neill. *Enough Is Enough: Building a Sustainable Economy in a World of Finite Resources.* San Francisco: Berrett-Koehler, 2013.

Dlugozima, Hope, James Scott, and David Sharp. *Six Months Off: How to Plan, Negotiate & Take the Break You Need without Burning Bridges or Going Broke.* New York: Henry Holt, 1996.

Dominguez, Joe, and Vicki Robin. *Your Money or Your Life: Transforming Your Relationship with*

Money and Achieving Financial Independence. New York: Viking, 1992.

Durning, Alan. *How Much Is Enough? The Consumer Society and the Future of the Earth.* New York: W.W. Norton, 1992.

Ehrenhalt, Alan. *The Lost City: Discovering the Forgotten Virtues of Community in the Chicago of the 1950s.* New York: Basic Books. 1995.

Elkind, David. *The Hurried Child: Growing Up Too Fast Too Soon.* Reading, MA: Addison-Wesley, 1988.

Ellul, Jacques. *The Technological Society.* New York: Vintage Books, 1964.

Elwood, J. Murray. *Not for Sale: Saving Your Soul and Your Sanity at Work.* Notre Dame, IN: Sorin Books, 2000.

Etzioni, Amitai. *The Spirit of Community: The Reinvention of American Society.* New York: Crown, 1993.

Folbre, Nancy. *The Invisible Heart: Economics and Family Values.* New York: New Press, 2001.

Frank, Robert H. *Luxury Fever: Weighing the Cost of Excess.* New York: Free Press, 1999.

Frank, Thomas. *One Market under God: Extreme Capitalism, Market Populism, and the End of Economic Democracy.* New York: Doubleday, 2000.

_____. *Pity the Billionaire: The Hard-Times Swindle and the Unlikely Comeback of the Right.* New York: Metropolitan Books, 2012.

Fromm, Erich. *The Anatomy of Human Destructiveness.* Greenwich, CT: Fawcett, 1973.

_____. *The Heart of Man: Its Genius for Good and Evil.* New York: Harper & Row, 1964.

_____. *Marx's Concept of Man.* New York: Frederick Ungar, 1971.

_____. *The Sane Society.* New York: Rinehart, 1955.

_____. *To Have or to Be?* New York: Bantam, 1982.

Fukuyama, Francis. *Trust: The Social Virtues and the Creation of Prosperity.* New York: Free Press, 1995.

Galbraith, John Kenneth. *The Affluent Society.* Boston: Houghton Mifflin, 1998.

Geoghegan, Thomas. *Were You Born on the Wrong Continent? How the European Model Can Help You Get a Life.* New York: New Press, 2010.

Gilding, Paul. *The Great Disruption: Why the Climate Crisis Will Bring on the End of Shopping and the Birth of a New World.* New York: Bloomsbury, 2011.

Goldberg, M. Hirsh. *The Complete Book of Greed: The Strange and Amazing History of Human Excess.* New York: William Morrow, 1994.

Goodwin, Neva R., Frank Ackerman, and David Kiron, eds. *The Consumer Society.* Washington, DC: Island Press, 1997.

Garon, Sheldon. *Beyond Our Means: Why America Spends While the World Saves.* Princeton, NJ: Princeton University Press, 2011.

Gore, Al. *Earth in the Balance: Ecology and the Human Spirit.* Boston: Houghton Mifflin, 1992.

Hacker, Jacob S. *The Great Risk Shift: The New Economic Security and the Decline of the American Dream.* New York: Oxford, 2006.

Hawken, Paul. *The Ecology of Commerce: A Declaration of Sustainability.* New York: Harper Business, 1993.

Hawken, Paul, Amory Lovins, and Hunter Lovins. *Natural Capitalism: Creating the Next Industrial Revolution.* Boston: Little, Brown, 1999.

Hayden, Anders. *Sharing the Work, Sparing the Planet: Work, Time, Consumption, and Ecology.* London: Zed Books, 1999.

Hayden, Tom. *Reunion: A Memoir.* New York: Random House, 1988.

Hertsgaard, Mark. *Earth Odyssey: Around the World in Search of Our Environmental Future.* New York: Broadway Books, 1998.

Heymann, Jody, and Alison Earle. *Raising the Global Floor: Dismantling the Myth That We Can't*

Afford Good Working Conditions for Everyone. Stanford, CA: Stanford University Press, 2010.

Hill, Steven. *Europe's Promise: Why the European Way Is the Best Hope in an Insecure Age*. Berkeley, CA: University of California Press, 2009.

Hochschild, Arlie Russell. *The Time Bind: When Work Becomes Home and Home Becomes Work*. New York: Metropolitan, 1997.

Hoffman, Edward. *The Right to Be Human: A Biography of Abraham Maslow*. Wellingborough, UK: Crucible Press, 1989.

The Holy Bible: New International Version.

Hunnicutt, Benjamin Kline. *Free Time: The Forgotten American Dream*. Philadelphia: Temple, 2013.

_____. *Kellogg's Six-Hour Day*. Philadelphia: Temple, 1996.

_____. *Work without End: Abandoning Shorter Hours for the Right to Work*. Philadelphia: Temple, 1988.

Illich, Ivan. *Energy and Equity.* New York: Perennial, 1974.

———. *Shadow Work.* Boston: Marion Boyars, 1981.

———. *Tools for Conviviality.* New York: Harper & Row, 1973.

Ivey, Bill. *Handmaking America: A Back-to-Basics Pathway to a Revitalized American Democracy.* Berkeley, CA: Counterpoint, 2012.

Jackson, Tim. *Prosperity without Growth: Economics for a Finite Planet.* London: Earthscan, 2009.

Jacobson, Michael F., and Laurie Ann Mazur. *Marketing Madness: A Survival Guide for a Consumer Society.* Boulder, CO: Westview, 1995.

Josephson, Eric, and Mary Josephson, eds. *Man Alone: Alienation in Modern Society.* New York: Dell, 1970.

Judt, Tony. *Ill Fares the Land.* New York: Penguin, 2010.

Kelly, Marjorie. *Owning Our Future: The Emerging Ownership Revolution.* San Francisco: Berrett-Koehler, 2012.

Klein, Naomi. *No Logo.* New York: HarperCollins, 2000.

Korten, David C. *When Corporations Rule the World.* West Hartford, CT: Kumarian, 1995.

Lafargue, Paul. *The Right to Be Lazy.* Chicago: Charles Kerr, 1989.

Lanchester, John. *Whoops! Why Everyone Owes Everyone and No One Can Pay.* London: Penguin, 2010.

Lane, Robert E. *The Loss of Happiness in Market Democracies.* New Haven, CT: Yale University Press, 2000.

Lasch, Christopher. *The Culture of Narcissism: American Life in an Age of Diminishing Expectations.* New York, W.W. Norton, 1978.

———. *The Minimal Self: Psychic Survival in Troubled Times.* New York, W.W. Norton, 1984.

———. *The Revolt of the Elites and the Betrayal of Democracy.* New York: W.W. Norton, 1995.

———. *The True and Only Heaven: Progress and Its Critics.* New York, W.W. Norton, 1991.

Lasn, Kalle. *Culture Jam: The Uncooling of America.* New York: Eagle Brook, 1999.

Layard, Richard. *Happiness: Lessons from a New Science.* New York: Penguin, 2005.

Lerner, Michael. *The Politics of Meaning: Restoring Hope and Possibility in an Age of Cynicism.* Reading, MA: Addison-Wesley, 1996.

Levering, Frank, and Wanda Urbanska. *Simple Living: One Couple's Search for a Better Life.* New York: Viking, 1992.

Levine, Madeline. *The Price of Privilege: How Parental Pressure and Material Advantage Are Creating a Generation of Disconnected and Unhappy Kids.* New York: HarperCollins, 2006.

Linden, Eugene. *The Future in Plain Sight: Nine Clues to the Coming Instability.* New York: Simon & Schuster, 1998.

Linder, Staffan Burenstam. *The Harried Leisure Class.* New York: Columbia, 1970.

Louv, Richard. *Childhood's Future.* New York: Houghton Mifflin, 1990.

_____. *The Web of Life: Weaving the Values That Sustain Us.* Berkeley, CA: Conari Press, 1996.

Luttwak, Edward. *Turbo-Capitalism: Winners and Losers in the Global Economy.* New York: Harper-Collins, 1999.

Mack, Burton L. *The Lost Gospel: The Book of Q and Christian Origins.* San Francisco: Harper San Francisco, 1993.

_____. *Who Wrote the New Testament? The Making of the Christian Myth.* San Francisco: Harper San Francisco, 1995.

Macy, Joanna, and Molly Young Brown. *Coming Back to Life: Practices to Reconnect Our Lives, Our World.* Gabriola Island, BC: New Society, 1998.

Madrick, Jeff. *Age of Greed: The Triumph of Finance and the Decline of America, 1970 to the Present.* New York: Alfred A. Knopf, 2011.

Marchand, Roland. *Advertising the American Dream: Making Way for Modernity, 1920–1940*. Berkeley, CA: University of California Press, 1985.

Marcuse, Herbert. *An Essay on Liberation*. Boston: Beacon, 1969.

_____. *One-Dimensional Man*. Boston: Beacon, 1964.

Martineau, Pierre. *Motivation in Advertising: Motives That Make People Buy*. New York: McGraw-Hill, 1971.

Marx, Karl. *Capital: A Critique of Political Economy, Volume III*. Edited by Friedrich Engels. New York: Modern Library, 1906.

_____. *Economic and Philosophical Manuscripts of 1844*. Moscow: Progress, 1974.

Marx, Karl, and Friedrich Engels. *Basic Writings on Politics and Philosophy*. Edited by Lewis S. Feuer. Garden City, NY: Anchor Books, 1959.

McCarthy, Eugene, and William McGaughey. *Nonfinancial Economics: The Case for Shorter Hours of Work*. New York: Praeger, 1989.

McElvaine, Robert S. *What's Left? A New Democratic Vision for America.* Holbrook, MA: Adams Media, 1996.

McKenzie-Mohr, Doug, and William Smith. *Fostering Sustainable Behavior: An Introduction to Community-Based Social Marketing.* Gabriola Island, BC: New Society, 1999.

McKenzie, Richard B. *The Paradox of Progress: Can Americans Regain Their Confidence in a Prosperous Future?* New York: Oxford University Press, 1997.

McKibben, Bill. *The Age of Missing Information.* New York: Random House, 1992.

_____. *The Comforting Whirlwind: God, Job, and the Scale of Creation.* Grand Rapids, MI: Eerdmans, 1994.

_____. *Deep Economy: The Wealth of Communities and the Durable Future.* New York: Times Books, 2007.

_____. *Hope, Human and Wild: True Stories of Living Lightly on the Earth.* New York: Little, Brown, 1995.

McNeal, James U. *Kids as Customers: A Handbook of Marketing to Children.* New York: Lexington, 1992.

Meadows, Donella H., Dennis Meadows, and Jørgen Randers. *Beyond the Limits: Confronting Global Collapse, Envisioning a Sustainable Future.* Post Mills, VT: Chelsea Green, 1992.

Meyer, Dick. *Why We Hate Us: American Discontent in the New Millennium.* New York: Random House, 2008.

Mick, David Glen, Simone Pettigrew, Cornelia Pechmann, and Julie L. Ozanne, eds. *Transformative Consumer Research for Personal and Collective Well-Being.* New York: Routledge, 2012.

Miller, Perry, ed. *The American Transcendentalists: Their Prose and Poetry.* Garden City, NY: Anchor Books, 1957.

Molnar, Alex. *Giving Kids the Business: The Commercialization of America's Schools.* New York: Westview, 1996.

Morton, A.L., ed. *Political Writings of William Morris.* New York: International, 1973.

Myers, David. *The American Paradox: Spiritual Hunger in an Age of Plenty.* New Haven, CT: Yale University Press, 2000.

Nabhan, Gary Paul, and Stephen Trimble. *The Geography of Childhood: Why Children Need Wild Places.* Boston: Beacon, 1994.

National Conference of Catholic Bishops. *Economic Justice for All: Pastoral Letter on Catholic Social Teaching and the U.S. Economy.* Washington, DC: U.S. Catholic Conference, 1986.

Naylor, Thomas H, and William H. Willimon. *Downsizing the USA.* Grand Rapids, MI: Eerdmans, 1997.

Naylor, Thomas H., William H. Willimon, and Rolf V. Ostenberg. *The Search for Meaning in the Workplace.* Nashville, TN: Abingdon, 1996.

Needleman, Jacob. *Money and the Meaning of Life.* New York: Doubleday Currency, 1991.

New Road Map Foundation in partnership with Northwest Environment Watch. *All-Consuming Passion: Waking Up from the American Dream.* Seattle: New Road Map Foundation, 1998.

The New York Times. *The Downsizing of America.* New York: Times Books, 1996.

Northwest Earth Institute. *Discussion Course on Deep Ecology.* Portland, OR: Northwest Earth Institute, 1998.

Northwest Earth Institute. *Discussion Course on Voluntary Simplicity.* Portland, OR: Northwest Earth Institute, 1997.

O'Connell, Brian. Civil Society: *The Underpinnings of American Democracy.* Hanover, NH: Tufts University Press, 1999.

O'Hara, Bruce. *Working Harder Isn't Working.* Vancouver, BC: New Star, 1993.

Oldenburg, Ray. *The Great Good Place: Cafés, Coffee Shops, Community Centers, Beauty Parlors, General Stores, Bars, Hangouts, and How They Get You Through the Day.* New York: Paragon House, 1991.

Olds, Jacqueline, and Richard S. Schwartz. *The Lonely American.* Boston: Beacon, 2009.

O'Neill, Jessie H. *The Golden Ghetto: The Psychology of Affluence.* Center City, MN: Hazelden, 1997.

Oppenheim, James. *The Nine-Tenths: A Novel.* New York: Harper & Brothers, 1911.

Packard, Vance. *The Hidden Persuaders.* New York: Pocket, 1973.

_____. *The Status Seekers.* New York: Pelican, 1961.

_____. *The Waste Makers.* New York: McKay, 1960.

Perucci, Robert, and Earl Wysong. *The New Class Society: Goodbye American Dream?* Lanham, MD: Rowman & Littlefield, 1999.

Phillips, Kevin. *The Politics of Rich and Poor: Wealth and the American Electorate in the Reagan Aftermath.* New York: Random House, 1990.

Postel, Sandra. *Dividing the Waters: Food Security, Ecosystem Health, and the New Politics of Scarcity.* Vol.132 of Worldwatch Paper. Washington, DC: Worldwatch Institute, 1996.

Postman, Neil. *Amusing Ourselves to Death: Public Discourse in the Age of Show Business.* New York: Viking, 1986.

_____. *Conscientious Objections: Stirring Up Trouble about Language, Technology and Education.* New York: Vintage Books, 1988.

Putnam, Robert D. *Bowling Alone: The Collapse and Revival of American Community.* New York: Simon & Schuster, 2000.

Rampton, Sheldon, and John Stauber. *Trust Us, We're Experts! How Industry Manipulates Science and Gambles with Your Future.* New York: Jeremy P. Tarcher, 2001.

Rath, Tom, and Jim Harter. *Well-Being: The Five Essential Elements.* New York: Gallup, 20210.

Rifkin, Jeremy. *The Age of Access: The New Culture of Hypercapitalism, Where All of Life Is a Paidfor Experience.* New York: Jeremy P. Tarcher, 2000.

_____. *The Empathic Civilization: The Race to Global Consciousness in a World in Crisis.* New York: Jeremy P. Tarcher, 2009.

_____. *The End of Work: The Decline of the Global Labor Force and the Dawn of the Post-Market Era.* New York: Jeremy P. Tarcher, 1995.

———. *Time Wars: The Primary Conflict in Human History*. New York: Simon & Schuster, 1987.

Robbins, John. *Diet for a New America: How Your Food Choices Affect Your Health, Happiness, and the Future of Life on Earth*. Tiburon, CA: H.J. Kramer, 1998.

Robbins, Ocean, and Sol Solomon. *Choices for Our Future: A Generation Rising for Life on Earth*. Summertown, TN: The Book Publishing Company, 1994.

Robinson, Joe. *Don't Miss Your Life: Find More Joy and Fulfillment Now*. New York: Wiley, 2011.

Röpke, Wilhelm. *A Humane Economy: The Social Framework of the Free Market*. Indianapolis: Liberty Fund, 1971.

Rosenblatt, Roger, ed. *Consuming Desires: Consumption, Culture, and the Pursuit of Happiness*. Washington, DC: Island Press, 1999.

Rubin, Lillian B. *Families on the Fault Line: America's Working Class Speaks about the Family, the Economy, Race, and Ethnicity*. New York: Harper Perennial, 1994.

Ryan, John C. *Seven Wonders: Everyday Things for a Healthier Planet.* San Francisco: Sierra Club Books, 1999.

Ryan, John C., and Alan Thein Durning. *Stuff: The Secret Lives of Everyday Things.* Seattle: Northwest Environment Watch, 1997.

Rybczynski, Witold. *Waiting for the Weekend.* New York: Viking, 1991.

Sachs, Jeffrey D. *Common Wealth Economics for a Crowded Planet.* New York: Penguin, 2008.

Sakaiya, Taichi. *The Knowledge-Value Revolution; or, a History of the Future.* Translated by George Fields and William Marsh. New York: Kodansha America, 1991.

Saltzman, Amy. *Downshifting: Reinventing Success on a Slower Track.* New York: HarperCollins, 1991.

Sanders, Barry. *A Is for Ox: The Collapse of Literacy and the Rise of Violence in an Electronic Age.* New York: Pantheon, 1994.

Schleuning, Neala. *Idle Hands and Empty Hearts: Work and Freedom in the United States.* New York: Bergin & Garvey, 1990.

Schlosser, Eric. *Fast Food Nation: The Dark Side of the All-American Meal.* Boston: Houghton Mifflin, 2001.

Schor, Juliet B. *Born to Buy: The Commercialized Child and the New Consumer Culture.* New York: Simon & Schuster, 2004.

_____. *The Overspent American: Why We Want What We Don't Need.* New York: Basic Books, 1998.

_____. *The Overworked American: The Unexpected Decline of Leisure.* New York: Basic Books, 1992.

_____. *Plenitude: The New Economics of True Wealth.* New York: Penguin, 2010.

Segal, Jerome M. *Graceful Simplicity: The Philosophy and Politics of the Alternative American Dream.* New York: Henry Holt, 1999.

Seiter, Ellen. *Sold Separately: Children and Parents in Consumer Culture.* New Brunswick, NJ: Rutgers University Press, 1995.

Sessions, George, ed. *Deep Ecology for the 21st Century.* Boston: Shambala Press, 1995.

Sessions, Robert. *Becoming Real: Authenticity in an Age of Distractions.* North Liberty, IA: Ice Cube, 2011.

Shames, Laurence. *The Hunger for More: Searching for Values in an Age of Greed.* New York: Times Books, 1989.

Shi, David E. *The Simple Life: Plain Living and High Thinking in American Culture.* New York: Oxford University Press, 1985.

Shorris, Earl. *A Nation of Salesmen: The Tyranny of the Market and the Subversion of Culture.* New York: Avon, 1994.

Shrady, Nicholas. *Sacred Roads: Adventures from the Pilgrimage Trail.* San Francisco: Harper San Francisco, 1999.

Slater, Philip. *The Pursuit of Loneliness: American Culture at the Breaking Point.* Boston: Beacon Press, 1970.

Sobel, David. *Beyond Ecophobia: Reclaiming the Heart in Nature Education.* Great Barrington, MA: Orion Society and Myrin Institute, 1996.

Speth, James Gustave. *America the Possible: Manifesto for a New Economy.* New Haven, CT: Yale University Press, 2012.

Steingraber, Sandra. *Living Downstream: An Ecologist Looks at Cancer and the Environment.* Reading, MA: Addison-Wesley, 1997.

Stiglitz, Joseph. *Freefall.* New York: W.W. Norton, 2010.

Strasser, Susan. *Satisfaction Guaranteed: The Making of the American Mass Market.* New York: Pantheon, 1989.

Suzuki, David. *Earth Time: Essays.* Toronto: Stoddart, 1998.

Swenson, Richard A. *Margin: Restoring Emotional, Physical, Financial, and Time Reserves to Overloaded Lives.* Colorado Springs: Navpress, 1992.

———. *The Overload Syndrome: Learning to Live Within Your Limits.* Colorado Springs: Navpress, 1998.

Thompson, William Irwin. *The American Replacement of Nature: The Everyday Acts and Outrageous Evolution of Economic Life.* New York: Doubleday Currency, 1991.

Thurow, Lester C. *The Future of Capitalism: How Today's Economic Forces Shape Tomorrow's World.* New York: Penguin, 1996.

Twitchell, James. *Adcult USA: The Triumph of Advertising in American Culture.* New York: Columbia University Press, 1996.

Wachtel, Paul L. *The Poverty of Affluence: A Psychological Portrait on the American Way of Life.* New York: Free Press, 1983.

Wallis, Jim. *The Soul of Politics: A Practical and Prophetic Vision for Change.* New York: New Press, 1994.

Walsh, David. *Designer Kids: Consumerism and Competition—When Is It All Too Much?* Minneapolis: Deaconess, 1990.

_____. *Selling Out America's Children: How America Puts Profits before Values—and What Parents Can Do.* Minneapolis: Fairview, 1995.

Wann, David. *The New Normal: An Agenda for Responsible Living.* New York: St. Martin's, 2011.

_____. *Simple Prosperity: Finding Real Wealth in a Sustainable Lifestyle.* New York: St. Martin's, 2007.

Weil, Andrew. *Eating Well for Optimum Health: The Essential Guide to Bringing Health and Pleasure Back to Eating.* New York: Alfred A. Knopf, 2000.

Weil, Michelle M., and Larry D. Rosen. *TechnoStress: Coping with Technology @Work @Home @Play.* New York: John Wiley, 1997.

Wilkinson, Richard, and Kate Pickett. *The Spirit Level: Why Greater Equality Makes Societies Stronger.* New York: Bloomsbury, 2009.

Williams, Terry Tempest. *Leap.* New York: Pantheon, 2000.

_____. *Refuge: An Unnatural History of Family and Place.* New York: Vintage Books, 1991.

Willimon, William H., and Thomas H. Naylor. *The Abandoned Generation: Rethinking Higher Education.* Grand Rapids, MI: Eerdmans, 1995.

The Worldwatch Institute. *State of the World.* 19 vols. (by year). New York: W.W. Norton, 1995–2013.

The Worldwatch Institute. *Vital Signs.* 6 vols. (by year). New York: W.W. Norton, 1995–2000.

Zablocki, Benjamin. *The Joyful Community: An Account of the Bruderhof, a Communal Movement Now in Its Third Generation.* University of Chicago Press, 1980.

ABOUT THE AUTHORS

JOHN DE GRAAF is a documentary filmmaker who has produced more than a dozen national PBS specials, including *Affluenza*. He is the co-author of *What's the Economy for, Anyway? Why It's Time to Stop Chasing Growth and Start Pursuing Happiness*, and editor of *Take Back Your Time*. He is the Executive Director of Take Back Your Time, co-founder of The Happiness Alliance, Senior Well-Being Advisor for Earth Economics and a member of the Earth Island Institute board of directors. He has taught at The Evergreen State College and lives in Seattle, Washington.

DAVID WANN is the author of ten books and a speaker on sustainable lifestyles and designs. He has produced twenty-five documentaries, several of them award winners. He is president of the Sustainable Futures Society and a designer of the cohousing neighborhood he has lived in for seventeen years, where he coordinates the community garden. He's now at work on a book of essays called *Letters to the Future*.

THOMAS NAYLOR is professor emeritus of economics at Duke University, where he taught for thirty years. He has also taught at Middlebury College. He is a writer and social critic and has consulted with governments and major corporations in more than thirty countries. In 1993 he moved to Charlotte, Vermont, where he writes about the search for meaning and community and for simplifying all aspects of our lives His articles have been published in the *New York Times*, the *International Herald Tribune*, the *Los Angeles Times*, the *Boston Globe*, the *Christian Science Monitor*, the *Nation*, and *Business Week*. He has appeared on ABC, CBS, CNN, NPR, and the CBC. He is the author or co-author of thirty books.

Berrett–Koehler Publishers

Berrett-Koehler is an independent publisher dedicated to an ambitious mission: *Creating a World That Works for All.*

We believe that to truly create a better world, action is needed at all levels—individual, organizational, and societal. At the individual level, our publications help people align their lives with their values and with their aspirations for a better world. At the organizational level, our publications promote progressive leadership and management practices, socially responsible approaches to business, and humane and effective organizations. At the societal level, our publications advance social and economic justice, shared prosperity, sustainability, and new solutions to national and global issues.

A major theme of our publications is "Opening Up New Space." Berrett-Koehler titles challenge conventional thinking, introduce new ideas, and foster positive change. Their common quest is changing the underlying beliefs, mindsets, institutions, and structures that keep generating the same cycles of problems, no matter who our leaders are or what improvement programs we adopt.

We strive to practice what we preach—to operate our publishing company in line with the ideas in our books. At the core of our approach is stewardship, which we define as a deep sense of responsibility to administer the company for the benefit of all of our "stakeholder" groups: authors, customers, employees, investors, service providers, and the communities and environment around us.

We are grateful to the thousands of readers, authors, and other friends of the company who consider themselves to be part of the "BK Community." We hope that you, too, will join us in our mission.

A BK Currents Book

This book is part of our BK Currents series. BK Currents books advance social and economic justice by exploring the critical intersections between business and society. Offering a unique combination of thoughtful analysis and progressive alternatives, BK Currents books promote positive change at the national and global levels. To find out more, visit www.bkconnection.com.

Berrett–Koehler Publishers
A community dedicated to creating a world that works for all

Dear Reader,

Thank you for picking up this book and joining our worldwide community of Berrett-Koehler readers. We share ideas that bring positive change into people's lives, organizations, and society.

To welcome you, we'd like to offer you a free e-book. You can pick from among twelve of our bestselling books by entering the promotional code BKP92E here: http://www.bkconnection.com/welcome.

When you claim your free e-book, we'll also send you a copy of our e-newsletter, the *BK Communiqué*. Although you're free to unsubscribe, there are many benefits to sticking around. In every you'll find

- A free e-book
- Tips form famous authors
- Discounts on spotlight titles
- Hilarious insider publishing news
- A chance to win a prize for answering a riddle

Best of all, our readers tell us, "Your newsletter is the only one I actually read." So claim your gift today, and please stay in touch!

Sincerely,

Charlotte Ashlock
Steward of the BK Website

Questions? Comments? Contact me at bkcommunity@bkpub.com.

Index

A

1 percenters,
    See wealthiest,
    1 percent,
3 EStrategies, *360*
30-40 now work plan, *334*
1984, *243*
abortion, effect on crime rates, *109*
acquisitive society, *95*
activity-limiting diseases, U.S. ranking, *151*
Adams, John, *180*
Adbusters, *319*
addictions,
    accumulating things, *27*
    See also hoarding,
    alcohol, *25*
    coffee, *23*
    gambling, *25*
    generosity, *163*
    illegal drugs, *25*
    pathological buying, *29*
    psychology of, *29*
    shopping, *25*
    similarities among, *29*
    social factors, *27*
    tobacco, *25*
adolescent pregnancy, U.S. ranking, *151*
advertisements,
    See also commercialism; marketing; television advertisements,
    anti-ads, *319, 321*
    billboards, *223*
    brand recognition, *223*
    Internet, *226*
    media literacy, *323*
    outdoor, *223*
    over the phone, *226*
    placement, *223, 226*
    protection from, *63, 65, 323*
    in schools, *67*
    telemarketing, *226*
    ubiquity of, *223*
    uncommercials, *319, 321*

advertising,
See also PR (public relations),
   Buy Nothing Day, *321, 322*
   hypercommercialism, *226*
   purpose of, *221*
   resistance to, *319, 321*
affluence, history of, *15*
affluenza,
   beginnings of, *169*
   conservatives vs. liberals, *95*
   curing, *260, 263, 265, 268*
   downshifters, *268*
   Patient Zero, *169*
   a self test, *252, 256*
   vaccinating children against, *323, 326, 328*
Affluenza (film),
   causes of gang violence, *109*
Agassi, Andre, *226*
AIDS, U.S. ranking, *151*
air travel,
   baggage, *38*
   trends, *38*
AirBnB, *309*

alcohol, addiction to, *25*
Alliance for Sustainability and Prosperity (website), *374*
Alone Together, *75, 78*
aluminum cans, recycling, *385*
Amador County, CA, *336, 338, 340*
Amazon, *79*
American Mania, *326*
American Revolution, *180, 182*
Andrews, Cecile, *271, 273, 277, 279*
Andrews, Paul, *19*
anti-ads, *319, 321*
anti-consumerism,
   See simplifying your life,
anti-smoking advertisements, *319, 321*
antidepressants, U.S. consumption of, *147*
antimaterialism,
   law of progressive simplification, *280*
   living off the grid, *265*

resisting consumerism, *321, 322*
techniques for, *279, 280*
ultra-small houses, *265*
World War II era, *214, 216*
antisocial behavior in pursuit of a product, *65, 67*
apodments, *265*
aquatic gyres, *142*
Aristotle, *175*
articles,
    See books and publications,
Atwater, Lee, *89*
automobiles,
    See cars,
autonomous cars, *36*
A Humane Economy: The Social Framework of the Free Market, *95*

B

baggage, air travel, *38*
Bangladesh textile factory fire (2013), *101*
banking,
credit default swaps, *230*
credit unions vs. banks, *301*
derivatives, *230*
financial collapse of 2008, *228, 230, 231*
Glass-Steagal Act, *230, 231*
in a new economy, *301, 303*
Barnes & Noble, *79*
Bartolini, Stefano, *23*
Beavan, Colin, *265, 268*
Beck, Glenn, *326*
bees, mass death of, *282, 284*
Begley, Ed, Jr., *326*
Bernays, Edward, *241*
Beverly Cooperative Bank, *301*
Beyond Ecophobia, *293*
Beyond Our Means: Why America Spends While the World Saves, *23*
Beyond the Limits, *153*
Beyond the Purchase (website), *328*

Bhutan, happiness rating, *363, 366, 367, 374*
bicycles, sharing, *311*
big-box stores, See chain stores,
bigwigs, *180*
billboards, *223*
Bingham Canyon Mine, *122*
Blackwell, Lucien, *333*
Blake, William, *180*
Blakely, Edward, *81*
Blanchard, Chuck and Joy, *205*
Bloomberg, Michael, *311*
Boe, Vivia, *252*
Boesky, Ivan, *221, 230*
book stores, chain stores, *79*
books and publications
    1984, *243*
    Adbusters, *319*
    The Age of Missing Information, *291*
    Alone Together, *75, 78*
    American Mania, *326*
    Beyond Ecophobia, *293*
    Beyond Our Means: Why America Spends While the World Saves, *23*
    Beyond the Limits, *153*
    Born to Buy, *63*
    'Bread and Roses', *196*
    Catholic Charities Review, *198, 200*
    The Circle of Simplicity, *273*
    Coming Back to Life, *380*
    Coming Home, *363*
    Common Sense, *299*
    The Communist Manifesto, *182*
    Consuming Kids, *63*
    Culture Jam, *317, 319*
    The Economic and Philosophical Manuscripts of 1844, *184*
    The End of Nature, *127*
    The End of Patience, *46*
    Flow, *158*
    Fortress America, *81*
    Free Time, *198*

The Future: Six Drivers of Global Change, *237*
Genetic Roulette, *144*
The Geography of Nowhere, *74*
The Greening of America, *216*
Grist, *116*
The Hidden Persuaders, *216*
A Humane Economy: The Social Framework of the Free Market, *95*
Kellogg's Six-Hour Day, *205*
The Ladies Home Journal, *194*
Last Child in the Woods, *284*
Life without Principle, *187*
Living Downstream, *135*
The Lonely American, *54*
'Love Global Warming', *239*
Luxury Fever, *346*
Marketing Madness, *223*
Motivation in Advertising, *221*
Natural Capitalism, *118, 348*
The New Normal, *38*
Nickel and Dimed, *107*
The Nine Tenths, *194, 196*
Our Stolen Future, *142*
Owning the Future, *301*
The Paradox of Choice, *46*
Port Huron Statement, *93*
Prodigal Sons and Material Girls: How Not to Be Your Child's ATM, *323*
Rerum Novarum, *198, 346*
'The Right to Be Lazy', *192*
Satisfaction Guaranteed, *209, 210*
Selling Out America's Children, *63*

The Simple Life, *175, 194*
The Spirit Level, *111*
The Status Seekers, *216*
'The Road Not Taken', *190*
This Ugly Civilization, *200, 201*
Toxic Deception, *137*
Toxic Sludge is Good for You, *235*
Turbo-Capitalism, *70*
Voluntary Simplicity, *271, 279*
Walden, *187*
The Waste Makers, *216*
The Wealth of Nations, *299*
'The Welfare of Children in Rich Countries', *59*
When Corporations Rule the World, *111*
Whoops!, *230*
Work Without End, *198*
Working, *93*
Your Money or Your Life, *260, 354, 355*
boredom among children, *59*
Born to Buy, *63*
Borsodi, Ralph, *200, 201, 203*
bottled water, *140*
Boyte, Harry, *88*
brain,
    examining under MRI, *163*
    nucleus accumbens, *160*
    reward center, *160*
Brancacio, David, *334*
brand recognition, *223*
'Bread and Roses', *196*
Bread and Roses Strike, *196*
Bretton Woods Agreement of 1944, *374*
Broder, David, *107*
Brower, David, *3*
Brown, Kirk Warren, *268*
Brown, Lester, *124*
Brune, Michael, *127*
Buffett, Warren, *306, 309, 389*

Bullitt Center, *313*
bumblebees, mass death of, *282, 284*
Bush, George W.,
    Do Not Call legislation, *226*
    working hours, *336*
Bushmen of the Kalahari, *112*
Buy Nothing Day, *321, 322*

C

caffeine in the water supply, *140*
campaign finance reform, *350*
Canadian Index of Well-Being, *374*
Cancer Alley, *109*
carbon taxes, *348*
carcinogens, environmental, *135, 137*
cars,
    annual model change, *210*
    autonomous, *36*
    driving rates, *21*
    non-drivers, *74*
    self-driving, *36*
    sharing, *309, 311*
    size trends, *17*
    traffic, *36*
Carter, Jimmy, *217*
Carver, Thomas Nixon, *200*
Cashman, Kate, *68*
Catholic Charities Review, *198, 200*
CCC (Civilian Conservation Corps), *88*
Celente, Gerald, *109*
cell phones,
    being buried with, *84*
    role in community, *78*
cement industry, CO_2 emissions, *313*
Center for a New American Dream (website), *268*
CEO compensation,
    See also wages,
    Disney, *107*
    Eisner, Michael, *107*
    Exxon, *127*
    Nike, *105*
    Parker, Mike, *105*
    Tillerson, Rex, *127*

vs. worker compensation, *105, 107*
chain stores,
   See also malls; shopping centers; specific stores,
   book stores, *79*
   coffee shops, *79*
   divider effect, *79*
   home improvement, *79*
   localization of food industry, *84*
   loss of locally-owned shops, *78, 79*
   resistance campaign, *79, 84*
   restaurants, *79*
charitable contributions by the wealthiest 1 percent, *103, 389*
chemicals,
   See also drugs; GMOs (genetically engineered organisms),
   in bottled water, *140*
   caffeine in the water supply, *140*
   dead zones, *140*
   environmental carcinogens, *135, 137*
   formaldehyde, *137*
   orphan molecules, *140*
   rate of discovery, *137*
   the Starbucks effect, *140*
   synthetic, *135*
   toxic house, *137*
   toxicity, *135*
Chevy Suburban, *17*
Chiaramonte, Loan, *61*
child welfare, worldwide rankings, *59*
childbirth leave, *334, 336*
children,
   antisocial behavior in pursuit of a product, *65, 67*
   boredom, *59*
   depression, *68*
   effects of television, *63*
   exposure to PCBs (polychlorinated biphenyls), *142*
   marketing to, *61, 63, 65, 67, 348, 350*
   mental health, *67, 68, 70*

protecting from commercialism, *63, 65*
self-centeredness, *70*
spending by, *61, 63*
suicidal thoughts, *68*
values held by, *68, 70*
choice, effect on anxiety, *46*
church attendance vs. mall attendance, *7*
Citi Bike program, *311*
Citizens United (Supreme Court decision), *350*
civil disobedience, See nonviolent civil disobedience,
Civilian Conservation Corps (CCC), *88*
classless society, *107, 109*
climate change,
    average planetary temperature, *127*
    cement industry, CO2 emissions, *313*
    denying, *239*
    effects on insurance industry, *118*
clinical depression, See depression,
clutter, sources of, *39*
coffee, addiction to, *23*
coffee shops, chain stores, *79*
cohousing, *315*
Colburn, Theo, *142*
Collins, Judy, *196*
Colman, Ronald, *362*
Coming Back to Life, *380*
Coming Home, *363*
commercialism
    protecting children from, *63, 65*
    in schools, *67*
Common Sense, *299*
community,
    duties and obligations, *74*
    fraternal organizations, *75*
    gated communities, *81, 84*
    great good places, *74*
    isolation, *74, 75, 78, 81, 84*
    loss of locally-owned shops, *78, 79*
    See also chain stores,
    role of cell phones, *78*

safety, *84*
social capital, *74, 75*
third places, *74*
compulsive buyers, mental states, *25*
conservatives vs. liberals, on affluenza, *95*
conspicuous consumption, role of department stores, *194*
Consumer Jungle (website), *323*
consumer loans, World War II era, *209, 210*
consumer spending, as percentage of overall economy, *7*
   See also shopping, consumerism,
     education, *323*
     resisting, *321, 322*
     World War II era, *209*
Consuming Kids, *63*
consumption,
   conspicuous, role of department stores, *194*
   definition, *190*
   European attitudes vs. American, *43*

Coontz, Stephanie, *57*
cooperative investing, *309*
copper, mining, *122*
Corrections Corporation of America, *111*
Costanza, Robert, *374*
credit default swaps, *230*
credit unions vs. banks, *301*
crime rates,
   effects of abortion, *109*
   imprisonment in the United States, *109*
crowdfunding, *309*
crowdsourcing, *309*
Csikszentmihalyi, Mihaly, *158*
Culture Jam, *317, 319*
curing affluenza,
   admitting the problem, *378, 380*
   campaign finance reform, *350*
   downshifting, *265, 268*
   fighting consumerism, *321, 322*

flexible work schedules, *333, 334*
key actions, *330, 333*
maternity leave, *334, 336*
maximum wage, *346* See also minimum wage,
new lifestyle paradigm, *380, 383, 385*
reducing spending, *260, 263*
single-payer health care, *341*
standardizing work hours, *333*
taxation, *348*
time protections, *334*
curing affluenza, work reduction,
    30-40 now plan, *334*
    childbirth leave, *334, 336*
    forty-hour week, *333*
    four-day week, *336, 338, 340*
    graduated retirement, *343*
    limiting overtime, *334, 336*
    paid sick leave, *334, 336*
    six-hour day, *333*
    thirty-hour week, *333*
    thirty-two-hour week, *333*
    time off for family illness, *336*
    time protections, *334*
    U.S. ranking, *334, 336*
    work reduction, *336, 338, 340, 341*
    work sharing, *336, 338, 340, 341, 343*
Cynic tradition, *175*

D

Daly, Herman, *370*
dead zones in the oceans, *140*
debt crisis, The Story of Broke (video), *326*
DeChristopher, Tim, *126, 127*
department stores, role in conspicuous consumption, *194*
depletion taxes, *348*

depression (clinical),
   among children, *68*
   rates of, in the United States, *75*
depression (economic), *203*
   See also Great Recession,
derivatives, *230*
development paradigm, *367*
development vs. growth, *370*
Disney, CEO compensation, *107*
divider effect, *79*
divorce rates, *59, 151*
Do Not Call legislation, *226*
Doherty, William, *57*
domestic servants, *107, 109*
Dominguez, Joe, *260, 263*
downshifting, *265, 268*
drilling for oil and gas,
   nonviolent civil disobedience, *126*
   See also fracking (Hydraulic Fracturing),
drug use, U.S. ranking, *151*
drugs (illegal), addiction to, *25*
drugs (prescription),
   antidepressants, U.S. consumption of, *147*
   deaths from, *150*
   sleep aids, *147*
Dubai Mall, *11*
Dungan, Nathan, *323*
Dunkin' Donuts, *79*
Durning, Alan, *160*

E

Earle, Alison, *50*
Earth, compressed time line of, *3, 5, 7*
Earth Day, *217*
Easterlin Paradox, *370*
Ebell, Myron, *239*
ecological footprint,
   for the average person, *118*
   definition, *118*
   in market analysis, *362, 363*
   reducing, *265*

vs. ecological handprint, *328, 329*
ecological handprint, *328, 329*
economy,
  collapse of, See depression (economic); Great Recession,
  community-based, *301, 303, 305, 306*
  cooperative investing, *309*
  crowdfunding, *309*
  crowdsourcing, *309*
  leasing vs. owning, *306, 309, 311*
  local living economies, *305, 306*
  postconsumer disruption, *350, 352*
  shaping for affordability, *385, 388*
  sharing-based, *306, 309, 311*
  sustainability, *301, 303*
ecophobia, *293*
Ehrenreich, Barbara, *107, 109*
eight-hour day, *198*
Eisenhower, Dwight D., *212*
Eisner, Michael, CEO compensation, *107*
Elgin, Duane, *271, 279*
energy companies, federal subsidies, *127*
Engels, Friedrich, *182, 186*
(En)Rich List, *322, 323*
ethics among low-income youths, *109*
  See also morality; values,
Europe, attitudes towards consumption, *43*
European Union, productivity, *53*
expenses, cutting, *260, 263, 265, 268*
extended producer responsibility, *124, 311, 313, 348*
extinctions,
  See species extinctions,
Exxon, CEO compensation, *127*

F

Faber, Ronald, *25, 29*
FAIR (Fairness and Accuracy in Reporting), *245*
Fair Labor Standards Act, *198*
family life,
    child welfare, worldwide rankings, *59*
    divorce rates, *59*
    marriage rates, *59*
    solitary living, *59*
    television and exposure to advertisements, *57*
    time pressures and strain on marriages, *57, 59*
    time spent together, *57*
    unmarried parents, *59*
family values,
    held by children, *68, 70*
    vs. market values, *70*
farm land, demand for, *124*
farmer assurance provision, *237*
federal subsidies, energy companies, *127*
financial collapse of 2008, *228, 230, 231*
    See also Great Recession,
First, Fred, *284*
five-day week, *203*
flexible work schedules, *333, 334*
Flow, *158*
flying,
    See air travel,
food,
    insects as food source, *126*
    trends, *17, 19*
food industry, localization, *84*
food insecurity, *103*
    See also hunger,
Ford, Gerald, *217*
Ford, Henry, *209, 210*
Ford, William, *17*
Ford Excursion, *17*
formaldehyde, *137*
forms of capital, *367*
Fortress America, *81*

forty-hour week, *198, 205, 333*
Forward on Climate rally, *127*
four-day week, *336, 338, 340*
Fox, Josh, *246*
fracking (Hydraulic Fracturing), *245, 246*
franchises,
   See chain stores,
Francis, Pope, *89, 91*
Frank, Robert, *29, 346*
Frankenfood,
   See GMOs (genetically engineered organisms),
Franklin, Benjamin, *180*
fraternal organizations, decline in, *75*
Free Time, *198*
freedom, a European view, *111*
freeway system, *212*
Fromm, Erich, *95*
front groups, *237, 239*
Frost, Robert, *190*
frugality, *260, 263, 265, 268*
Furlong, Edward, *140*

G
Galbraith, John Kenneth, *15, 216*
gambling, addiction to, *25*
Gandhi, Mahatma, *378*
gang violence, causes of, *109*
garage size, *30, 32, 33*
gardening, *295*
gas,
   See oil and gas,
Gasland, *246*
gated communities, *81, 84*
Gates, Bill, *105, 389*
GDP (gross domestic product), *357, 359, 360, 362, 363*
generosity, addiction to, *163*
Genetic Roulette, *144*
Genuine Progress Indicator (GPI), *359, 360, 362, 363*
glass bottles, recycling, *385*
Glass-Steagal Act, *230, 231*
global warming,
   See climate change,

GMOs (genetically engineered organisms), See also chemicals,
   crop yields, *144*
   farmer assurance provision, *237*
   mandatory product labeling, *146*
   Monsanto, *142, 144, 146*
   Monsanto Protection Act, *237*
   overview, *142, 144, 146*
   patenting, *142*
   pesticide use, *144*
   Roundup Ready crops, *142, 144*
goals,
   commonly expressed, *155*
   Maslow's hierarchy of needs, *156, 158*
   universal human, *158, 160*
   wanting what we have, *163*
Goodman, Ellen, *39*
Goran, Sheldon, *23*
Gore, Al, *237*
GPI (Genuine Progress Indicator), *359, 360, 362, 363*
GPI Plus, *374*
graduated retirement, *343*
grain, demand for, *124*
Grayson, Alan, *52*
great good places, *74*
Great Recession,
   credit default swaps, *230*
   credit unions vs. banks, *301*
   depression (economic), *203*
   derivatives, *230*
   financial collapse of 2008, *228, 230, 231*
   Glass-Steagal Act, *230, 231*
   role of the housing market, *230*
Green, David, *388*
Green, William, *198*
green taxes, *348*
greenest office building, *313*
Greenway, Robert, *293*
Grist, *116*

gross domestic product (GDP), *357, 359, 360, 362, 363*
Gross National Happiness Index (website), *366*
growth vs. development, *370*
gun industry, *84*
Guzman, Monica, *19*
gyres, *142*

H

Hanauer, Nick, *346*
Handprinting (website), *329*
happiness,
    material wealth and, *153, 328, 329, 370*
    measuring, *340*
    United Nations Happiness Report, *370, 371*
    U.S. ranking, *371*
    vs. well-being, *370*
    on weekends vs. workdays, *340*
Happiness Initiative, *374*
happiness skills, *371*

Harmony Village, *315*
Hawken, Paul, *348, 380*
Hayden, Tom, *93*
Hayes, Sylvia, *360*
Healey, Ron, *334*
health care,
    as percentage of GDP, *53*
    single-payer plan, *341*
health consequences of poverty, *109*
health issues, among wealthy people, *153*
heart disease, U.S. ranking, *151*
Heller, Rick, *268*
Helliwell, John, *371*
Heschel, Abraham, *175*
Heymann, Jody, *50*
Hightower, Jim, *350*
hoarding,
    problem scope, *32*
    sources of clutter, *39*
hog waste, *146*
Holst, Carol, *326, 328*
Home Depot, *79*
home improvement, chain stores, *79*
home shopping, *13*

hoodia plant, *112*
Hoover, Herbert, *203*
Horsey, David, *328*
houses,
  apodments, *265*
  average size, *15, 30, 32, 207, 209*
  garage size, *30, 32, 33*
  off the grid, *265*
  ultra-small, *265*
housing,
  cohousing, *315*
  designing a neighborhood, *315*
  short-term rentals, *309*
housing market, role in the Great Recession, *230*
Howell, Ryan, *328*
Hummer, *17*
hunger, *103*
  See also food insecurity,
Hunnicutt, Benjamin, *198, 205*
hunter-gatherers, *169, 170, 173, 177*
Hurdle, Annette, *284*
Hydraulic Fracturing (fracking), *245, 246*
hypercommercialism, *226*

I

imprisonment,
  as a business, *111*
  in California, *111*
  Corrections Corporation of America, *111*
  in the United States, *109, 151*
impulse buying, *11*
income distribution, *101, 103*
  See also wealth distribution; wealthiest 1 percent,
income levels, role models, *23*
industrial accidents,
  Bangladesh textile factory fire (2013), *101*
  demands for safe working conditions, *194, 196*
  Thai toy factory fire (1993), *99, 101*

Triangle Shirtwaist Factory Fire (1911), *101*
workplace safety, *194, 196*
Industrial Revolution, working hours, *182*
infant mortality, U.S. ranking, *151*
insecticides, bee deaths, *282, 284*
insects, as food source, *126*
insomnia, *147*
Internet advertisements, *226*
interstate highway system, *212*
isolation,
    in communities, *74, 75, 78, 81, 84*
    de-individualization, *97*
    loneliness, *59*
    overcoming, *93*

J

Jacobson, Michael, *9, 223*
Japanese culture, *155*
Jesus, *177*
Johnson, Allen, *170, 173*
Johnson, Beth, *32*
Johnson, Brad, *223*
Johnson, Lyndon B., *216*
Johnson, Samuel, *190*
Jones, Van, *306, 309*

K

Kasser, Tim, *93, 153*
keeping up with the Joneses downside of, *95*
    the Jones family today, *252*
    The Status Seekers, *216*
    trends, *21*
Kellogg, A.K., *203, 334*
Kellogg's, working hours, *203, 205*
Kellogg's Six-Hour Day, *205*
Kelly, Marjorie, *301, 303, 306*
Kelly, Michael, *303*
Keltner, Dacher, *388*
Kennecott Copper Mine, *122*
Kennedy, John F., *93*
Kennedy, Robert F., *217*

Kerry, John, *336*
Keynes, John Maynard, *303*
Keystone XL Pipeline
environmental impact of, *114, 116*
   nonviolent civil disobedience, *127*
Korten, David, *111, 112, 151*
Kubiszewski, Ida, *374*
!Kung Bushmen, *169, 170*
Kuntsler, James, *74*
Kurnit, Paul, *65*
Kuznets, Simon, *360, 362*

L

Lafargue, Paul, *192*
Lakota Sioux tribe, *177*
Lanchester, John, *230*
land, demand for, *124*
Lasn, Kally, *235, 317, 319, 321, 322*
Last Child in the Woods, *284*
law of diminishing marginal utility, *27*
law of progressive simplification, *280*
Layard, Richard, *109*
laziness, as a right, *192*
leaded gasoline, PR (public relations), *239, 241, 243*
leasing vs. owning, *306, 309, 311*
leisure class, time pressures, *46*
leisure time,
   effects on business, *200, 201, 203*
   wealth as disposable time, *184, 186, 187, 188*
Leo XIII, Pope, *198, 346*
Leonard, Annie, *323, 326*
Lerner, Michael, *91, 93*
levels of sufficiency, *370*
Levittown development,
   average house size, *15*
   World War II era, *207, 209*
liberals vs. conservatives, on affluenza, *95*
life expectancy, American, *53*
life-satisfaction scores, *374*

Life without Principle, *187*
Linder, Staffan, *46, 48*
Linn, Susan, *63*
Living Downstream, *135*
localization of food industry, *84*
   See also chain stores, resistance campaign,
logging industry, *129*
loneliness, *59*
   See also isolation,
Los Angeles, traffic, *36*
Louv, Richard, *284, 285*
'Love Global Warming', *239*
Lovins, Amory and Hunter, *348*
Lowe's, *79*
lung disease, U.S. ranking, *151*
Luntz, Frank, *334*
Luttwak, Edward, *70*
luxuries vs. necessities, *19*
Luxury Fever, *346*

M

Machiguenga tribe, *170, 173*
Mack, Burton, *175*
Macy, Joanna, *378*
magnetic resonance imaging (MRI), brain imaging, *163*
mail order shopping, *13*
Mall of America, *11*
malls,
   See also chain stores; shopping centers,
   attendance, *7*
   cost in lost farmland, *7*
   decline in, *13*
   Dubai Mall, *11*
   Mall of America, *11*
   New South China Mall, *11*
   Phoenix City Market Mall, *11*
   Potomac Mills, *9, 11*
   Super Mall, *9*
   vs. houses of worship, *7*
Mander, Jerry, *163*
Marcuse, Herbert, *95*

market values, vs. family values, *70*
Marketing Madness, *223*
marketing to children, *61, 63, 65, 67, 348, 350*
  See also advertisements,
marriage rates, *59*
Martineau, Pierre, *221*
Marx, Karl, *182, 184, 186*
Maslow, Abraham, *156, 367*
Maslow's hierarchy of needs, *156, 158*
mass production, deindividualizing the worker, *97*
maternity leave, *334, 336*
Matthews, Vince, *122*
Max-Neef, Manfred, *367*
maximum wage, *346*
Mazur, Laurie, *223, 226*
McDonald's, *79*
McDonough, William, *285*
McGinn, Anne Platt, *137*
McKibben, Bill, *126, 127, 291, 323*
Mead, Margaret, *275*

Meadows, Donella, *153, 246, 247, 323, 380*
media literacy, *323*
medieval times, working hours, *182*
mental health, among children, *67, 68, 70*
Merry Maids, *107*
Mexico, community forests, *303*
Meyer, Jim, *114, 116*
military spending, U.S. ranking, *151*
mindfulness, *268*
minimum wage,
  garment workers in Bangladesh, *101*
  papal call for, *198*
  U.S. ranking, *346*
moderation, *175, 177*
Molnar, Alex, *67*
money,
  buying happiness, See happiness;
  well-being,
  vs. time, *188*
monitoring employees, *50*
Monsanto, *142, 144, 146, 237*

Monsanto Protection Act, *237*
morality,
   See also ethics; values, codes through history, *175, 177*
   direction of a consumer society, *95*
Morris, William, *192*
Mosaic, *309*
Mother Teresa, *88, 89*
Motivation in Advertising, *221*
Mount Rainier National Park, *86, 88*
MRI (magnetic resonance imaging), brain imaging, *163*
Musikanski, Laura, *374*
Myers, David, *27*
Myers, Norman, *126*

N

Nader, Ralph, *348, 350*
Naisbitt, John, *39*
Natural Capitalism, *118, 348*
natural gas drilling, See fracking (Hydraulic Fracturing),
natural resources, See resources (natural),
nature,
   a child's view of, *284, 285, 287*
   ecophobia, *293*
   for educators, *289*
   for individuals and families, *287*
   restorative properties of, *289, 291, 293, 295*
   separation from, *291, 293*
necessities vs. luxuries, *19*
neighborhoods, See community,
Netherlands, work reduction, *340, 341*
New Development Paradigm, *367, 370*
New South China Mall, *11*
Nickel and Dimed, *107*
Nike, CEO compensation, *105*

No Impact Man, *265*
No Impact Project (website), *265*
No-Vacation Nation, *50*
Nomad community, *315*
nonviolent civil disobedience,
   drilling for oil and gas, *126*
   Forward on Climate rally, *127*
   Keystone XL Pipeline, *127*
   Sierra Club, *127*
Norman, Al, *79*
Norris, Margaret, *109*
Northwest Earth Institute (website), *277*
nucleus accumbens, *160*
Nussbaum, Karen, *50*

O

Obama, Barack, *336*
obesity, U.S. ranking, *151*
Occupy Wall Street,
   forerunners of, *194, 196*
O'Connor, Terrance, *380*
off the grid, *265*
oil and gas, drilling for,
   declining petroleum production, *124*
   fracking (Hydraulic Fracturing), *245, 246*
   nonviolent civil disobedience, *126*
oil and gas industry, PR (public relations), *245, 246*
oil sands, *114, 116*
Oldenburg, Ray, *74*
Olds, Jacqueline, *54, 57, 70*
O'Malley, Martin, *362*
Omega Boys Club, *109*
On-Going community, *315*
1 percenters,
   See wealthiest 1 percent,
online resources,
   See also specific resources,
   Alliance for Sustainability and Prosperity, *374*
   Beyond the Purchase, *328*
   Center for a New American Dream, *268*
   Consumer Jungle, *323*

Gross National Happiness Index, *366*
Handprinting, *329*
No Impact Project, *265*
Northwest Earth Institute, *277*
Postconsumers, *328*
PRWatch, *235*
Redefining Progress, *118*
Share Save Spend, *323*
Sprawl Busters, *79*
The Story of Broke (video), *326*
The Story of Stuff (video), *326*
online shopping, growth in, *13*
Oppenheim, James, *194, 196*
orphan molecules, *140*
Orwell, George, *243*
Our Stolen Future, *142*
outdoor advertisements, *223*
overconsumption, stimuli for, *38, 39*
overtime, limiting, *334, 336*
Owning the Future, *301*
owning vs. leasing, *306, 309, 311*

P

Packard, Vance, *216*
Paine, Thomas, *299*
parents, in television advertisements, *65*
parents as gatekeepers, *65, 67*
Parker, Mike, CEO compensation, *105*
patenting GMOs, *142*
paternity leave, *334, 336*
pathological buying, *29*
Patient Zero, *169*
Paul, Alexandra, *326*
PCBs (polychlorinated biphenyls), *142*
petroleum, declining production, *124*
pharmaceuticals, See drugs,
Phoenix City Market Mall, *11*
phone advertisements, *226*
Pickett, Kate, *111*
Piersall, Alex, *32*

pig waste, *146*
Pinkerton, David and Mary, *137*
planned obsolescence, *209, 210, 216*
pollution taxes, *348*
polychlorinated biphenyls (PCBs), *142*
Port Huron Statement, *93*
Porter, Lana, *295*
possession overload, *41, 43*
Post-Growth Institute, *322, 323*
Postconsumers (website), *328*
Potomac Mills, *9, 11*
Potvin, Noelle, *84*
poverty,
    1980s, *103*
    2010, *105*
    environmental contaminants, *109*
    health consequences of, *109*
    worldwide, *112*
poverty-level wages, *107*

Powers, Bill and Melissa, *265, 268*
Poyntz, Juliet Stuart, *198*
PR (public relations),
    See also advertising,
    definition, *235*
    fracking, *245, 246*
    front groups, *237, 239*
    history of, *239, 241, 243*
    influence on policy, *235, 237*
    for leaded gasoline, *239, 241, 243*
    oil and gas industry, *245, 246*
    scientific feedback, *246, 247*
    spin doctors, *243, 245, 246*
    for tobacco, *239, 241, 243*
pregnancy, adolescent, *151*
Prodigal Sons and Material Girls: How Not to Be Your Child's ATM, *323*
productivity, European Union, *53*

progressive consumption tax, *346*
PRWatch, *235*
psychology, of addiction, *29*
publications,
  See books and publications,
Publix Supermarkets vs. WalMart, *79*
Putnam, Robert, *74, 84*

Q
Quakers, *180*

R
Rand, Ayn, *89, 95*
rare earth elements, demand for, *122, 124*
Reagan, Ronald, *219*
recession,
  See Great Recession,
recycling,
  See also waste disposal,
  advocacy vs. performance, *277*
  aluminum cans, *385*
  extended producer responsibility, *124, 311, 313, 348*
  glass bottles, *385*
Redefining Progress (website), *118*
Rees, William, *118*
Reich, Charles, *216*
Reich, Robert, *81*
religious observances, time for, *198, 200*
reports,
  See books and publications,
Rerum Novarum, *198, 346*
resource pyramids, *122*
resources (natural),
  See also specific resources,
  learning from the past, *116, 118*
  oil sands, *114, 116*
  waste production for an average family, *118*
  water consumption in an average lifetime, *118*
resources (sources of help),

See books and publications; online resources,
restaurants,
    chain stores, *79*
    portion creep, *27*
retirement, graduated, *343*
reward center of the brain, *160*
Riederer, Susan, *389*
Rifkin, Jeremy, *190*
'The Right to Be Lazy', *192*
Robin, Vicki, *260, 263, 268, 354, 355*
Roosevelt, Franklin D., *203*
Röpke, Wilhelm, *95, 216, 226, 228*
Roundup Ready crops, *142, 144*
Roy, Dick and Jeanne, *275, 277, 279*
Ryan, John, *198*
Ryan, Richard, *93, 153*

S

safety,
    community, *84*
    workplace, *194, 196*
    See also industrial accidents,
Saint Monday, *182*
Saltzman, Amy, *268*
Satisfaction Guaranteed, *209, 210*
savings rates, trends, *23*
Schilke, Jacki, *246*
schools, commercialism in, *67*
Schor, Juliet,
    American workload, *48*
    children as consumers, *63*
    on productivity, *52, 53*
    television as a role model, *21*
    values held by children, *70*
    on working hours, *333*
Schumacher, E.F., *323*
Schwartz, Barry, *46*
Schwartz, Richard, *54, 57, 70*
Seeds of Simplicity, *326*
Segal, Jerome, *175, 180*

Seiple, Robert, *88, 89*
self-centeredness,
   in American culture, *88, 89, 91*
   among American children, *70*
self-driving cars, *36*
Selling Out America's Children, *63*
Share Save Spend (website), *323*
sharing,
   bicycles, *311*
   cars, *309, 311*
   housing, *315*
   work, *203, 336, 338, 340, 341, 343*
sharing-based economies, *306, 309, 311*
Shenk, David, *46*
Shi, David, *175, 194*
shopping,
   addiction to, *25*
   consumer spending, as percentage of overall economy, *7*
   from home, *13*
   impulse buying, *11*
   by mail order, *13*
   online, *13*
shopping centers,
   See also chain stores; malls. vs. high schools, *7*
   World War II era, *212, 214*
sick leave, paid, *334, 336*
Sierra Club, nonviolent civil disobedience, *127*
Sillivan, Mike, *17*
Simon, Scott, *9, 223*
simplifying your life,
   antimaterialism, World War II era, *214, 216*
   law of progressive simplification, *280*
   living off the grid, *265*
   resisting consumerism, *321, 322*
   techniques for, *279, 280*
   ultra-small houses, *265*
single-payer health care, *341*
Sismondi, Jean Charles de, *186, 187*
Sitting Bull, *177*
six-hour day, *203, 333*

sleep aids, *147*
Smith, Adam, *299*
Smith, Jeffrey M., *144*
smoking, vs. stress, *50*
Sobel, David, *293*
social capital, *74, 75*
socialism, working hours, *186*
solar projects, *309*
solitary living, loneliness, *59*
species extinctions, *126, 129*
Speck, Sarah, *50, 52*
Spencer, Miranda, *245*
spending,
    by children, *61, 63*
    reducing, *260, 263, 265, 268*
spin doctors, *243, 245, 246*
Sprawl Busters, *79*
Starbucks, *79*
Stauber, John, *235*
Steingraber, Sandra, *135*
Steves, Rick, *43*
Stone Age cultures, *169, 170, 173*
Strasser, Susan, *194, 209, 210*

stress,
    effects of, *50, 52*
    resulting from work, *50*
    vs. smoking, *50*
stress clinics, *91, 93*
study circles, *271, 273, 275, 277, 279, 280, 326*
suicidal thoughts among children, *68*
suicide rates, Indian Farmers, *144*
Super Mall, *9*
support groups, forming, *277, 279*
survival of the kindest, *388, 389*
sustainability,
    Alliance for Sustainability and Prosperity (website), *374*
    balanced with growth, *352*
    of economies, *301, 303*
Suzuki, David, *323*
Swenson, Richard, *41, 43, 177*
Swofford, Mike, *328*

synthetic chemicals, *135*
See also chemicals,

T

The Age of Missing Information, *291*
The Circle of Simplicity, *273*
The Communist Manifesto, *182*
The Economic and Philosophical Manuscripts of 1844, *184*
The End of Nature, *127*
The End of Patience, *46*
The Future: Six Drivers of Global Change, *237*
The Geography of Nowhere, *74*
The Greening of America, *216*
The Hidden Persuaders, *216*
The Ladies Home Journal, *194*
The Lonely American, *54*
The New Normal, *38*
The Nine Tenths, *194, 196*
1984, *243*
The Paradox of Choice, *46*
the realm of necessity, *186*
The Simple Life, *175, 194*
The Spirit Level, *111*
the Starbucks effect, *140*
The Status Seekers, *216*
The Story of Broke (video), *326*
The Story of Stuff (video), *326*
Tawney, R.H., *95*
tax share (2004), wealthiest 1 percent, *103*
taxes,
  carbon, *348*
  curing affluenza, *348*
  depletion, *348*
  green system, *348*
  pollution, *348*
  progressive consumption tax, *346*
Taylor, James, *239*
telemarketing, *226*
television,
  effects on children, *63*
  as a model for standard of living, *21*

World War II era, *214*
television advertisements,
   See also advertisements; commercialism; marketing,
   cost of, *223*
   increasing exposure to, *57*
   lifetime exposure to, *221*
   parents as gatekeepers, *65, 67*
   portrayal of parents, *65*
temperature of the planet, average change, *127*
Terkel, Studs, *93*
test for affluenza, *252, 256*
texting, and traffic accidents, *78*
Thai toy factory fire (1993), *99, 101*
'The Road Not Taken', *190*
Thinley, Jigmi, *366, 374*
third places, *74*
thirty-hour week, *203, 205, 333*
thirty-two-hour week, *333*
30-40 now work plan, *334*
This Ugly Civilization, *200, 201*
Thoreau, Henry David, *187, 188*
3 EStrategies, *360*
Tillerson, Rex, CEO compensation, *127*
time,
   See also working hours,
   to know God, *198, 200*
   vs. money, *188*
   as wealth, *184, 186, 187*
time famine, *43, 44, 46*
time off for family illness, *336*
time pressures,
   of the leisure class, *46*
   strain on marriages, *57, 59*
time protections, *334*
timesickness, *293*
tobacco,

addiction to, *25*
anti-smoking advertisements, *319, 321*
PR (public relations), *239, 241, 243*
Toxic Deception, *137*
toxic house, *137*
Toxic Sludge is Good for You, *235*
toxicity, of common chemicals, *135*
Toynbee, Arnold, *280*
traffic, *36*
  See also cars,
traffic deaths, U.S. ranking, *151*
Triangle Shirtwaist Factory Fire (1911), *101, 194*
Truman, Harry, *214*
Turbo-Capitalism, *70*
Turkle, Sherry, *78*
Turner, Ted, *389*
The Waste Makers, *216*
The Wealth of Nations, *299*

U

uncommercials, *319, 321*

United Nations Happiness Report, *370, 371*
United States,
  activity-limiting diseases, *151*
  adolescent pregnancy, *151*
  AIDS, *151*
  as a bad example, *23*
  child welfare, worldwide rankings, *59*
  divorce rate, *151*
  drug use, *151*
  heart disease, *151*
  imprisonment, *109, 151*
  infant mortality, *151*
  lung disease, *151*
  military spending, *151*
  obesity, *151*
  traffic deaths, *151*
  wealth, worldwide rankings, *150, 151, 153*
unmarried parents, *59*
'the Uprising of the Thirty Thousand', *196*
Ura, Dasho Karma, *366*

V

vacation time,
  average, *50*
  guaranteeing, *52, 334, 336*
  perils of not taking, *52, 53*
values,
  among students, *93*
  moral codes through history, *175, 177*
  moral direction of a consumer society, *95*
values, family,
  ethics among low-income youths, *109*
  held by children, *68, 70*
  vs. market values, *70*
Van Boven, Leaf, *328*
van den Haag, Ernest, *97*
Voluntary Simplicity, *271, 279*
voting in presidential elections, *75*

W

Wachtel, Paul, *15*
Wacker, La Nita, *30, 32*
Wackernagel, Mathis, *118, 362*
wages,
  See also CEO compensation,
  maximum, *346*
  poverty-level, *107*
  stagnation, *228*
wages, minimum,
  garment workers in Bangladesh, *101*
  papal call for, *198*
  U.S. ranking, *346*
Wal-Mart,
  annual revenue, *79*
  resistance campaign, *79, 84*
  vs. Publix Supermarkets, *79*
Walden, *187*
Walsh, David, *63, 65*
Wangchuck, Jigme Singye, *366*
Wann, David, *38*
waste disposal,
  See also recycling; specific wastes,
  aquatic gyres, *142*
  hog waste, *146*

reducing personal waste, *275, 277*
at sea, *140, 142*
waste production,
  for an average family, *118*
  ecological footprint, *118*
water consumption,
  in an average lifetime, *118*
  ecological footprint, *118*
Waters, Alice, *84*
wealth,
  from within, *155*
  accumulating, motives for, *153*
  as disposable time, *184, 186, 187*
  flaunting, *29*
  U.S. rankings worldwide, *150, 151, 153*
wealth distribution, *103, 105*
  See also CEO compensation; income distribution,
wealthiest 1 percent charitable contributions (1980s), *103*
  charitable contributions (today), *389*
  income distribution (1980s), *101, 103*
  tax share (2004), *103*
  wealth distribution (1999), *103*
wealthy people, health issues, *153*
Weber, Max, *182*
Webster, Donovan, *146*
'The Welfare of Children in Rich Countries', *59*
well-being, measuring,
  Canadian Index of Well-Being, *374*
  community level, *357, 359, 360, 362, 363*
  development paradigm, *367*
  Easterlin Paradox, *370*
  forms of capital, *367*

GDP (gross domestic product), *357, 359, 360, 362, 363*
GPI (Genuine Progress Indicator), *359, 360, 362, 363*
GPI Plus, *374*
Gross National Happiness Index, *366*
Happiness Initiative, *374*
levels of sufficiency, *370*
life-satisfaction scores, *374*
national level, *357, 359, 360, 362, 363, 366, 367, 370, 371*
New Development Paradigm, *367, 370*
personal level, *355, 357*
United Nations Happiness Report, *370, 371*
well-being vs. happiness, *370*
West Coast Trail, *129*
When Corporations Rule the World, *111*
Whoops!, *230*
Whybrow, Peter, *326*
Wicks, Judy, *305*
Wilkinson, Richard, *111*
Williamson, Marianne, *299*
Wilson, E.O., *126*
wind rights, *303*
Woll, Matthew, *198*
Woolman, John, *180*
work,
    pace of, *48, 50*
    sharing, *203*
    stress resulting from, *50*
Work Without End, *198*
working hours,
    See also time; vacation time,
    30-40 now plan, *334*
    childbirth leave, *334, 336*
    during the depression, *203*
    eight-hour day, *198*
    Fair Labor Standards Act, *198*
    five-day week, *203*

forty-hour week, *198, 205, 333*
four-day week, *336, 338, 340*
graduated retirement, *343*
Industrial Revolution, *182*
at Kellogg's, *203, 205*
limiting overtime, *334, 336*
medieval times, *182*
movement to shorten, *198*
paid sick leave, *334, 336*
the realm of necessity, *186*
Saint Monday, *182*
six-hour day, *203, 333*
under socialism, *186*
thirty-hour week, *203, 205, 333*
thirty-two-hour week, *333*
time off for family illness, *336*
time protections, *334*
trends, *48*
U.S. ranking, *334, 336*
work reduction, *336, 338, 340, 341*
work sharing, *203, 336, 338, 340, 341, 343*
work week, prediction for (1965), *44*
workplace,
monitoring employees, *50*
safety, demands for, *194, 196*
See also industrial accidents,
World War II era,
antimaterialism, *214, 216, 217*
consumer loans, *209, 210*
consumerism, *209*
Levittown development, *207, 209*
planned obsolescence, *209, 210, 216*
shopping malls, *212, 214*
television, *214*
voices of discontent, *214, 216*
Wuerthele, Suzanne, *135*

Y

Yalom, Irvin, *355*
Your Money or Your Life, *260, 354, 355*

Z

Zipcar franchise, *309*

www.ingramcontent.com/pod-product-compliance
Ingram Content Group UK Ltd.
Pitfield, Milton Keynes, MK11 3LW, UK
UKHW041208180426
11947UKWH00023B/1939